THE DEVIL
I KNOW

THE DEVIL I KNOW

My Haunting Journey with Ronnie DeFeo
and the True Story of the Amityville Murders

JACKIE BARRETT

BERKLEY BOOKS, NEW YORK

THE BERKLEY PUBLISHING GROUP
Published by the Penguin Group
Penguin Group (USA) Inc.
375 Hudson Street, New York, New York 10014, USA

Penguin Group (Canada), 90 Eglinton Avenue East, Suite 700, Toronto, Ontario M4P 2Y3, Canada
(a division of Pearson Penguin Canada Inc.) • Penguin Books Ltd., 80 Strand, London WC2R 0RL,
England • Penguin Group Ireland, 25 St. Stephen's Green, Dublin 2, Ireland (a division of Penguin
Books Ltd.) • Penguin Group (Australia), 250 Camberwell Road, Camberwell, Victoria 3124, Australia
(a division of Pearson Australia Group Pty. Ltd.) • Penguin Books India Pvt. Ltd., 11 Community
Centre, Panchsheel Park, New Delhi—110 017, India • Penguin Group (NZ), 67 Apollo Drive,
Rosedale, Auckland 0632, New Zealand (a division of Pearson New Zealand Ltd.) • Penguin Books
(South Africa) (Pty.) Ltd., 24 Sturdee Avenue, Rosebank, Johannesburg 2196, South Africa

Penguin Books Ltd., Registered Offices: 80 Strand, London WC2R 0RL, England

This work is a true and accurate report of the events described. For reasons of privacy,
however, the author has in some instances disguised or altered the identities of certain individuals.
The publisher does not have any control over and does not assume any responsibility
for author or third-party websites or their content.

THE DEVIL I KNOW

A Berkley Book / published by arrangement with the author

PUBLISHING HISTORY
Berkley premium edition / August 2012

Copyright © 2012 by Jackie Barrett.
Cover photo of author by Joanne Agnelli.
Cover design by Oyster Pond Press.

ISBN: 978-0-425-25042-6

BERKLEY®
Berkley Books are published by The Berkley Publishing Group,
a division of Penguin Group (USA) Inc.,
375 Hudson Street, New York, New York 10014.
BERKLEY® is a registered trademark of Penguin Group (USA) Inc.
The "B" design is a trademark of Penguin Group (USA) Inc.

PRINTED IN THE UNITED STATES OF AMERICA

10 9 8 7 6 5 4 3 2 1

Most Berkley Books are available at special quantity discounts for bulk purchases for
sales, promotions, premiums, fund-raising, or educational use. Special books, or
book excerpts, can also be created to fit specific needs.

For details, write: Special Markets, The Berkley Publishing Group, 375 Hudson Street,
New York, New York 10014.

ALWAYS LEARNING   PEARSON

To William, Joanne, and Jude

ACKNOWLEDGMENTS

To I. J. Schecter, no words could ever express my sincere appreciation for all your hard work, dedication, and enormous talent! My editor, Shannon Jamieson Vazquez, at The Berkley Publishing Group, you have my deep appreciation on such a complex and twisted tale of murder/possession, a project that many couldn't handle. You are truly a step above and beyond excellence! Jim McCarthy, my literary agent with Dystel and Goderich, your strength and leadership has been a gift to me—you're amazing.

To my husband, William, who has never left my side, you are my guard in the dark and my shade in the light, you have opened every door and pulled me through loving you always. My fearless daughter and co-partner, Joanne Agnelli, we have lived what others could only imagine. There is no one prouder of you and your strength of steel. Embrace your gift, it belongs to you! Uncle Ray, who can always find a smile and a sandwich, you are loved.

To Victoria Laurie, author and intuitive, my true sister beyond blood, who stood by my side in the dark and gave me light. My love forever. Jude Weng, a phenomenal executive producer, director, writer, and co-founder of brand-new entertainment productions. You made it possible for me to break my chains and face the devil more times than I can count. I am forever grateful to such a powerhouse of a woman, and am honored to work with you. Scott Morgan, producer and head cameraman, my otherworldly partner, we have shared what lies beyond. I'm truly thankful for your wisdom and knowledge.

And in loving memory of my dog Max. Forever and after.

Mirror, mirror on the wall, who's the one to see you all . . .

Just when I think it's done, the mirror cracks, and out you come.

—JACKIE BARRETT

Dear Jackie

    I hope this finds you well.
We really have to do this, I'm ready, I hope
you are! You have it all, free my family
and your mother!
See you in HeLL.

        High Hopes! Get this out of me
please!

  Becareful and Thank you
  may God Be with you you'LL need it
This thing is real and Strong
          R.D.
          Butch

One of the first letters Ronnie wrote me. After this, I knew I couldn't just walk away.

ONE

———

The drowned teenager's name was Kieran McCaffrey.
His body, bloated and waterlogged, had been found
floating on Long Island's south shore several months earlier. But a recovered body, as I had observed countless
times, gives little comfort to a grieving family if all the
other circumstances of death remain shrouded in mystery.
When the questions surrounding a child's death go unan-
swered, families seek information like starving people seek
food: with blind desperation. The only kind of comfort
left to them is knowledge—"closure," as it's often referred
to. But the wounds don't ever close. They just get filled
in bit by bit, answer by answer. The families may hope
these wounds will heal, but in their hearts, they simply
crave whatever fact, whatever truth, they can acquire.
Because at the end of the day, it's at least better than
guessing. You accept whatever bits and pieces might provide the illusion of someday making you whole again.

On a chilly morning in March 2009, I stood with Adam Quinn, NYPD's recently retired captain of Cold Case Homicide and head of Search and Rescue, on the deck of the thirty-foot boat *Victory* off the coast of Long Island, New York. I watched Adam pull on his diving gear as rain needled into the water. Cameramen fixed their tripods in place and adjusted lighting levels as we set out along the south-shore canal and crawled past coveted beachfront properties and boathouses.

The evening before, I'd felt exhilarated. For several days, Adam and I had been shooting scenes for the pilot of a proposed A&E reality show called *Medium P.I.*, a series that would follow us in our quest to fill in the gaps of unsolved deaths. The network had high hopes for the show, so the fact that it had rained every day of the shoot hadn't bothered us. We were determined to try to help families in pain while hopefully creating a good piece of entertainment.

I'd done lots of TV before, including, a couple of years earlier, a show called *America's Psychic Challenge*, which pitted psychics against each other. I hadn't wanted to do it, since it shot in California and meant being away from my home and family in New York, so I agreed to do the pilot only. But my agent, and the producers, helped change my mind by telling me about the $100,000 prize. My plan was to win the thing and then donate the money to the Red Cross and an animal shelter in Louisiana.

I was told just to be myself. They didn't have to tell me that; I don't know any other way to be. Viewers seemed to like me. I think I must have differed from whatever stereotype they had in mind for a psychic.

I finished second—but in this case, losing was more like winning. I may have walked away without the $100,000, but between the end of the finale and my flight home to New York, my phone rang multiple times with producers offering me my own series. One of those calls turned into *Medium P.I.*

But what Adam and I were doing here wasn't just cooked up for the cameras—we'd worked together for twenty years on various cases, and we'd conducted this type of exercise dozens of times before. More often than not, we'd been successful—via logic and steely resolve on Adam's side, instinct and perception on mine—in unearthing evidence that had escaped others. We were a formidable team and an interesting contrast for the cameras. For years, Adam and others in the world of law enforcement had used my psychic gifts to help them untangle cases that had seemed unsolvable. Now, for TV, they were finally revealing me as the secret weapon they'd kept in the background for so long.

During our time together, Adam and I had seen just about everything. You would be hard-pressed to surprise either of us, even if you were trying to put together the strangest or most grisly murder imaginable. Still, as Adam prepared to dive off the boat that day, I couldn't shake the feeling of apprehension curling through me.

It was first thing that morning that I'd awakened with a feeling of disquiet. I'd sat up in my bed to discover I wasn't alone. And I don't mean my husband, Will. I had company of the most unpleasant kind. This kind of feeling is difficult to describe but unmistakable; it's as obvious as if someone threw a bucket of ice water on you the moment you woke up. For me, the experience is particular. The air becomes still. My insides shift. Anxiety prickles me like an itch occurring from the inside out.

I told Adam not to dive—I felt sure that there was no evidence to be found in the canal that day, and I knew the water would be frigid. My equal in stubbornness, Adam told me he was going anyway. Despite the firmness of his words, I knew that he was as unsettled as I was. I also knew he would never admit it.

In our years together dissecting homicides, I'd never seen Adam fazed or nervous. This is a guy who sprinted into the burning towers on 9/11 to save others, heedless of his own safety. Once, in 1994, while a member of SWAT, Adam was called to a skyscraper on the Upper East Side where a woman with five children and no job stood on the roof. He tried to talk her in, with no luck. She edged forward until only her heels were touching the edge. Adam quickly tied one end of a rope around his waist, the other around the air-conditioning unit, and then, an instant before the woman launched herself, jumped also, catching her in midair and holding her there, dangling twelve stories above the ground, until help arrived.

Now, on the boat, as we continued to prepare—checking the tank gauges, making final equipment adjustments, assessing the level of debris in the canal—Adam tried to assure me that it was okay for him to dive. I saw his mouth moving, but suddenly his voice trailed away and was replaced by a series of rapid shotgun blasts searing my eardrums. I looked around, asking if anyone else—the camera crew, the captain of the yacht, the safety divers—had heard. I was met with expressions of confusion. Puzzled, I asked a second time, "Didn't anybody else hear those shots?" People only shook their heads and looked at me curiously. I looked to Adam, assuming that if anyone else had heard, it would be him. His training had conditioned him to be hyper-attuned to every stimulus, allowing him to assess crime scenes and dissect witness accounts in seconds. But I realized, as his voice slowly reemerged in my ears, that he hadn't heard the shots either.

Normally, Adam and I would dive in tandem. Today, he insisted on diving solo. I should stay on board and spot, he said. I looked at the thermometer bobbing on the surface of the water. Fifty-eight degrees Fahrenheit. No one should be diving today, I told him again. Again he objected.

Then he looked at me, gave the thumbs-up, executed the same slow backflip I'd seen him perform countless times, and disappeared over the edge of the boat.

I moved quickly to the side and assumed the spotter's position. Adam became a gray silhouette beneath the dark water; then, as he dived farther, a specter. The only sound was the patter of rain on the surface of the water. My unease intensified. I suddenly had the sensation of being watched by something more than just the cameras.

Minutes passed uneventfully as Adam explored the dark canal, and I started to wonder whether my concern was unfounded. But then he popped up.

Because of the uncommonly bitter temperature—this was cold even for March in Long Island—Adam had worn a dry suit, made of different material than a traditional wet suit and as a result considerably heavier. The weight of his suit, not to mention the muscular bulk of the man himself, should have been more than enough to keep him under. But up he came, needing more mass. I looped a rope around my ankle, leaned out over the platform, and added weighted cubes to Adam's diving belt.

Back into the murk he dove, but a few minutes later, he popped up again, like a stubborn cork. Again he had to return to the boat to acquire more weight. Again I looped the rope around my ankle and added cubes to his belt.

It kept happening. Adam would beat downward into the darkness of the water, then break the surface once more, tired from the effort but still too buoyant. It was like the water was trying to reject him.

And then, at a remove, I heard myself say these words: "Ronnie's coming."

I didn't know what the words meant or why I'd said them.

"Ronnie DeFeo," I heard myself say this time, and now I was twice as puzzled. I'd never heard this name, and I couldn't understand why it was surfacing on my lips.

A new feeling came over me, one I recognized but have never quite become accustomed to—a kind of intense focus that's also a kind of haze. As I said this mysterious name, the boat's motor began to sputter loudly. Within a few minutes, we had stopped dead, and the baffled captain was apologizing, claiming this had never happened before.

Through my fugue, I felt the rain step up its force, becoming colder and razor-sharp. One of the cameramen dropped his equipment and began to vomit over the side of the boat. I asked someone what was wrong with him. No one knew. As had happened earlier, all the sounds around me collapsed into a vacuum and were replaced by a series of shotgun blasts as loud as thunderclaps. Again I asked if anyone had heard, but their faces were no different than they had been the first time.

It was then that I realized Adam was acting odd, disoriented in his swimming and uncharacteristically jerky in his movements.

I shook myself from the trance and saw immediately the reason for his alarm. He was losing air. None of us understood how this could be. Prior to a dive, you don't check tanks once; you check them three or four times. That's exactly what we had done. Adam's air should have lasted an hour. Instead it had depleted in minutes. I yelled at the group to get Adam the hell out of the water and us off the canal.

I don't scare easily.

I was scared.

I dashed onto the deck, snatched a ten-foot aluminum rod from its clips, then hurried back to the side of the boat and climbed out onto the platform. I held out the rod to Adam with one hand and clung to the boat with the other as rain stung my eyes.

Adam grasped the rod, and I started to pull. I saw his panic growing as his limbs started to flail. Something was pulling against me—something more than Adam's weight. I stretched farther toward him, yelling for someone to grab my legs and hold on. Someone did. I pulled with every muscle in my small frame, dragging Adam around the side of the boat and toward the metal ladder. Towing him through the water, I also registered that his mask had somehow become a poor fit for his face, despite our having checked and double-checked every piece of equipment prior to the dive.

Finally, Adam, gasping, reached the side of the boat. With the help of three other crew members, I hauled him up and over the gunwale, then climbed back into the boat myself, my knuckles scraped and bleeding. We attended to Adam, feeling relief as his breathing returned to normal. I kept my arms wrapped around his torso and could feel his heart hammering in his chest. As I wrung water from my coat, I repeated to the crew that we needed to get off the canal. I also told Adam I was going to have to walk away from the show. He nodded, knowing I had a sense of something greater coming—something not meant for the cameras.

Then I heard the strange blasts again, this time accompanied by the image of a young man cradling a shotgun at his hip. I looked across the canal, where Joanne, my daughter and assistant, stood with the producer of *Medium P.I.* at the edge of a dock, perhaps a football field away. Joanne is the one who keeps me on the ball. When I'm working, I'm focused on the objective at hand and nothing else. If it wasn't for her, I wouldn't remember to change my flip-flops to boots in January.

Though only in her late twenties, Joanne has both the wisdom and the resourcefulness of someone twice her age. She does it all—research, paperwork, reports—while letting me know where I'm supposed to be and when. People tell *me* I'm always working. That's how I feel about Joanne. She's the gas in my tank.

I sensed something powerful blowing in Joanne's direction. Something malevolent. Joanne is not a good swimmer. I looked at her, then at the icy water. She waved at me through the rain.

"Let's *move*," I said to the crew. I kept my arms wrapped around Adam and my gaze fixed on Joanne as the boat's engine chugged to life again. We carved slowly through the water, finally reaching the other side, and the dock where Joanne and the producer stood, after what seemed like an eternity. They stepped onto the boat and saw the shared unease on our faces. Then we all got the hell out of there.

When the day's shoot was done and the pilot wrapped, we all retreated into ourselves. There was little talking, little interaction. Adam's body language had changed. The man whose chin was usually held high and confident stood with his shoulders slumped, his eyes a million miles away. We all felt something dark and oppressive. No one talked about it. We just went our separate ways.

As we waited to hear whether the show would be

picked up, I tried to return to my normal life: dealing with my long list of clients, doting on my pets, and continuing to quietly assist the police in solving homicides to help grieving families. But returning to normal proved impossible when I promptly came down with pneumonia. It's rare that I get sick. But this bug took me down hard. I felt like I'd fallen into a black hole.

And the longer I lay there in bed, the more that strange sensation I'd felt at the canal lingered. It had followed me home and was starting to envelop me like a cloak I didn't want. Will, a tender bear of a man, tried to rouse me from my inertia, but I still felt cold, empty, and anxious. Joanne talked to me reassuringly, telling me I'd be better soon. If I was going to believe anybody, I'd believe her. Though we'd never really talked about it, I'd often suspected that Joanne's psychic abilities were as strong as my own. I'd never brought it up because she'd never brought it up. That was fine with me. I felt lucky not only that my daughter worked alongside me everyday but that she did it willingly. It was more than a lot of mothers could ask for. My mother certainly hadn't—she'd had me working for her from the time I was a child, but *willingly* isn't the word I'd have used to describe my part in it.

Joanne was a born researcher, a logical sleuth, and relentless when it came to accessing information fast. It was a perfect working relationship. My work haunted me as much as it gratified me. If she did have the instincts, I was just as happy for her never to have to use them.

Adam, my partner and confidant, saw my trepidation and was confused by it. He had always seen in me the same unwavering strength I had seen in him. He asked me what was wrong. I could tell him only that I was feeling something sinister.

Or, rather, I was fighting an instinct I've had many times before and was hoping would go away if I ignored it long enough. This instinct isn't particular to psychics or mediums. We all experience it. It's the voice telling you there's something you're going to have to deal with, whether you like it or not.

I called Joanne into my room. She asked how I was feeling and offered me a cold washcloth for my head. "Never mind that," I said. "I need you to find out everything you can about someone named Ronnie DeFeo—including where I can reach him."

TWO

I was twelve years old on Wednesday, November 13, 1974. My family had settled in a plantation-style house in Nola, Louisiana—though for us, *settled* was always a relative term. My mother, Mary Palermo, was a high priestess in the occult, and there are still many people who believe they can gain strength from her grave. Paranormal groups, ghost hunters, those who claim to be occult specialists—all of them have tried to learn where she lies. I won't tell.

Some people still claim they can spot her spirit walking along the roads, trying to get home. This doesn't surprise me. Her presence was powerful, but her soul was pulled by darkness. She never allowed me to call her mom—only Mary. When she would turn away, I would whisper "Mommy," even as an adult. Even if out of earshot, she would turn and shoot me a look. I made her a card when I was six. It was simple, a picture of her and me holding hands. She looked at it, slapped me off the chair, and said, "No soft stuff in this house," then threw the card away.

Mary lived in the spirit world but liked to anchor her existence to the physical realm by purchasing properties in different places. She'd buy them for the purpose of doing her rituals. We'd go from the bayou, with its streams and marshes, to the Garden District, with its mansions and old Creole money, then land elsewhere for a little while before starting the loop anew.

Just as she felt the need to spread her physical imprint as far as possible, so too did Mary straddle both sides of the spiritual existence, the good and the bad. She would put money in the poor box at church by day, and at night raise Cain. I would sit and watch her, nervous but compelled. By that time, I already knew I had many of the same abilities. I had discovered early that I could, for reasons unknown to me, make the same kinds of connections that she could to people's inner selves, their before and after. It frightened me, just as I imagined my mother's talents frightened her, but I also recognized, just as she must have, that such a gift couldn't simply be pushed aside.

I'd watch her perform her rituals. She would be dressed in black, wearing a veil and gloves, one celebrity after another in our house, connecting with her spirit, being absorbed by her until she released them back into the normal. I'd feel something blowing in—blowing through—the walls.

Mary and her own mother, Josephine Maria, who lived with us, operated a funeral parlor out of our house. There was an embalming room in the rear of the place that was always occupied by one corpse or another. After a while, you got used to it. People would say Mary's embalming work was so fine it looked as though she brought people back to life unmarred by death. She would prepare the bodies with the mirrors covered and music playing.

Sometimes, when she wasn't working, she'd play the piano, and I would watch from the top steps. My father, Andrew Palermo (he used her name)—the tranquil Blackfoot medicine man to her Sicilian voodoo priestess, the diligent Canadian steelworker to her hot-blooded Creole—would sit and listen. His tough features would be softened by her sweet chords.

They called Dad "The Bull." He wore a size sixteen shoe and walked like a silverback, but he never raised his voice. Dad had once shot himself in the foot just to see if it would hurt. Another time he'd had a piece of metal pierce his shoulder clean through, and he still made it home for dinner. The man was *tough*. But when Mary touched the keys, he changed. He'd just sit, listening. In Creole he would murmur, "My beloved," and she would keep playing, a smile on her face.

Joanne had done her usual digging, and had unearthed the story of a nightmare.

On November 13, 1974, in Amityville, New York, Ronnie DeFeo had been taken into police custody after it was discovered that both of his parents and all four of his younger siblings, ages nine to eighteen, had been killed in cold blood in the early hours of that same morning. The kids had all been found facedown on their beds, bloody holes in their backs. Ronnie was twenty-three at the time, an employee in his father's Buick dealership and a known delinquent.

It was a story I'd been only vaguely aware of, since I was so young at the time it had happened, and it was so far away from my home in Louisiana. Even as an adult, I knew no more of the Amityville murders than most people, which is to say I was generally aware of the case because of all the horror movies and books that had come out in the years since the gruesome event had occurred.

Most of my work is accomplished through feel and rare perception, but a deep curiosity was still gnawing at me, and this time I felt I needed more facts to validate the sensations. Sometimes I see things happening long before they actually occur, and I know I have to follow the path set out before me and begin to try to fill in pieces of the puzzle. This time felt different. It was as though I was seeing both ahead and behind.

As Joanne continued to research the case and report to me, I learned that most of what I'd picked up about the story from all of these movies and books could essentially be ignored. The slim paperback that had started the sensation, *The Amityville Horror*, had nothing to do with the crime itself. It was a chronicle of the alleged horrors experienced by George and Kathy Lutz, who moved into the DeFeos' house after the murders and moved back out less than a month later, claiming the house was a source of intense paranormal activities. The book, a runaway bestseller, became a movie, and it was the movie that had transformed Ronnie DeFeo from an ordinary criminal doing his time to an altogether different kind of figure: a celebrity monster on par with fictional serial killers Freddy Krueger and Jason Vorhees, equally abhorred and scrutinized by a public that had become enthralled by his tale.

Apparently, the fascination hadn't abated. *The Amityville Horror*, despite the self-assured subtitle *A True Story*, had long ago been exposed as a hoax. William Weber, the lawyer who had defended Ronnie DeFeo at his trial, had admitted that he'd dreamed up the story with the Lutzes one evening over some wine—despite the Lutzes having stood firmly by the story's authenticity until their deaths two years apart soon after the turn of the twentieth century. These conflicting assertions aside, the stream of books and movies devoted to the subject had stayed constant over the years. *The Amityville Horror*, though built on a ruse, had become the stuff of pop culture.

I read as much as I could about the facts of the original case, about Ronnie DeFeo, the crime, the trial, and his ongoing imprisonment. Most of what I read seemed driven by bias, hyperbole, or both. Or it just went in circles. There was enough speculation about what had really happened in the DeFeos' home that night to populate a library.

And soon I realized why this man's name had come to my lips in the middle of the canal. At the time, we'd been only a few hundred meters from the DeFeos' now-famous address, 112 Ocean Avenue. We'd been a stone's throw from the place where an entire family had been slaughtered.

One night, I was doing research on the case online. I had regained some of my strength following my bout with pneumonia, but the aftereffects weren't quite gone, and I was still pretty run-down. I was about to switch off the computer and turn in for the night when something stopped me cold. I was looking at one of the mug shots snapped of Ronnie DeFeo on the night of the murders. I suddenly realized, with the force of a punch, that it was the same face that had floated into my bedroom more than forty years ago.

It was 1966, and I was four. My older brother Billy had been told to look after me that day, as was often the case. When you're the youngest sibling of six, you're always the one being taken care of. I didn't yet know that I was the strongest of any of us.

My father was at the steel factory, my mother at a client's. Billy was in his room with a girl. A thirteen-year-old boy, even a smart one like Billy, has only one thing on his mind. My mom had a rule: no girls in the house when he was taking care of me. But the minute she drove off, it seemed a girl would appear instantly, like she'd merely been hiding in the closet. Maybe she had, for all I knew.

Billy was showing this girl an Elvis album and trying to warm her up for a kiss. I knew this because I was spying on them from the edge of my bedroom, down the hall. They were sitting on his bed. She had braces and shoulder-length blonde hair. When I got too curious for my own good and crossed the hall to get a better vantage point, Billy spotted me and told me to go back to my room—he'd come get me when it was time for lunch. But he said it with affection, not annoyance. Billy had a big heart. He would save his comics for me, teach me how to put a worm on a hook. He taught me how to write my name, *Jackie*.

I went back to my room and picked up a doll. I had started having a conversation with the doll when the feeling of being watched made my nerves jump. I looked up and saw an enormous face materialize on the white wall of my bedroom. Along with the face came a torso and two arms whose hands were held outward, as though the wrists were bound together. As the figure lifted off my wall and began floating toward me, I sat paralyzed by fear. It drifted slowly toward me and hovered a moment, looking directly at me, expressing nothing. My voice felt choked at first, in the way one can never seem to produce a sound during a terrifying dream, but then my silence broke and I shrieked.

Yelling my name, Billy burst through the doorway of my bedroom, the girl trailing him. My brother was big for his age, built solidly, like our father. As I reached for Billy, I saw a portal open on my wall, a swirling field of gray. Billy must have seen it, too, because he paused halfway across the room to look back at the wall. The floating figure, which had reached my bedside, suddenly darted its arms out, reaching for me. I felt its touch, shadowy but horrifyingly real. Billy's girlfriend was immobile, her hand over her mouth, tears streaming down her fine cheekbones.

Billy grabbed my hand, tugged me hard, and we ran— out of my bedroom, down the stairs, and out the front door. Then we kept going, all the way to the edge of the lake a quarter of a mile away.

As we caught our breath, Billy looked at the girl and told her never to tell anyone else about what had happened. Together we walked her home. I never saw her again in our home or with Billy.

Though Billy had told the girl to stay mum, with our own family, we hid nothing. My parents had taught us not to keep secrets from one another. That night, when we told them what had happened, my mother sat silent. In Creole, my grandmother, sitting in the next chair, whispered, "The devil finds his way."

There was something else my parents taught: don't show fear. If we had a bad dream, we weren't allowed to go to their bed seeking a reassuring cuddle. We were supposed to stay in our own beds and deal with the fear. If we felt anxious in the dark, no one went out and bought us a night-light; they told us to find the inner strength to cope. After listening to my story, my mother sent me back to my room and told me to go to sleep.

That was eight years before the Amityville murders occurred, forty-three years before I first set foot on the south shore of Long Island. Now, as I peered at the mug shot taken on that distant night, I realized I was looking into the features of the same face that I'd last seen in my bedroom while a small, frightened girl.

The feeling I'd brought home with me two weeks earlier from the canal still seemed to cling. And now, the same evening I'd recognized Ronnie DeFeo's face as the one that had terrified me years before, that feeling seemed to manifest in tangible forms. Our brand-new refrigerator, in perfect working order, abruptly failed, ruining everything inside. Eggs cracked and oozed yolk; meats became rancid; bread purchased the day before turned immediately to mold.

Our longtime housekeeper, Abby, was at a loss. She'd been coming for several years, three times a week, morning till evening. She was a cleaning whirlwind, and we all respected the work she did and tried not to mess it up too badly or too quickly. But now we couldn't do anything about it. She'd come on Monday morning, clean everything from top to bottom, then return on Wednesday to find the place a sty. We could only shrug our shoulders and apologize, explaining that we'd had nothing to do with it. But Abby dealt in reason. Like many, she believed only in what she could see.

That's fine when the things you can see are explainable. But what do you do when they aren't? Abby would hear my voice coming through the intercom even when I wasn't home. Other times, she would hear children's giggles that chilled her blood. Our pets, normally affectionate with her, would suddenly take to hiding when she was around, and she would have to spend hours looking for them all. And the damn beds. She'd make one, go clean a different room, then return to find it unmade again. Finally, she walked up to me one day and said simply, "There's something evil here." A few days later, I found a cross and a protection medal between Joanne's mattress and box spring.

Finally Will and I decided to go to the store and stock up on nonperishables, then investigate the issue once we got back. But as we were preparing to leave, we looked at Joanne, and both of us had the same thought. We need to stay right here. Even a slight tremor of anxiety in one's child, no matter her age, is like an earthquake inside the heart of a parent.

"What's wrong?" I asked her.

"Nothing."

"Something's up," Will said. "Talk to us."

"I'll be fine," Joanne said, pushing us out the door as though we were going on a date. "Go. I'm just going to run a bath."

"I'll get you some coffee," I said. We left, but I kept my phone close. Will and I didn't need to say anything to each other. Our eyes said it: *Let's just get what we need as quickly as possible and get back home.* At the grocery store he rushed up and down the aisles as though he were on a game show.

We were gone just short of an hour, our anxiety snowballing with each minute that passed. When we arrived back home and came through the door, a feeling of alarm seized me. I called for Joanne, but she didn't answer. Will and I saw her bathroom door ajar. Will dropped the shopping bags he was carrying and ran toward the bathroom. I'm not as big or as fast as Will, but I was close behind. I was the first to notice the washcloth floating in the tub. Will was the first to spot Joanne.

She was curled up in the corner of the bathroom, sobbing, her white robe tied loosely at the waist. Her head was on her knees, the phone clutched in her fist. On the other end, I could hear Adam's voice and his attempts to comfort her.

Will scooped up Joanne and carried her to her bedroom. I told Adam we'd call him back and then followed Will and Jo to the bedroom, where he lay her down on the bed and stroked her hair, asking what happened. After a few minutes the sobs began to subside, and she was able, in brief gasps, to explain the vision that had accosted her.

She had just slipped into the bath when she'd thought she heard us come through the door. But it couldn't be us, since we'd only been gone a few minutes. There were noises coming from the kitchen—clattering of pots, spoons banging. Then voices, rising in tandem. Neither of the voices was ours, Jo realized. She had grabbed the robe and stepped out of the bath, still dripping, then sneaked toward the kitchen and peered into the dining area. That was when one of the figures turned: a woman, her face covered in blood, her eyes wild, saying she was coming back. That she was going to get her. Joanne had shut her eyes against the horror and ran.

I asked Jo to describe the figure. Attractive, even through the blood, she said. Medium height, graying hair. Italian looking. Wearing a red dress and pearls.

"Wait," I said, and rushed to my office. I grabbed the DeFeo file Joanne had started to assemble and scoured the pictures she'd gathered so far. There it was. An aging but beautiful Italian woman in a red dress and pearls. Louise DeFeo. Ronnie's mother.

The next morning, I went directly to my office and took out a sheet of paper. You can only ignore things for so long. I started to compose a note, but I was still dizzy, and too weak to finish. So I went back to bed.

Every day I kept taking out the paper to write, and every day the pneumonia, which had returned, reminded me who was boss. Finally, after another week of cold sweats and a liquid diet, I felt strong enough. I got out of bed and sat at my desk. I didn't know what I was supposed to say or why I was supposed to write this letter. I began anyway, because if I've learned only one lesson in all my years doing what I do, it's this: at the end of the day, the only true guide you have is your own instincts.

I stared at the paper, my own thoughts reflecting its blankness. The fever had mercifully broken a few days before, but now it had come back with a vengeance, and I was a tangle of mental cobwebs.

Dear Mr. DeFeo, I finally wrote.

"Jackie?"

I looked up to see Will in the doorway. Will is the kind of person who is almost always smiling out of nothing more than the feeling of wanting to smile. The expression on his face was far from a smile. I asked him what was wrong.

"That day," he said. "When you were on the canal."

"What about it?" I said.

He walked over to my side. "I saw something. A big man. In a black coat. I saw him standing in our living room."

I looked back at the paper. My feeling of unease had taken root on the boat and wormed its way deeper and deeper through me while I scuffled with the virus. Now, the feeling was morphing into something else. Instead of someone felled by an unknown hand, I felt more like a creature quietly steeling itself for battle.

What do you want? I wrote. *What's my part in this?*

"I've got the address." Joanne was in the doorway, a piece of paper in her hand. "Green Haven Correctional Facility, in upper New York State," she said. "Maximum security."

I added my name and phone number and handed her the letter. There was no need to write more. "Mail it," I said.

Uncle Ray, our permanent houseguest, is old-school Italian. For a sausage-and-pepper hero, he'd give you his unending loyalty. Uncle Ray isn't really an uncle. He's a friend of my brother's. He started staying with us years ago, the initial arrangement a trade involving his caring for the pets—between his shifts at Whole Foods—and our providing him a roof and a bed. Even as our addresses changed, Uncle Ray always came with. It became a running joke whenever we considered a new place: where would Ray's room be?

Ray—fifty-five but still a perpetual teenager, still sleeping on a pull-out couch in the basement, still caring for the pets, still doing his own thing—and Joanne are like brother and sister, even though he's nearly twice her age. They love each other and bicker the way siblings do, yet in the end are thick as thieves. For years Ray has talked about saving up and moving to Nevada, but it's never happened, and that's just fine with us. His sincerity and integrity bring light to any room he's in. He's the cheerful one when everyone else is down, the guy telling you to put a smile on your face just because it's fun to be alive. He takes care of the pets, not because he has to but because he adores them.

There were six of them when he moved in: one dog, Max, a bichon frise just sixteen inches off the ground but fearless as a pit bull; and five cats: Ernie, our Egyptian tabby and the elder statesman, who would sit alongside every ritual as though overseeing it; Toby, the forty-five-pound pixie bobcat; Dilly, a domestic cat, and Will's shadow—he called her his "favorite girl"; Oreo, a Hemingway (that is, she had extra toes); and Puss 'N' Boots, the tuxedo cat, who, since the day we'd brought him home, I'd always felt had an old soul and a warrior spirit. Puss 'N' Boots had found his way to my side years before, and the moment we met, I had the sense that we'd met before on these crossroads. Cats do have a sense; there's a reason they gravitate to people like me. It goes beyond a bowl of food and water.

The other thing we love about Ray, the thing that serves as a moderating element in our lives, is his quiet respect for the work I do and the world in which I do it.

Most people get their information about the occult and the paranormal from sensationalist books or movies. Ray is in the thick of it, along with the rest of my family. He's seen the real stuff again and again and hasn't once turned from it.

Ray went to Catholic high school and college but doesn't follow any organized religion. If you ask him what he believes in, he'll say he believes in himself and other living creatures, and that's that. His main concern is that the pets are cared for and treated well. When Toby, who'd been as healthy as an ox for nine years and then suddenly got sick, had to be put down, Ray tried to hail a cab from Whole Foods so he could get to the vet's to say good-bye. When he couldn't get a cab, he ran the three miles instead. During Toby's last moments, Ray bawled like a little boy.

Sensitive though he is, Uncle Ray is also stone-cold resilient. His life has not been the easiest, yet he displays serious bounce-back again and again. His hide is thick, and his spirit stalwart. Despite the fact that he lives in the basement and generally keeps to himself, he is in many ways the quiet core of strength in our home.

But when he called me on the house intercom the morning after Joanne's experience in the kitchen, I felt like I was speaking to a scared kid.

I'd never heard Ray sound worried, much less panicked. When his voice burst through the speaker, I jumped. He was calling for help. I asked him what was wrong. He screamed that the basement door to the upstairs wouldn't open. Through the speaker I could hear him pounding on it.

I ran downstairs, and indeed found the door to the basement, strangely, locked. I unlocked it and he ran upstairs. The fear I'd heard in Ray's voice was in his eyes, too. He was like a child who'd just been forced through his first haunted house.

It took time, but eventually, Will, Joanne, and I got Ray to calm down. I made him some tea. He sipped at it slowly, then started to tell us about the dream he'd had.

There was a dark, dingy room he didn't recognize. Someone appeared before him—an old priest, maybe— dressed in black from head to toe, face concealed. No, it wasn't a priest, he said—something different. It shifted form, but remained covered in black. A strong wind had gusted from behind, lifting Ray off the ground. He kept talking about the wind, which was not quite a wind, he said, but a force. "It was blowing into me from the back, forcing me up, not letting me back away. I couldn't move," he said. "I couldn't speak."

Whatever the thing was, moved from a standing position to a sitting one, then from a sitting one to a reclined one. Fearfully, Ray walked over, reached down, grabbed the material covering the thing's face, and yanked upward. He caught a glimpse of something terrifying, then woke up.

After that day, Ray slept with the radio on. He began to frequently get sick, something that had seldom happened before. He began to hear voices and footsteps, and scratching at the walls. He didn't want the three of us to go out and leave him alone, whereas before he'd always been thrilled with the idea, the perpetual teen having the

run of the house, our treasured pets his preferred company. He became too frightened to be alone.

Uncle Ray also made an important, recent decision.
His fear of being alone aside, he thought it might be time
to get his own place. It would be the lesser of two evils.

Perhaps the pets picked up on Uncle Ray's vibe, or perhaps he picked up on theirs. Or maybe they and he were
sensing the same thing. Either way, it wasn't only Ray
whose behavior changed in the days after I mailed the
letter to Green Haven. The pets, who usually clung to
me, refused to enter my bedroom. They began acting
skittish around me. Like Ray, even the hardiest of them
started getting sick.

This illness transferred itself to the rest of us. Will, who
looks like he's carved from stone, came down with a high
fever and began sensing an oppressive weight on his body
every night as he slept. Joanne started acting delirious,
retreating to her room, talking in her sleep. The three of
us shared a dream: a figure walking toward us, shrouded
by dense fog, burned-down trees around us, the growling
of animals filling the space.

We would wake up bruised. On one morning, I woke
up with half a dozen blue-black marks on my chest and
back. I went to my doctor, who asked me what I'd done.
"I fell," I lied.

"Where?" he asked. "Every corner of the house?"

The truth was that things in our house were moving
around of their own accord, devices turning on and off,

furniture being displaced. A song would blast out of my iPod after I'd turned it off. Artwork hanging on double hundred-pound hooks that had been in one location on the wall one night would be in another the next day. Terence, our nineteenth-century straw clown doll, would seem to shift position, as though following our movements.

My mother taught me to respect the spirits and the world of the transcendental. People like Adam taught me to look for rational explanations. I operate in a world that lies outside the norm, but all the same, when someone approaches me claiming a laundry list of paranormal activity, my first reaction is skepticism. I wanted to be able to explain away the strange activity in my own home. I had no explanations—so I chose instead to ignore it.

On another morning, I stepped into the shower and turned the knob to hot. Though we kept the thermostat at seventy-eight, the house had become perpetually frigid. I turned the shower handle expecting the soothing feeling of warm water on my head and over my skin. Instead, I felt a series of sharp sensations, like pellets. I looked up to see pebbles coming out of the showerhead.

I turned the handle in the opposite direction, stopping the flow of pebbles. Still choosing the side of the rational, I turned on the bath faucet instead, to see if the issue might be plumbing-related. The water began flowing normally, filling the tub. I knelt at the edge and flicked my fingers under the water.

Whatever it was that shoved me from behind did it unseen. My torso and head jerked forward, my forehead smacking against the marble wall. As the water continued to pour out and the tub continued to fill, I staggered backward. Will found me there, a bright welt on my forehead, steam rising out of the tub. He turned off the water and carried me to my room.

But it was Joanne who seemed most caught in the crosshairs of our suddenly whipped-up environment. The house had become a violently shaken snow-globe, and her room, it appeared, was at the center of it, a fact that quietly worried me. Any mother would rather be a target than her child. Several times Jo had woken up to see a large, shadowy figure sitting at the foot of her bed, wordless but unmoving. Once, the figure had come to the side of her bed and attempted to crawl in. She had jumped out of bed screaming and nearly flown to my room.

One day Joanne sat in her bedroom reading, an attempt to distract herself from the troubled atmosphere. She has an antique wooden rocking chair in her bedroom. In it sits an old doll from Louisiana. Suddenly the chair began to rock—slowly at first, then faster. The shutter doors of her walk-in closet swung open, and several articles of clothing flew out. That was it. She was in my room seconds later, and all three of us crowded into our bed.

The pets nuzzled close underneath at first. Then Puss 'N' Boots got up, marched toward the bedroom door, chose a spot near the middle of the doorway, and settled back down onto the floor, gently defiant. Soon the other pets followed suit, with Max, the bichon, last. They remained together at the threshold of the room, a row of furry sentries, united in their resolve. As I looked at them and smiled, my eyelids started to flutter. Eventually, sleep found me.

* * *

I woke to a pounding head, as I had every morning since Joanne had mailed the letter to Ronnie DeFeo. Will's stomach ached. Joanne hadn't slept a wink and was stiff all over. Worse, we were faced with a large mess to clean up—Joanne's room looked like it had been tossed—and no one to help do it. Abby had left running from the house the night before, vowing never to return. To this day, she still calls regularly, pleading for us to leave, too.

For Will, the closest thing to a religious temple is the gym. He bartends, often at night, and his usual morning ritual involves an early, intense workout before tackling the day. On this morning, he was supposed to be at an early meeting at the Sheraton, but he couldn't muster the strength to go either to the gym or to the meeting. I understood his bailing on the meeting; I was stunned at his bailing on the gym.

I heard Joanne on the phone with Adam. She was supposed to send him a homicide report on a case I'd asked to have reopened based on certain things I'd felt and seen. She hadn't delivered the report, and Adam, understandably, was concerned. Joanne never misses deadlines. She was exhausted, I heard her telling him. She just couldn't get herself going. Adam was asking if she'd been hurt. No, she said. He asked if she was okay, if anything had happened. "No," she said. "Everything's fine. I'm just tired."

"Fine," he said. "I'll come to you."

As I tried to get myself together, I looked over at Will

and Joanne, then at Joanne's room, and I knew it would be several hours before any of us could go anywhere. I told Joanne to cancel my appointments for the rest of the day.

It was around ten in the morning when the phone rang. Joanne looked for me and found me sitting up on the edge of her bed, sound asleep. I'm not much of a sleeper—on a good night I get maybe four or five hours—but I'm also not usually a sleep*walker*. Yet somehow I'd made my way to Joanne's bed and sat down on it unaware.

Joanne ignored the conventional advice about never waking a sleepwalker and bent down in front of me. "It's from Green Haven," she said. I woke up with a start. She handed me the phone, and I heard the operator ask if I would accept the charges. I told her yes.

After a pause, I said, "Is this Ronnie DeFeo?"

"Yes."

I inhaled deeply. "What do you want me to do?"

"Help me make it stop," came the response, spoken in a reedy, childlike voice. Then the voice immediately changed to a huskier one, and this voice said, "I've been waiting for you, Jackie. All grown up now." Then a third intonation, sharper and more cutting: "Oh, before I forget, poor Mommy says hello." A nasty chuckle followed, then humming. The humming turned to singing. I recognized the tune—"I Remember You," a song my mother used to sing around the house. The man on the other end of the line asked if I remembered him. He told me I was the only one who could handle what was inside. A darker voice told me I couldn't save him.

And then he mentioned the Surf Hotel.

* * *

Most children are taught to read and write, ride a bike, throw a ball, do fractions. Not me. My parents' interests for me lay outside most children's scope of the normal.

Mary recognized my abilities as early as I did. She would watch me paying close attention to the stream of socialites and entertainers who flocked to our back door hoping to be assured of fame and fortune. By the time I was five, she saw my gift, and she would have me participate in her séances, eventually assigning me the role of medium. But the responsibility came with stern warnings. This was not child's play; it was serious business. There is no God without the devil, she would tell me. You can't be on both sides.

It wasn't long before she and I both realized that my powers surpassed even hers. I was able to do something other mediums couldn't: I could absorb and pass along the spirit of the dead into the person yearning for connection. I was able, for a period, to become the person whom the other had lost. My mother made me her partner before I knew how to tie my shoes. I was able to witness her grimmest rites and the severity with which she warned people not to treat the spirits lightly.

One day, when I was ten, I heard a solemn hymn begin to flow through the house. I knew a ritual had begun. Mary, dressed completely in black, left through the back door and drove down the road.

Half an hour later, she returned, her face thoroughly bandaged, barely visible through the black veil. She wore small black gloves and carried a straw suitcase. Tears were rolling down her cheeks.

My grandmother opened the back door. "Joanie," she called to my mother. "Please come in." I didn't understand why she'd called her by a different name. She made tea and sat at the table, trying to offer words of comfort to the woman who, I now saw, my mother had become. It's going to be okay, my grandmother said. I sat there, quietly, and observed. A few days before, Mary had traveled to meet with a woman, Joanie, looking to escape an abusive marriage. And now she had turned into her.

My mother looked up at me, though it wasn't her face. Out of her mouth, in an uncharacteristically soft tone, came the words, "Who is this sweet child?" Then she began to remove the bandages, and I sat horrified. Her face was a map of black and blue, and her nose looked like it had decided to follow a different direction halfway down.

I knew what it meant. Mary had absorbed the woman utterly, in order to try to free her. She had taken on her pain with as much fullness as she could handle. The tears continued to roll, my grandmother continued to soothe, and I continued to watch, saying nothing.

Four days later, a headline on the front page of the newspaper reported a terrible car accident. The woman's husband was the victim. My mother, again returned to herself, read the story over her morning coffee with my grandmother. "Silly man," she said, shaking her head.

"Too bad nothing was left of the body. We could have done his wake, too." They shared a laugh.

On November 12, 1974, a séance was held in my house in Nola, and I, at the appointment of my mother, was the medium. She had been preparing for several days—placing candles on the altar, blessing the tablecloth in a ritual of music and dance, and preparing offerings for the spirit like liquor, cigars, coffee, money, and fruit. I had my own way of preparing: listening to Jim Morrison.

For a few nights before the séance, I couldn't sleep. News of my talents had spread quickly, and many people had come to our door curious about the young medium with the power to conduct the dead. But it wasn't the pressure of my odd rising stardom that was keeping me up. It was the nightmares.

I would constantly feel myself running from a creature that made hideous animal sounds. I would run down a series of endless steps toward a constantly receding hiding place, the wind stinging my face as I struggled to reach it. The ground shifted from concrete to mud to sand, and with every step I felt myself sinking as the creature gained. Soon I could feel a claw swiping at my legs, accompanied by the sound of howls coming from faces that were nearby but shrouded.

Finally, I would reach the shelter, a windowless space with the sensation of a tomb. Through the thick walls I could still hear the painful moans, which now merged with the animalistic growls that had pursued me.

I crouched in the corner of the room and began to sob. As one will in dreams, I tried to break out of it, wish myself back into reality. But something was pulling me back. I saw myself look up. My face was somewhat my own, but not completely. "Mommy, I'm scared," I said. I couldn't know it then, but it wasn't my face at all. It was Joanne's.

I tried to leap into the dream from that outside place, tried to break down the walls of logic and consciousness to rescue the crying little girl in the corner of the room. I didn't reach her, but something else did, and began to drag her down. Down she went, through the floor, into darkness. The last thing I would see was her face vanishing downward, followed by an upward spurt of blood. I screamed.

The nightmares alone were not the source of my anxiety. It was exhausting for a twelve-year-old girl to have to regularly invite, hold, and deliver the spirits of the dead. "It's your cross to bear, Jackie," Mary would say. "Learn both sides of the Bible. Those who want and those who need."

The sensation is hard to describe. Plus, I was only starting to become familiar with it. The spirit would enter me like a sudden wind, a kind of rush containing the adrenaline but not the pleasure. A flip-book of snapshots would roll through my head, a lightning series of images of a life I didn't know.

At some point—I couldn't predict whether it would be quick or slow—I would experience their deaths. To be their proper conduit, I needed to open myself fully. I would face their last moments, suffer their last breaths. If it had been a murder, I became both victim and killer, feeling fear and bloodlust together.

I was a powerhouse of energy, sometimes conducting energy among three people at once. When the spirit had been fully taken in, it could then be released and passed along. I would have answers, and the spirit would have solace. Hopefully.

That night, a family of five quietly filed into the room and took their seats. I didn't know any of their names, and I preferred it that way. I had learned not to interact any earlier than I had to. It wasn't yet dark out, but that didn't matter, since the room had no windows.

I could sense their fear as they passed me. A woman dressed in black handed my mother a picture. With tears in her eyes, she said, "Please, Momma, I need to feel him and see him." Though I wasn't allowed to call Mary "Mommy," she was "Momma" to everyone else.

My mother looked at me and said, "When you're ready, Jackie. Bring this young man through." She put the picture down at the head of the table, where I sat, then took her own spot off to the side. She lit three black candles and three white, and I started moving around the room. I picked up the picture. Soon I felt my body leaving as a vision of the woman's son, who had died from an overdose, visited me. His life had passed too quickly. I was falling now. I went to reach for the boy's mother. The ground below my feet seemed to disappear. I felt as though I was suspended in air. The family members all got up from their chairs and stumbled into a protective huddle.

My mother stepped between me and the family and commanded the entity, "Leave my child!" The candles lifted and smashed into the wall. I felt myself unable to respond as Jackie. Through the barrier of this other consciousness, I sensed my father trying to open the door of the séance room from the other side. It was splintering inward with his blows but not breaking. And I could feel my mother still standing before me, yelling commands.

I sensed that I was no longer inside my house or the séance room. I had been transported to a darker place, where I was now trying to get my bearings. I saw a wasteland of smoking trees burned to the stumps. Yet it was cold, my breath visible in front of me. I sensed many pairs of eyes peering at me, blurred faces, sobbing. I couldn't make a sound.

From opposite ends of the billowing smoke, two men walked toward me. One wore a jumpsuit; the other, gleaming-eyed, wore a dark business suit and had his hair slicked back into a short ponytail. He handed the man in the jumpsuit a piece of paper and a pen. I could see their mouths move but couldn't hear their words. As the man in the jumpsuit turned to walk away, the pen he'd used turned into a shotgun.

I turned, and the bright-eyed man suddenly grabbed me by my throat. "Remember me," he said. He threw me across the room, and I staggered several times trying to get up. Then he disappeared, and I was in a different room, where everything was upturned and broken. It was a different house, unfamiliar. I grabbed for a banister to right myself, but my hands only slipped off. A streak of blood stained the banister where my hands had been. The walls began to shake, jarring pictures from their hooks and a chandelier from its mounting.

As the crystals of the chandelier shattered against the floor, I heard laughter from the top of the steps. The man in the jumpsuit was there, yelling down to me.

"You're too late!" he shouted. "I'll be back!"

I felt the house was going to cave in. Gun blasts echoed off the walls. I covered my ears, then my eyes. When I opened my eyes again, I was back at the séance, crumpled on the floor. The members of the family were no longer there. They had all run out screaming.

My father ran over and picked me up. I saw my mother standing in the corner of the room, a fevered expression on her face. She was rambling, spouting words I didn't recognize. My father took me to my room and lay me down in bed.

There was a room in our house that usually stayed padlocked. It was opened only when Mary felt an exorcism needed to be carried out. The room had a small pull-out bed, lots of religious relics, a large Sicilian Bible, a wooden chair whose straps made it look eerily like an electric chair, and a chalked circle around the bottom of the chair lined with candles, open jars, and mirrors.

I wasn't supposed to see the exorcisms at that age, but like any child, I was often too curious for my own good. I knew when they happened because the special door would be unlocked, the atmosphere in the house would change, and my mother would sit alone for hours, pre-paring.

One day, I sneaked over and watched. A man was brought in, along with a priest and the local doctor. The man was strapped to the chair, terror stamped on his face. My mother, calm but intense, began the rite, chanting, moaning, growing in fervor and volume. This lasted until the following morning, when she finally declared the spirit cast off. I wasn't frightened by my mother's behavior or by the presence of the priest and the doctor. What I still carry with me, however, is the terrible look on the man's face.

Mary knew I had watched. Had probably meant for it to happen. She took me aside the next day. "Respect both sides, Jackie," she told me. "The dead warrant the same respect as the living."

As I got older, she insisted that I graduate from séances to exorcisms. Prepare to endure, she would say. The spirit or the demon rushes through you before it is expelled, and you must house that evil. Some of us are vessels; we don't choose it. Spirituality is a two-sided coin, Jackie. Never forget that. Doors open, and we must choose whether to walk through them.

She died walking through one of those doors. During the storm. Katrina. Both of them, I always said, she and my dad. Both passed in the storm.

At least, that's what I've always told people.

She didn't, of course.

THREE

Sometimes I'm pulled into a situation for reasons I'm not aware of, and all I can do under such circumstances is arm myself with information. That's where Joanne comes in. There are people who research because they have to do it for their jobs, and there are people who do it because they love it. Joanne is the second type, and I'm grateful every day.

The energy drawing me toward Ronnie DeFeo was powerful, but it was also frightening, setting me on edge somewhere deep down in my bones. Before I pursued the conversation with him any further, I wanted facts.

Joanne had jumped in with both feet, as she always does. The good news was that there was no shortage of information on the Amityville murders; the bad news was that it was from a great variety of sources, most of them unreliable.

But that's another thing she's good at: separating the

wheat from the chaff. Her bullshit meter is at least as keen as mine, if not more so. Much of the information she came across, she discarded immediately. Instead, she assembled as much information as she could that she felt passed the test of trustworthiness, then laid it all out and fused the different parts into the most consistent story she could. It would at least give me some context.

This much seemed clear: Ronnie DeFeo had been a spoiled young man who used drugs regularly and got in trouble often, probably for lack of a better idea. He worked a vague job at the family's car dealership in Brooklyn, cruised the Amityville River in a personal speedboat his parents had given him, and got abused regularly by his hotheaded father.

Ronnie had been born and raised in Brooklyn. When he was thirteen, in 1964, the DeFeos had moved into the majestic, four-thousand-square-foot Dutch Colonial on the shores of Long Island, at 112 Ocean Avenue. Their new house was a postcard of the American Dream: two stories, a big attic that served as a third floor, a finished basement, a heated in-ground pool, a sun porch—the whole nine yards, including a boathouse on the river. Along with Ronnie, there were three other siblings: Dawn, five years his junior, Allison, herself five years younger than Dawn, and Marc, a year younger than Allison. The year after the DeFeos moved into their new home, another brother, John Matthew, would be born. The two young boys would share a bedroom, as would Dawn and Allison. Ronnie, as the eldest child, had the benefit of being the only family member with his own room. And Ronald DeFeo Sr., Ronnie's dad, would pound into the ground, on the front lawn, a now-famous sign containing two simple words: *High Hopes.*

On the evening of November 13, 1974, the DeFeos went to bed. In the morning, they were all dead, except Ronnie. Two shots had killed Ronald DeFeo Sr., one through his kidney and one into his spine, lodging in his neck. His wife, Louise, had also been shot twice, one shattering her rib cage, the other puncturing her right lung. The brothers, Marc and John, had each been killed by a single shot to the back as they lay prone in their beds, the bullets having ripped through their bodies and become lodged in their mattresses. The sisters, Allison and Dawn, must have stirred or tried to defend themselves, because they'd gotten parts of their faces blown off. It had all happened within minutes, around three in the morning.

And that's where the story gets cloudy. It was clear Ronnie had burst into his local watering hole late the next day—nearly a full day after the deaths—and shouted about something having happened to his family. It was known that some friends had accompanied him to the house, broke in through a window, and discovered his family dead. It was fact that Ronnie had been questioned by the police in his kitchen, then at the neighbors', then at the precinct, first for his own protection—he'd named a local Mafia figure as the likely killer, and they were worried the guy might be after him, too—then as a suspect. And once the police found shell casings matching Ronnie's gun, they'd decided the more likely murderer was the one sitting in front of them. Plenty of others had been questioned, too, but ultimately released. Only one man would have to stand accused.

The trial that put Ronnie behind bars forever started nearly a year after the murders and lasted just over two months. He had, at the direction of his lawyer, William Weber, tried to act insane, but it didn't fly, and the prosecutor had eventually worn him down, just as he would wear down the series of psychological experts the defense would call to the stand to try to paint a picture of Ronnie DeFeo as someone unaware of his actions at the time of the murders. He'd done it, Ronnie had admitted in court. He'd killed them all, then had discarded the evidence, gone to work, gotten high with some friends, and, eventually, run into the bar trying to act his way out of it all.

That story hadn't worked, either, because of the shell casings. They'd matched one of the many guns Ronnie owned—a .35-caliber rifle, the same type of gun that had been responsible for the killings. The discovery of the shell casings had prompted a search for the gun itself, which had been recovered by divers in the shallow waters by the DeFeos' boathouse. It was a slam dunk. Ronnie DeFeo was given six consecutive life sentences. Since the murders were deemed one continuous act, he could serve the terms concurrently and be eligible for parole in 1999. He'd had parole hearings since, which, predictably, had gone nowhere.

Were it not for George and Kathy Lutz—and Ronnie's lawyer, Weber—he might eventually have been forgotten, just another briefly notorious killer left to rot in jail. Instead, a few years after the killings, *The Amityville Hor-*

ror was released. The book went gangbusters, a movie followed, and 112 Ocean Avenue became a character all its own. With it, Ronnie DeFeo's legend grew.

The Lutzes became minor celebrities. But people started to question the claims made in the book, in particular the fact that it seemed to contain a virtual kitchen sink of nasty paranormal entities, from beds rising up off the floor to a sixty-seven-piece marching band led by a pig with red eyes. The most fantastic parts of the story were picked apart again and again, until finally Weber admitted they had fabricated the story for commercial interests. The Lutzes, who stood by their story until the end, would soon vanish from public memory. But not Ronnie DeFeo. More books and movies followed over the years, some dissecting the crime, others examining the life of the DeFeos, still others delving into the personality and character of the alleged killer himself.

Three questions from the original trial seemed to persist. First, reminiscent of Lee Harvey Oswald, was the question of whether Ronnie DeFeo had acted alone. Certain individuals, like Herman Race, a private investigator hired by Ronnie's grandfather on his mother's side, Mike Brigante, believe that one person *couldn't* have killed six people in their beds that night with a high-powered rifle, execution-style.

The second question had to do with the police procedure surrounding the murders. Several witnesses suggested that the police had done everything they could to secure a confession from the young delinquent, ultimately beating it out of him.

Finally, and most puzzling, was the fact that no one ever reported having heard a shot fired in the house, even though no fewer than five different people in the neighborhood said they heard the DeFeos' dog, Shaggy, barking like mad that night while he was tied to the boathouse.

Regarding Ronnie himself, no single theory had ever really taken hold, mostly because he had changed his story numerous times over the years, starting with that very first conversation after the murders, in which he'd implicated a local mobster. Later, at the precinct, Ronnie admitted to participating in the killings but named different accomplices at different times. By the time the case got to trial, Weber had advised him simply to act as crazy as he could in order to try to get off on insanity. But only people who are truly insane genuinely come off that way.

In later years, Ronnie would suddenly point the finger at Dawn, eighteen at the time of the murders, as the mastermind of the whole thing. A major question in the courtroom had been what to make of the unburned gunpowder found on Dawn's nightgown after the killing. Some pointed to this as evidence that she had fired a gun. But the question had been explained away by experts showing that gunshot residue can appear not only on the shooter but also the victim, if she is close enough. Still later, Ronnie DeFeo would tell the parole board he simply couldn't remember the events of that night at all.

I, like the rest of the world, didn't know what to believe.

FOUR

I can usually tell a lot from people's voices—sometimes everything. But the first time I heard Ronnie DeFeo's voice, it seemed strangely shrouded. The voice was high and slightly rasping, the agitated voice of someone trying to make a point and hoping anyone within earshot will listen. Even during our first phone call, I learned one thing quickly about Ronnie DeFeo. It wasn't easy to keep him on track. At least, not on one track.

It's hard to remember everything we talked about on that first call. Even saying "we" is a bit inaccurate, since it was mostly him doing the talking. He spoke fast and urgent, like a little kid desperately trying to make sure he doesn't lose your attention. The voice was like a pinched hose that had been released, the words coming furiously. He spoke about being older and in poor health. He spoke about needing to tell the truth. He spoke about release—not from prison but from pain. I didn't say much, yet at the end of the conversation, when his allotted time was up, I somehow felt we'd shared about the same amount with each other.

After that, he began calling every day. I came to understand that our most productive mutual rhythm involved letting Ronnie talk while I toggled between two roles: facilitator, pushing him to go on when he got quiet; and moderator, calming him down when he got too overwrought and needed to be reined back in.

During our conversations, there would be periods of several minutes where I said nothing, only listened or offered words of acknowledgment to let Ronnie know that I was still there. Much of the time, when he got especially distressed, I wasn't even sure he was aware of someone listening at the other end. He was venting to the air.

Of course, what goes up must come down. His feverish tone could only last so long. There were many times he would end one conversation abrasive and edgy only to begin the next one quiet and subdued. I soon learned that this pattern would become normal. On a given day, I wasn't sure which Ronnie I would get—the tense, aggressive one; the somber, sad one; or something in between. Listening to him was a roller-coaster ride, though his expressiveness never failed to surprise me.

Speaking to a man convicted of killing six of his family members, I tried to place any bias or preconception aside. When I didn't know whether someone was being straight with me, I trusted my psychic sense, which had been my sole true guide since I was a child. I'd had enough crazies contact me over the years that I approached every conversation with caution. Ronnie knew things about me, but not the kinds of things people find on the Internet. He knew about the Surf Hotel. Almost no one knew about that.

I had two tools available to me: my intuition and my willingness to listen. Sometimes you need to pull words out of the person you're talking to. Other times, those words come in an unremitting stream. With Ronnie, my task wasn't to elicit the words; it was to try to make sense of them.

I listened, paid attention, and looked for the trigger points. One morning, a few weeks after our first conversation, I asked him, as I had in my original letter, why he felt we were meant to connect. There were two reasons, he told me. First, it was time for the world to know the truth about what happened in that house, and I was the one to tell them.

Second, he needed my help. "I'm being haunted," he told me.

"Who's haunting you?" I asked.

"He's back," Ronnie said. "He wants to finish the job."

"Ronnie, what are you talking about?" I said.

"All my life that bastard was beating me up, and now he wants to finish the job. The week before everything happened, he busted a pool stick over my head. I come in the room and bam, right over my head. That shit hurt. He almost knocked me out. Now all this happening in my cell. It's him. He hasn't had enough."

There was little linearity but plenty of consistency in Ronnie DeFeo's stories. I knew that each of his rants, each little snippet, were pieces of a larger mystery. I tried to remain indifferent as Ronnie unveiled his secrets. I knew bullshit the moment it appeared, and I did not suffer fools. His words, though bizarre, felt authentic.

"Slow down, Ronnie," I said. "Tell me about what's happening in your cell."

"I had to put a towel over my mirror after what happened last night. Four o'clock in the morning. My cell, you know, isn't that big, so I got up out of the chair, was writing you a letter, I passed the mirror, all of a sudden I saw his face, my father's face. If eyes were daggers, I'd be dead, I swear. His mouth was moving but I couldn't hear anything. That son of a bitch."

Thanks to Joanne's expert briefing, I knew Ronnie's father, Ronald DeFeo Sr., quite well. He had been, in many ways, the picture of the American dream, a second-generation Italian American who had scrounged up enough to buy into a modest Buick dealership with his wife Louise's family, the Brigantes, and eventually had moved his family into one of the country's posh spots, Long Island's south shore. The quaint-looking *High Hopes* sign he'd placed in the ground on the front lawn was a message to the rest of the world that he wanted the dream to continue.

He'd employed his son Ronnie, who he'd nicknamed "Butch," at the dealership, not because of Butch's work ethic or desire to start a career but to try to keep him out of trouble, something for which he showed an unfortunate knack.

"Why did your father call you Butch?" I asked Ronnie.

"That was my name growing up," he replied. "No one called me Ronnie. I only became Ronnie after all that shit happened with my family, after I got to jail. Until then I was Butch DeFeo to everyone. I guess he probably did it so we wouldn't share a name. It was a serious mistake me telling my friends my name was Ronnie, because people would call the house and my father would answer the phone and start getting pissed. 'Your name is Butch; your name isn't Ronnie.' My grandparents, everybody. None of them called me by my real name."

"Why do you think the face in the mirror is your father's?" I asked. "What business does he have with you now?"

Ronnie went on without answering my question, a move that would become typical. "I started screaming for the guard, I swear to God. Then I realized the guard ain't coming. I'm locked in this cell; I gotta deal with it. Drove me nuts, I'm telling you. He's really back."

I'd learned that I had two choices when Ronnie went off on one of his restless tangents. I could either try to pull him back, or—at moments like this, when his speech accelerated and the tension in it climbed—I could simply go along and wait for him to come back to the story. Eventually, he always did.

"He used to say about a dozen times a week, 'I brought you into this world, I can take you out of it.' You knew exactly what he was saying. I had to hear this everyday. He drove me to use the fucking drugs, I'm telling you."

Whenever I spoke to Ronnie, I did two things: I recorded our conversations—I'd gotten his permission during the first phone call—and I kept Joanne's research files in front of me. If Ronnie mentioned something noteworthy, unfamiliar, or both, I'd make a note to myself to come back to it later. It was the only way to keep him even slightly focused.

"Last night I was brushing my teeth, and one fell out.

It's next to the one that got knocked out when the bastard threw a chair at me when I was eleven and hit me in the face. Those two things happened at the same exact time, 9:35. I remember that, because you remember when your father throws a chair at you and knocks your teeth out. A wooden high chair, he bought it in the lumberyard. That thing was solid oak."

"Did it happen a lot?" I asked. But Ronnie was no longer listening. He was on to a new topic that would come to demand the same recurring airtime as his father's abuse: his mother's supposed affairs.

"No wonder he was so mad, the way my mother was running around. Who knows how many there were? I only knew about the hairstylist, that she was doing once a week, and Brother Isaac, who was my gym teacher, if you can believe that. But maybe there were other ones, too. Who knows?"

"Hold on. Leave your mother aside for now."

"My father made me bury the garbage bag with the heart in it, for Christ's sake. I'll never forget it. I stayed in the shower for a half hour, I swear to God, scrubbing myself."

"I've got to go, Ronnie," I said at this point, hanging up and shutting off the tape. His time limit was approaching. Plus, I wasn't ready for the new direction he had started to take. I was still considering what he'd said about an evil entity in his cell. Though I had lengthy experience with evil, I needed to take things slowly. Ronnie was a spout you couldn't turn off if you let it go too long. It was easier to take in everything he had to say in small doses.

As I hung up the phone, a lovely scent hit my nostrils—

something clean, fresh, and mildly spicy. I walked downstairs, found Joanne at her computer, and asked if she was burning something, eucalyptus maybe. She shook her head no.

The next morning, Ronnie called early, just after daybreak. The first thing he said was, "I was in the day room last night, and suddenly I got hit in the shoulder. Twice."

"What do you mean, Ronnie?"

"Just what I said. I'm standing in the day room, and something clips me in the shoulder, hard, two times. When I look up, nothing's there. Then suddenly there was this clean, fresh smell, really strong, whooshes right underneath my nose. Like a spirit playing tag or something. Boom, I got you."

A spirit playing tag. Maybe.

"Tell me more about your dad, Ronnie."

"I was trying to tell you yesterday. They made me bury the garbage bag with the heart in it. From Brother Isaac. I mean, come on."

"We'll get to that, Ronnie. I want you to put it aside for a bit. Tell me when your father started hitting you."

"Forever. Three, four. The guy took me on whenever he felt like it. There was plenty of beatings, for no reason at all. None whatsoever. You ask me if I knew what I did wrong. How could I know? I was a kid." His voice was spiraling upward again. "It happened all the goddamn time. When I was nineteen, he busted my lips open. The top and the bottom. I ran to the forest."

Here he paused uncharacteristically. In my conversations with Ronnie DeFeo, I was normally able to get a word in only when I guessed at the right spot to jump in. Often he would still speak over me, desperate to relieve himself of all the anxious thoughts battling for space in his head.

I believe the reason for his pause now was the same reason for my not filling it. We had come to a mutual crossroads. In every relationship there comes a moment where both parties must decide how much they trust each other.

"You want proof?" he finally said.

"Proof of what?"

"You want to be able to trust me?"

"Yeah," I said. "I want to be able to trust you."

And that's how I found myself standing at the edge of a forest.

"I had a coin," Ronnie had told me. "He gave it to me when I was nineteen. Had an Indian head on it. I still had that coin before everything happened."

I hadn't yet asked him about the murders, partly because I was still trying to figure out why I'd been thrust into this strange association in the first place. The other reason was that I'd learned the need for patience. Killers were often victims, and victims were often killers. Ronnie DeFeo had told me plenty, and still only seemed to be warming up. I was confident he would tell me the truth when he was ready. The last thing I wanted to do was scare him away.

There was a third reason. I may not have known at that point what I was really meant to do for Ronnie DeFeo, but it's fair to say I had begun to suspect that there truly were dark entities afoot which had to do with him. And in order to fight evil, you need to first learn what tortures the soul of someone who has committed it.

Though *Medium P.I.* had never made it to air, I was still in touch with the production team that had been on the canal with me. They were aware of my peculiar relationship with Ronnie DeFeo. When I told them I'd be searching for a coin in the forest, they asked if I'd be willing to appear on a televised special about my journey with him. More important, they said, would *he* be willing to appear? I told them I would be okay with it as long as I felt it was done properly. When I put the question to Ronnie, he was okay with it, too. He was ready to talk, and was happy to have as large an audience as possible to hear his side.

As I approached the south shore forest with the cameras following me, I hoped I was wrong. I hoped Ronnie DeFeo would prove to be a liar, so I could dismiss everything he had told me, end our communications, and go on with my life. The cameras would be there to prove there was nothing to Ronnie's claims.

The forest lay three miles from 112 Ocean Avenue, near the corner of Ocean and Merrick Road. Behind it, Croons Lake, also called the Massapequa Water Reserve, sat undisturbed. At the opposite end, the so-called Bogeyman Park led to Bethpage State Park, a popular recreational site among teens and adults alike.

As I took the first step into the forest, a feeling immediately started to gnaw at me, something I wanted terribly to smother. It wanted out; I wanted it to stay in.

"It was before everything happened," Ronnie had said. Though at no point yet had he discussed the night of the murders in any detail, he had made several allusions, always referring to it as *when everything happened* or *when my family died*.

"One day he decided to give me a beating," he had said. I'd asked him why.

"I don't know why. How do I know why? That's what I'm trying to tell you. It was out of nowhere, like usual. He punched me in the face and busted my lips open. The top and the bottom. I took off. I ran to the woods near our house. I grabbed that goddamn coin and buried it. I didn't want anything to do with him, and that coin was part of him. He collected them, thirty, forty years, maybe more than that. He had every kind of coin. I buried it and left it there. You want to know you can trust me? Go dig up that coin."

At first I didn't know what to make of Ronnie's words. How was I going to find a single coin in a forest, not to mention one buried more than thirty-five years ago? It smacked of the kind of test a madman gives you for no reason other than to exert control. But a voice inside told me to go, and so I went. Now here I stood, steps inside the forest.

As I stared at the trees and the brush, I began to change. I always hesitate to try to describe the experience, because it rarely translates well into words, but I'll try, and you may judge it, and me, however you like. What happens is that my own spirit slips away for a while in order to make room for another, like taking a brief vacation from the space you usually occupy and temporarily subletting it to someone else. I feel this other spirit as something tangible, as though suddenly given a different pair of eyes to see with or a different body to master. Don't picture *Field of Dreams*. I'm not walking into a cornfield and disappearing. I very much remain physically. The part of me that becomes imbued with something else is spiritual. Some call it possession; some transformation. Me, I don't care what you call it. I just know what it feels like.

Moments after entering the forest, I sensed Ronnie's voice guiding me. I intentionally don't say I "heard" Ronnie's voice, because that isn't quite right. It isn't like wearing an earpiece and somebody talking into it. No—it's a feeling.

There were no footpaths or markers in the south shore forest. It was thick, enjoyable perhaps for squirrels and rabbits, but not a good place to search for an object no more than an inch around. I weaved my way through the dense foliage, along the uneven forest floor, around potential clusters of poison ivy, wondering how in the world I was supposed to unearth a single coin among the expanse. For nearly an hour I followed Ronnie's silent direction, not yet knowing whether to trust him.

Soon his voice told me to angle slightly in a particular direction and walk forward, to the base of a sugar maple. I knelt in the dirt and began to dig. As I clawed at the ground and tossed aside one small handful of dirt after another, a hulking spider, the kind I used to see in the swamps of New Orleans, crawled up my forearm and across my shoulders. I swept it off and continued.

A few minutes later, my knees damp, my fingernails caked with earth, I spotted it: a faded, round edge of something metal. I pulled it out.

An Indian-head coin. With dried blood on it.

FIVE

My father called his moonshine the best this side of the Mississippi. He would show me how to make it. It sat in an old bathtub with cut-up fruit and potatoes, an oversized wooden stick always at the ready for mixing. I would fill the old jelly jars with the stuff, place them into a pillowcase, and off I went, a five-year-old girl happy as punch to go play with the hobos by the tracks.

Dad made like he didn't know, but he did. I think his respect for the hobos made it okay. When I got older, he leaned down and said to me, "I knew you took my moonshine to those folks to make them happy. It isn't hard to spot the smile of a man who's just had a good sip." He'd laugh and smile at me in his big, warm way.

I would sit by the railroad tracks where he worked and play games with the hobos. I understood their nomadic souls. Sometimes I would go down there alone just to visit them. They were my secret family, always carrying a smile and a song.

One of the hobos, Old Mr. Johnny, could play the guitar like nobody's business. The rumor was that he'd come from the Mississippi swamp back in the day to see Momma, and she had granted him his wish, which was to be able to play and sing just like the King. The wish had come true, but Old Mr. Johnny had walked away without respecting the gift he'd been given. Momma had smiled and said, "Oh my, Old Mr. Johnny forgot to pay his dues. What a shame." And just like that, he'd lost his hearing. All those crowds clapping and yelling his name, him hearing none of it, unable even to hear his own music.

Sometimes I'd bring the hobos food, too, if it didn't seem the moonshine was enough. I would bring the outside world to them—newspapers, gossip from town—and they would soak it up happily. "I hear the steps!" they would say as I approached. "The young shall lead the old!"

They taught me the things that at the time were most important: how to skip a rock, how to open a can with a pocketknife, how to play the spoons on one knee, how to tell when the train was coming by listening to the ground, what to put on red ant bites. The rule among them was no shoes allowed, and to this day I prefer to be barefoot.

As soon as a train pulled up, the stories would fly. The hobos would talk about how one day we would all sit in the dining car like the rich folks with their fancy china. One day I sneaked onto a train heading north. It wasn't the way they'd imagined it. The dining cars didn't have china at all. But nowadays, I still use a china tea cup every morning.

The leader of the group was an old guy named Mr. Gramp. One evening I was helping them build a fire, and Mr. Gramp looked at me and said, "You a cowboy with no belt." Then he cut some rope, and that rope became my belt. I still have it. I would sit and take everything in, how they shared food, moonshine, smokes, music. They helped me find the human side of life, taught me real lessons. Crawl if you can't walk. Eat that pound of dirt if that's what there is to eat. But there was one cardinal rule you would violate at your own peril: never say Momma's name out loud. I saw the fear in their eyes. She'll get ya like she got Old Mr. Johnny.

One morning I came to the tracks to find that Mr. Gramp had passed in his sleep. I was seven. Mr. Gramp had always read the news to me from the papers I brought. But at some point I realized he could never actually read at all. He'd just been making up stories for my entertainment. When the train pulled in that late afternoon, we all put something in Mr. Gramp's pocket to carry on his journey, as was tradition. I gave him a stone that I'd carried for a long time—so he could make soup in the next domain—and a dried flower. Then I stood back and watched the others place Mr. Gramp comfortably in the laundry car, where he would be carried away—to where, we could only guess. Life changes form but doesn't die.

A few days later I was sitting in my bedroom reading, and when I looked up, I saw Mr. Gramp sitting in a chair in the corner. I knew he'd come to say good-bye. I walked over to him and felt the temperature in my room drop. With a smile, Mr. Gramp gestured me closer. I put my ear to his mouth. "I love you," he said. And then he was gone.

Whenever I travel back to New Orleans, I go by train. I take the sleeper car. It's a twenty-seven-hour journey from New York City, and I love every minute of it. Passing the lazy Mississippi, the shotgun houses, folks waving as the train slows down and passes. I watch my past sliding by me in slow motion.

That tough Canadian blood coursed hard through my father's veins. He never felt it necessary to wear a coat, not even in the middle of a winter storm. He'd carry his big, black lunch pail and bring down his sledgehammer with glory and pride. I would sit and watch the sparks jump with every blow.

He worked on pipelines, bridges. His hands were constantly dirty and bloody, and he liked it that way. He'd smile looking at the labor his hands had endured. A man's hands tell his life, he would say. He had a side-to-side swagger that said I'm unbothered, but don't be fooled. "Never put your head down, Jackie," he would tell me.

Once I was trying to climb the big oak in our front yard, and I fell, badly. My dad stood slowly up from the porch but didn't come over to rescue me. The blood dripped down my cheek, and my eye stung. I was ready to let out a howl of pain—but then, seeing him, I stopped. Instead I brushed the grass and leaves from my shorts and walked over to him. He took my hand tenderly and said, "Cowboys don't cry."

We went into the embalming room in the back of the house, and he sat me on the draining table, a flat tub with a drain and hoses where the corpses would be siphoned of any remaining fluids before being prepared. There was a wooden sign that hung above the door with the words *Out of this world into the next* burned in. Below the words was da Vinci's pentagram, the wheel of life, the five-point sign of protection.

My father wiped a damp cloth across my eye. "Ain't that bad," he said, then he took one of the sickle-shaped needles and some black thread that my mother would use to sew up the mouths of the dead. "Bite this," he said, handing me a rag. Then he stitched me up.

Often, when the day was done, I would sit on the edge of my bed and he would teach me the blues. Whereas my mother played her beguiling tunes on the piano, my dad's musical tools were more rural: the fiddle, the harmonica, the spoons. By the time I was six, I could play all of them, and they came to be my escape from the feeling of constant commune with otherworldly souls, walking around my bedroom, those spirits from this realm and the one beyond, lost, drifting, knowing I was there watching. I didn't know what they wanted.

My father believed in the spirit as profoundly as Mary, but he derived something different from it. His rituals were out in the light, pure, part of a tradition and a line. I would help him build a fire and then dance around it while thumping a canvas drum and chanting. He built those fires and did those dances and banged on those drums to call on our ancestors for guidance. He summoned the spirits to help him find his center and stay out of the shadows. My mother walked into those shadows and never returned.

I didn't know whether Ronnie DeFeo was bad from the inside out, whether his father had convinced him he was, or whether a dark spirit had invaded him at a vulnerable point in his existence. If it was the latter, perhaps I had been thrown on to this path to help. I had observed evil and its endless incarnations. I had seen demons in various forms occupy people and places, and I had learned of the terrible deeds they had sometimes done while swayed by darkness. I had seen it break individuals and families apart. And I had tried to outrun it. I was starting to wonder whether it was now cornering me in the form of a man who had been incarcerated for more than half his life.

Ronnie had been talking about his father almost constantly during our calls, and I got the sense that he'd keep on doing so unless I forced him in another direction.

"I was bad," Ronnie said. "I know I was bad. Certain people, I guess they're born that way. I wish I wasn't, but I guess I was."

"Ronnie, were you ever involved in the occult?" I didn't know why I was asking the question. My intuition told me to.

"I went to a meeting once," he said.

"How old were you?"

"When I was a kid, I ran away a lot to get away from that son of a bitch. I always went to Greenwich Village. I used to have dreams all the time, good ones, bad ones. Anyway, I had this dream that I was gonna run into a pretty girl with blonde hair that was gonna have a brand-new convertible, what kind of car I wasn't sure, but the bad thing about the girl in my dream was she was a member of the occult and very high up in the ranks. Well, when I ran away, I was going to Saint Francis Prep School at the time, I was either fourteen or fifteen, and I met this girl in the Village; her name was Wanda. She was attractive; she had, you know, it was a front, they try to lure people. She had an all-red Ford Galaxie convertible. Brand-new, with white interior and white top. And sure enough, she tried to recruit me."

"Recruit you for what?"

"She told me she was a priestess, and they worshipped the devil. I was already familiar with Lucifer—I went to Catholic school all my life. Supposed to be twelve years, but it was thirteen and a half, they held me back one. So I knew about religion. She wanted me to go to Ohio with her. She said, 'I practice here, too.' I said, 'Practice?' "

"Did you know what she was talking about?"

"How the hell would I know what she's talking about? Like I said, I learned that shit all through school, but that ain't the same as meeting a girl who says she's a priestess. She said, 'Tomorrow night there's gonna be a meeting here, and you're gonna come with me. Then we're gonna go to Ohio.' I said, 'You're not gonna use me as a human sacrifice.' 'Ha ha ha,' she says. 'We don't do that.' "

"Were you scared?"

"I don't know; I mean, she was pretty good-looking."

"She was good-looking, so you weren't scared?"

"Blonde, nice build, about five-seven. And she was up there, in her thirties, maybe. She had a carload of people."

"So you went?"

"I went to the first meeting. The local one."

"Where was this?"

"Down by the Meatpacking District, Tenth, near the Hudson."

I knew the area he was referring to, where, at night, a lot of the buildings turn into underground clubs. I also knew that it was an area where people had often gone missing. Many of the buildings there look shut down or boarded up. But after dark—long after—the place comes to life. Although maybe that isn't exactly the right way to say it, given the reason for a lot of these meetings.

"We drove. I took one of the cars."

"One of whose cars?"

"My father would let me use a bunch of different cars from the dealership, and they were all 100 percent good shape, didn't have to worry about breaking down or anything. Except I was a little nervous because the one I took had New York plates, which I figured would be strike one to the people we met if [we] went to Ohio. People outside of New York don't always like New Yorkers, you know what I mean?"

"I certainly do."

"And I had two antennas right next to each other, on the right front fender. One was a power antenna, went up and down electronically; the other one was solid-mass stainless steel, thirty inches, for my FM radio. That would probably be strike two, 'cause it made the car look like a cop car. And then I had a PBA badge in my wallet."

"The gold one?" I had one of those myself. A PBA— Patrolmen's Benevolent Association—badge is a card, an honorary one, indicating that the holder is part of the broader family of law enforcement, or at least that he or she is tight with someone on the force.

"Yeah, the gold one."

"How did you get a PBA badge?"

"My dad knew a lot of cops. Anyway, when we got there, I opened my wallet and they saw the PBA badge, and now they think I'm a cop. But I told them, 'Look, the cops ain't any friends of mine, and I ain't one. You can search me or the car if you want.' They did, and then they convinced themselves I was okay. They opened the door and let me in, and this guy named Wayne greets me. Right away he starts talking Satan this and Satan that. Behind him, there are people holding flares burning at both ends. It was a real circus."

"But you wanted to stay?" My question went ignored. As so often happened, Ronnie was caught up in the momentum of his own words.

"They were for real. They all had black gowns with hoods. Every one of them. They gave me one to wear. Everybody looks the same. There's a reason for that, so nobody knows who the other person is. So I went through that ordeal. But I didn't go to Ohio with her."

"Did you go to any more meetings?"

"One other one, that a different female took me to. Her name was Lauren. And I'm gonna tell you straight out, I saw shit go down in that meeting that scared me good. I don't even want to remember that stuff, okay? These guys went the whole nine yards is what I'm trying to say. And I couldn't just leave, because the girl I was with, God knows what coulda happened to her, and I really liked her, so I stayed. Later on I told her look, to each his own, but that shit ain't my cup of tea."

I didn't bother to ask more details about what Ronnie had seen or thought he'd seen. I already knew it wasn't easy trying to tease out the parts of Ronnie DeFeo's stories that made sense and the parts that, well, required a dose of skepticism. I was familiar with the world of dark practices, however, and I knew what went on behind its doors. I didn't know what he'd seen and what he hadn't, and I wasn't confident he knew, either. But I knew that world was real.

"I said hey, that coulda been you or me. But she wanted to be a part of it. So that was the end of that. Good-bye, Lauren."

In Louisiana, the police would come to our house asking to speak to the child with the strange gift. They were having some difficulty getting to the bottom of a certain case, they'd say, and they wondered if they might talk to her. I may have been a kid in numeric age, but I hadn't really been one for a long time, if ever.

"Please come in," Mary would say. They would sit at the kitchen table, and I'd be summoned. "Come on in here, Jackie. These gentlemen need to speak to you about something important. Try to help them."

Typically they would slide a picture under my hand. "Tell us, Jackie," they would say. "What do you see?"

There was one girl, a small girl, like me, but more innocent looking. A fat detective had come to our house with his partner and the girl's anguished father. The fat detective had passed her photo to me across the table, which I now held under my palm.

The transformation was almost immediate. I fell back on my chair, assaulted by the smell of burning flesh in my nostrils. I ran out the front door. My mother, the detective, and the girl's father followed.

I reached the lawn and stumbled. I was on the grass now, rolling around, trying to rid myself of the vision. The fat detective started to approach me, but Mary held him back. "Wait," she said. "Wait."

The smell subsided, and a pretty girl, slightly shorter than me, appeared at my side. It was the girl from the picture. I stood up slowly and looked at her. She held out her hand. I took it. Together we began to cry.

She leaned toward me, whispered something in my ear, and pointed toward her father. When I looked at him, he sprinted.

The pretty young girl had revealed everything to me. Her father had set her on fire in order to collect the insurance money on her life. When he took off around the side of my house, toward the backyard, the detectives ran after him, along with my mother and me. But he was fast for a big man. We were losing ground.

Then, suddenly, the man buckled, his legs giving way, and he started screaming. I turned around to see my father standing outside the back door, holding his revolver. He placed the gun down as casually as if he'd just shot a tin can, walked over to me, and laid his big, gentle hands on my shoulders as the detectives handcuffed the girl's father and recited Miranda.

"Enough of this," my father said, crouching down to me. "Jacks," he said, looking into my eyes. He called me Jacks after the playground game, because, he said, you never knew where I was going to land. "When you get old enough, go. Go far away, and don't let anyone in unless you have to." He pointed to my forehead.

But word was out, and the police kept coming. Detectives, district attorneys, the FBI. All of them wanted a piece of me, their secret junior recruit. They watched me closely and visited often. They would use my help but not talk about it.

They couldn't. Who would believe them? And, more important, they really didn't care who might believe them or who might not. In their line of work, as in mine, they saw things on a regular basis that most people don't ever see, and they cared about one thing only: whether I could help find, and place, missing pieces to all sort of different puzzles.

Ronnie and I had continued to talk about the occult meetings he'd attended close to home. But, as we talked, I got the sense that he had gone farther afield to explore the dark arts. My intuition told me to ask him if he'd ever visited my original stomping grounds. I asked.

"After what I saw and heard in those meetings, I wanted to go see what it was all really about," he said.

"And?"

"And there's only one place to do that. I was about twenty. I jumped in the car and went."

"To New Orleans."

"I was too curious not to go."

"What did you tell your parents?"

"Nothing. They didn't really keep tabs on me like that. I went down there and found the people who ran the meetings, who I'd been advised to talk to by the occult people here, and this one guy says okay, you have to drink blood to get the feel of this. So I did. He said a female's blood is sweeter than a male's blood. How true that is I don't know. I drank a glass of blood, probably four ounces. Didn't do anything to me."

"Did you feel anything in particular while you were there, Ronnie? Any sense of being pulled or conflicted?"

"You gotta be very careful down there," he said, bypassing my question in deference to his own path, like usual. "I mean, you'll just disappear. They check everybody when you go in there, for guns and whatnot. I had to go along with the game plan; I couldn't bring a gun in. They lock the place up like a vault. Steel bars came down on the door; they had to put a big lug nut, big wing nut on it. You ain't coming through that. The shutters were barricaded the same way. These people were for real; they don't play no games. If they even think you're in there for the wrong reasons, good luck to you. Man, that place is another world."

Was Ronnie DeFeo a bored, aimless suburban kid with too much money and too much time on his hands? Maybe. Was he drawn toward life's underbelly merely for lack of a more stimulating alternative? I'd certainly seen that syndrome play out lots of times. But the darkness in this man seemed deeper-set. As I spoke to the former small-time hood who had become a renowned mass murderer, I felt a fundamental energy in him that shook me to my core.

"Let's go back to your father, Ronnie," I said. "Why do you think he felt you were so bad?"

"Because I *was* bad," he said. "I was up to all kinds of stuff." For example, he said, he was sleeping around with the married neighbors. "There was a jealous husband a few houses away. And there was this cop named Eddie. I came home drunk one day, and at the time I was screwing, what's her name, the mother a few blocks away; she was beautiful; she had a son and a daughter. Anyway, I tried to get in the front door and the back door, but one window upstairs was open, and it was their bedroom window. I went into my boathouse and got the forty-foot extension ladder. I took the ladder, and I'm coming up the driveway. Eddie sees me with it, he stops, he says, 'What the hell, what are you doing?' I says, 'I ain't breaking the law, I'm going to get some pussy. You gonna shoot me? I got a gun, too, you know.' So we start talking for a while, I showed him my gun, a brand-new Colt Python, and he asks me where I got it. I gave him the gun, and then I says, 'We all done here?' I took the ladder. He says, 'Get out of here, you're crazy, you can't do that!' But guess who helped me put the ladder up in the end? Eddie."

"What time was this, Ronnie?"

"Real late. Or real early, I guess. Maybe four in the morning. I got to the top, I says, 'Baby, I'm here!' She woke up, the husband turned, she says, 'Are you crazy?' So I climb back down the ladder and Officer Eddie is still sitting there in his cruiser. I tell him, 'She wants me to go to the door.' Eddie helps me take down the ladder, you know, with the top part that collapses into the bottom part. We put it down on the ground and I head for the front door. When she sees me she says, 'You can't be coming here!' I pushed my way in anyway. I says, 'Honey, you gotta give me some now, this is bullshit.' I seen Officer Eddie on the news about six months ago. He rescued someone in Amityville from a burning house on his way home. I said, 'That son of a bitch is still on the force?' "

I had no way of knowing whether this story, or any of Ronnie's tales, for that matter, were true, and it's not as though the Amityville police were about to corroborate it. I had only my instincts as a guide. If Ronnie's stories *were* fabrications, they were impressive both in their vividness and consistency. Were all these things I was hearing day after day merely the products of a sociopathic mind spinning one tall tale after another for the simple purpose of having nothing better to do? I doubted this. Were they stories that he had long ago manufactured and had now come to believe were true, providing the reason for his conviction in the telling? That also seemed unlikely, if only for the reason that each served to paint an increasingly unflattering picture of him. If we make up stories about ourselves, it's usually to make ourselves feel better, not worse. Yes, a child who's getting in trouble will sometimes do something even worse in order to show his parents just how bad he can be, but a sixty-year-old man isn't likely to do the same. At least, I didn't think so.

"You were all over the place."

"If I woulda got caught, these guys woulda killed me. I used to go out and drink with a guy after screwing his wife. The police came up with all these enemies I had." He listed some names, including black guys in the Bronx from whom he said he would buy dope back in the day. "Where they lived, it was a rough neighborhood, Lewis Avenue, Hundred Thirty-Eighth Street. They don't like white people around there. They tried to take me out, they tried to murder me down there, I ain't gonna lie about it."

The stories often came rapid-fire. On one hand, they sometimes seemed to have nothing to do with each other. On the other hand, taken as a whole, over the course of many conversations, they began to form an overall picture: that of a lost, strung-out young man trying to get attention in a number of ways, many dangerous, all equally sad.

"Who tried to take you out?"

"Some jokers, I don't know who. I'm telling you they are not fond of white people. They blew the windshield out, brand-new Buick, it was my father's car, blew my windshield right out, that's how close they got. I had a

.357 Magnum, I pulled it out, Duchek was in there screaming."

I quickly flipped through the file and found the name Liam Duchek. A friend of Ronnie's, someone he used to run around with in the neighborhood. And, like Ronnie, apparently a big fan of recreational drugs.

"Duchek was with you?"

"Yeah, we used to get up to stuff together. Things could get a little wild. Like I'm trying to tell you, some of them are very leery about doing business with white guys. But in the end, everybody got to know me, and they told me, 'Look, you're safe, you ain't gonna have a problem.' Every day I had a new car, a different car, a new Buick. There was one guy I sold a Riviera to, a Gran Sport Riviera, the same color as my father's car, the one I was using; it was his favorite, burgundy with wine-color interior and a white top. I said to the guys at the dealership, 'Look, this is gonna sound crazy, but they got a Gran Sport Riviera, loaded, leather interior, sunroof; they paid cash for it.' Then my grandfather starts in with me: 'What are you doing with these drug dealers?' "

"Rocco DeFeo," I said, looking at my notes. Ronald Sr.'s father.

"Yeah. He was known as Rocky DeFeo. That's what we called him. The next morning I had to go to work early, we had to open it up, take it out of the showroom, make it ready. I undercoated the car, tank up with gas, it said three gallons, three gallons my ass. I got up to stuff all the time. I was no good. That's why they were planning to kill me."

"Who was planning to kill you, Ronnie?"

"Both of them. My father and my great-uncle, Pete DeFeo. Thanksgiving day."

I flipped through the file again. Peter "Pete" DeFeo, born March 4, 1902, died April 6, 1993. Known as "Philie Aquilino," a New York mobster who grew up in Little Italy and became a *caporegime* under a number of big-name bosses, including Frank Costello and Vito Genovese. After becoming a made man, Pete worked his way up the ranks, eventually achieving the rank of captain and operating his "businesses" out of various social clubs in the neighborhood and the Cuomo Cheese Corporation. At his peak, it seemed Pete DeFeo was one of the more respected bosses on the Lower East Side.

How ironic, then, that he didn't truly become known until November 1974, when his grandnephew was convicted of killing Pete's niece, Louise, along with her husband and their other four kids. Pete, along with, it seemed, everyone else in the vicinity, was considered an early suspect before the clamps came down on Ronnie.

"You think they were planning to kill you?"

"I don't think so, I know so. I overheard the whole conversation. My father says, 'He's using drugs, he's using heroin, we can't trust him. The kid knows too much; he's gonna take us down. He comes home late at night, drives his mother nuts.' They were gonna do it. Thanksgiving day. You gonna kill your own kid? I mean, come on."

SIX

No matter where they're from or what kind of lives they lead, all teenagers get restless. I was no different. Around my eighteenth birthday, I felt my spirit being pulled. If I think about it, I suppose it was different from the usual scenario, since the reason for my restlessness wasn't just the typical desire to escape my parents' rules and do my own thing.

It was something more than that. Voices were coming through to me, from multiple directions, asking for help. Some of them seemed near, some distant. But they were calling. The feeling overcoming me wasn't like wanderlust. It was a need to answer the voices.

I had always known my mother to travel—New York, California, elsewhere. She'd go almost monthly, sometimes for a week, sometimes two, usually scouting and buying properties in which she could perform her rituals. New York was the place that drew her most powerfully, and most often, and because of that, I'd always felt a kinship for the place, too, though I'd never been.

The voodoo community, especially the elders with whom my mother conferred, saw my need and understood it. You have to realize that Louisiana Voodoo is not just a practice; it's a religion, too. Some people are raised in the arms of the church or the synagogue or the mosque. I was raised in the arms of medicine men, dark priestesses, and warrior chiefs. That was my spiritual cocoon.

They agreed it was time for me to spread my wings, but they also needed to know I was up for the challenge. I would be assigned travels, forays into the outmost corners and darkest places, where my job would be to record and witness demonic possession, followed by, in some cases, exorcisms. If it wasn't too late, I would be charged with saving those who could still be brought back. The visits would require approval from the Vatican, the family's priest, or someone high up in their church.

I feel this bears repeating. Some teens are sent on church missions or youth retreats. Others are encouraged to do exchanges with those of like-minded faiths. Teenagers in New Orleans who have a talent for communing with the dead are sent around the globe to chase the devil. At least, this one was.

My parents agreed. I hadn't asked for the gift I'd been given, but, as my mother had told me, with the gift came responsibility. I set out for the world, to see how many lost souls I could help.

I would return home to the bayou regularly, especially when my mother needed, or wanted, more money. After all, despite her own gifts, for a long time I'd been her meal ticket, the strange and compelling child who could connect with the other side. She knew I could still bring people in for her, and I, still trying to win her approval, was happy to fulfill my role.

During one of these stops, in 1982, I was back in Nola preparing for a séance my mother wanted me to lead. A group of entertainers from California were flying in to see if they could make contact with someone who had passed to the next world, and my mother and I now stood with the five of them in a cemetery, invoking the gods. It was after midnight on a typical sticky Louisiana night. The banging of our drums, along with the crackling from our fire, were the only sounds filling the air. We were making offerings to Baron Semedi, the keeper of the dead and an important deity in the voodoo religion, a figure half in this world and half in the other.

I noticed someone at the side of the cemetery, watching. He was alone. Curiosity seekers aren't unusual, but the power I felt flowing from this person was different from normal. Seeing me catch his gaze, he walked forward. As he approached, I saw he was a muscular young man who looked to be in his late teens, like me. He stood as rigid as a cadet.

"Are you Jackie Palermo?" he said.

"Who wants to know?" I asked.

"My name is Adam," he said. "Adam Quinn. I'm from New York. I go to Saint John's, and I'm here for a national track meet this week. I'd like to talk to you."

"Who told you about me?"

"We're staying at the LSU dorms. Everybody there knows about you."

"What do you want?"

"Is it true what they say?"

"I don't know. What do they say?"

"They say you can show heaven and hell."

I didn't say anything.

"I want to know about voodoo," he went on. "I want to learn about what you do."

"No, you don't," I said.

"Yes, I do."

"Go away, for your own good," I told him. "And don't come back." I went back to the fire and continued to beckon the gods.

The more Ronnie talked about his father, the more transparent his feeling of rejection became. He hated the man with all his heart yet wished he could have found the secret to earning his love. I recognized in Ronnie's voice an awful and classic condition: that of the victim still desperately trying to win the affection of his tormentor. People denied their parents' love will spend their entire lives trying to get it, even after they're gone. This I knew from experience.

When I had picked up the coin in the forest, bolts of pain had shot across my arms and torso. Soon my entire body felt racked, and the trip out of the woods proved much more arduous than the trip into it.

"I wanted to be done with it," Ronnie had told me

after my return from the forest, as though picking up a conversation that had been paused only a minute. "I didn't want any part of him whatsoever. And that coin was his."

I had learned to listen, follow one door down a path that led to another. That was how you got Ronnie to slowly disentangle the different strands that would, I hoped, eventually lead to the truth.

As I gained his trust, the phone calls came to be supplemented by letters—an infrequent trickle at first, then temporary bursts of a handful or more at once, then, not long after that, a reliable stream. Soon I knew my mailbox would hold at least one letter from Ronnie every day. Some days there were five stuffed in there. Some weeks I received thirty. They were always in blue or red ink. Ronnie DeFeo, like many inmates, liked to write.

The letters were a curiosity unto themselves. They would take on a variety of forms and expressions, sometimes seeming to come from different people entirely. One letter would have messy penmanship similar to that of a child, as though Ronnie's handwriting had stopped developing when he was a youngster, and would be characterized by sloppy structure and simple thoughts and ideas. The next would have tight, measured script written by a sure hand, and its contents would contain real insight and intelligence.

I showed some of the letters to associates of mine who work in forensics. They were startled that some of the letters showed a distinctly left-handed slant, while others seemed obviously written by someone right-handed. In addition, they pointed out, the thrust of certain letters seemed more typical of a teenage girl than a grown man.

The letters continued to come in droves. I have boxes filled with them. And it wasn't just letters. Ronnie would send cards, drawings, musings, whatever happened to occur to him that day. Sometimes he would send me cartoons. A few weeks after the first letter he'd sent, a drawing arrived in the mail. It was a cartoon drawing of the Surf Hotel.

One morning, Ronnie called and simply said, without greeting, "I want you to have power of attorney." He seemed especially uptight.

"What?"

"I want you to have exclusive rights to the story and power of attorney over my estate, Jackie. I want to be cremated. I'm not being buried in that plot."

"What plot, Ronnie?"

"They bought nine plots. They bought the six for my family; then that scumbag Rocky DeFeo, 'cause he had no place to be buried, took more money from the estate—I'm the one that turned it into an estate—and bought three more, for him, my grandmother, and me."

Joanne, working in the same room, had already started to dig. She was still building the ever-growing file on Ronnie, and I'd gone through the material she provided me numerous times, but it was still hard to keep up with the catalog of characters Ronnie would casually drop, as though I was a fellow branch on the extended DeFeo tree and was familiar with all the players in this drama.

"Why don't you want to be buried there, Ronnie?"

"Why don't I want to be buried there? Let me tell you something. When I was in the county jail—"

"Exactly when, Ronnie?"

"What do you mean, exactly when? Right after all the shit happened with my family. As soon as I got up there, they sent Vinny Procita up to see me. He says we don't want all your money, but we need this signed."

"Who is Vinny Procita?"

"My aunt's husband. My aunt Phyllis. My father's sister is Phyllis Procita, and that's her husband. He's the same one who at the crime scene was saying, 'God only knows what people on drugs do.' This is what one of my family says? My aunt's husband says that? To make a long story short, he wanted me to make him administrator of the estate, because they couldn't pay for the funeral, they needed money."

"The funeral for your family?"

"Yeah, the funeral for my family. They didn't have the money for it. But listen, they had to be buried, didn't they? So now Rocky DeFeo has to pay for the caskets, but it isn't his money."

"Whose money is it, Ronnie?"

"It's my money! But he took it and paid for the caskets, the plots in the cemetery, and the stone."

"And you were upset that he spent too much of your money?"

"Too much? What are you talking about?"

"I assumed you were angry with him for taking control of the estate money that you were entitled to and then squandering it on expensive coffins and so on."

"What? No. He takes the money and buys white coffins. I mean, what is this guy doing? They were cheap boxes. It's not his money. White boxes. This came from the estate that wasn't an estate yet. Bank accounts and so on. This is because Rocky DeFeo wanted to make this an estate immediately so he could get the money."

"You were upset that the coffins weren't good enough."

"That's what I'm trying to tell you!"

It was when Ronnie would engage in these bizarre rationalizations that he would become the most agitated. He was angry at his grandfather for buying insufficient caskets for the family members *he'd* been accused of killing.

"I mean, you want to buy a plot, you go and buy a plot for the six people who were just, you know . . ."

"Killed."

"Right, killed. He goes and buys nine. They came in threes. He could have bought six. Nine people were not dead. The other three, according to him, was for my grandmother and him and me. But the deed for all of this is in my name. What are you doing taking the money and buying something for yourself and your wife? There isn't even an estate yet. And he throws me into the mix, for this third plot. 'Oh, yeah,' he says, 'one for you, too.' I said, 'What kind of garbage is this? This ain't your money. You can't do this.' I screamed at the guy. 'I wouldn't care if you spent all the money on the people who died.'"

The people who died.

"Maybe he just wanted to make sure you'd be at rest with your family when the time came," I said, "and that he and his wife would be buried with their son."

"That's horseshit. That ain't it. They just wanted to keep as much of that money as they could for themselves. I mean, when they were all buried, suddenly according to them there's no money for a stone. I said, 'Wait a minute here, there's no money for a stone?' That's what happened, this fucking Rocky DeFeo and his fucking daughter."

"Phyllis."

"Yeah."

"And her husband Vinny."

"That's what I'm saying. 'You went and bought you and your wife something. You can't do that! You want to pay for it, that's fine. But this isn't your money. This is a pure rip-off!' Then he turns all my letters and everything over to the DA, because they're worried about me coming back on an appeal, he's worried I'm gonna beat this on an appeal. And his daughter turns around and testifies against me?"

"Who, Ronnie?"

"Geraldine Gates."

"That's your father's other sister?"

"Yeah."

"So they wanted to make sure you stayed put and they'd get control."

"The cemetery knows that I'm the owner of those plots. The deed says Ronald Joseph DeFeo Jr. That's me. So the cemetery's well aware of the fact who owns it. But I don't know where the deed is now. Geraldine Gates got her hands on it; the Nanowitzes had it, maybe they still got it."

"Who are the Nanowitzes?"

"Our housekeepers. They were with us for seven years. We were real close to them."

"They might have the deed?"

"They were saying my grandparents had it, the Brigantes, and they gave it to my aunt."

"Your father's sister."

"My father's sister."

"I'm trying to keep up. How do you know the Nanowitzes might have had it or given it to your aunt?"

"They wrote me and came to see me in prison. They cared about me. They were good people. But giving it to my aunt, that don't make no sense. I don't want nothing to do with that woman. I didn't want anything to do with her before this case."

Maybe this oddly high-and-mighty stance was part of Ronnie's way of dealing with what had gone down that night, or his way of displacing the need to face it at all. Did he really feel cheated that he could no longer be in charge of the DeFeo estate? I wasn't sure. But he certainly sounded as sincere about this as he sounded about everything else. You couldn't accuse the man of not being passionate in his opinions. When Ronnie DeFeo expressed anger that the family he apparently killed was getting disrespected in death, you found yourself on some level understanding his point.

"I mean, that's the lowest thing you can do. Took the money and bought himself and his wife a burial plot. And throwing me in there. You can't do that crap."

I rifled quickly through Joanne's file. "They're both dead, is that right? Your paternal grandparents?"

"He died in 1983; my grandmother in 1984. They're in those plots now. Then an area where there's no name. That's for me. I'm not being buried there. I got news for you. When I go, I'm being cremated. I want nothing to do with them, no part of any of them. They're snakes with two heads. Phony hypocrites. I even heard they said some nasty shit to my father at the funeral, as they were lowering him into the ground. I heard Rocky DeFeo was at the grave the day he buried him, and he said some pretty bad shit. Sure, you can bury him with garlic and all that crap, but it's words that count. The man is disrespecting his own son as he's being put in the ground."

"How do you know that?"

"The Nanowitzes were right there. They heard it all, and they told me. I mean, I couldn't be there to hear it, of course, because the Suffolk County Police Department made sure I wasn't allowed to come."

"You think you should have been allowed to attend the funeral, Ronnie?"

"They made absolutely sure I wasn't gonna be there, oh yeah. He was an animal, but as dead as he was, I never got to go to the grave."

Hearing this victim-speak, even from someone who had allegedly perpetrated so heinous a crime, was heartbreaking. Nearly forty years after his father's death, Ronnie still stung from not having been given the opportunity to say good-bye to the man he so deeply loathed. The man he'd killed. I'm no psychologist, but I was intimately aware of the perverse phenomenon affecting Ronnie. It's overwhelmingly painful when the parent whose approval you crave finally goes away forever, because it means that approval will never come. You will always be a disappointment. You will eternally be ridiculed. You will forever be abused.

Adam drove the hour from the LSU campus in Baton Rouge to my home in Nola twice more that week in 1982, each time begging for further glimpses into my world. His manner never changed. He was straight up, nothing fake, just a young man too curious for his own good.

"Look," he said on the third visit, "I've come all the way here just to talk to you. The least you can do is talk."

So I let *him* talk. He was on a full sports scholarship at Saint John's. He was going to be a professional athlete one day, he said, a track athlete or maybe a football player. Once I let my guard down a little, I found I warmed to him. Despite my general suspicion of anyone who asked to speak with me, Adam seemed different. My intuition told me he was someone who was going to play an important part in my life.

"I have to get back to school soon," he said. "Will you let me watch?"

"Watch what?" I said.

"Something else. Anything. I just want to see what it's all about."

"Fine," I said. "You can watch. But remember, I warned you. You shouldn't knock on the door if you don't want to see what's on the other side."

I let him observe another preparatory ritual, a war dance around the fire. Another means to summon the dead.

* * *

"Ronnie, earlier, when I asked you why your father thought you were so bad, you told me that you *were* bad. Do you still feel that way?"

"I need to tell you something, I don't know if I should tell you. Me and two other guys robbed a bank. In 1973. Two black guys. One was a schoolteacher; the other one worked for my father. The whole thing was a dare. I was scared to death, I ain't gonna lie. I decided I'd jump right over the bank counter, like in Hollywood. I just said to myself, 'Let me see if this works.' I didn't even have no gun on me. The other guys, they had guns, 12-gauge shotguns, including the guy driving the getaway car. The shotgun was mine. I jumped over the counter with a paper bag. I didn't have no gun; I wasn't going to hurt nobody. I told the lady I had a bomb in the bag. There was a kid's clock inside; it went *tick-tock, tick-tock.* I told her, 'You press that button, I'll blow this whole bank up including myself; we'll all die together, right now. I got nothing to lose.'"

"What did you mean by that?" I still didn't have a reliable sense of whether Ronnie's stories were real, embellished, or completely fictitious. But each one provided a small opportunity to find out more about the man, and what had made him who he had become.

"Just what I said."

"You had nothing to lose."

"That's exactly what I had to lose. What did I have? That bastard beating me whenever he felt like it, and my mother screwing the hairstylist one day and the brother the next. That's what I got to lose?"

"So robbing the bank was a way of saying you didn't care what happened to you."

"I was happy to do it or not do it. It was a dare."

"What happened when you said that to the woman?"

"She says, 'Oh my god, oh my god.' I'd shaved my beard off, I had a blond wig. She starts screaming, 'Don't take it all, please!' So I left all the singles and all the change."

"Why did you do that?"

"I told you, for kicks. I was restless, I don't know. Came out of there with thirty-nine thousand. The other guys couldn't believe I'd did it. I gave them five grand apiece, kept the rest of the money. I didn't hurt nobody. I was never arrested, never indicted. It's ridiculous. I shoulda taken the singles. Probably another thousand or so. Manufacturers Hanover Trust, that was the name, it was on a corner. 1973."

I signaled to Joanne, who looked up the bank online and came up empty. With some more searching, she quickly found that it had closed in 1992.

"The one we hit was in Manhattan. Peter was with me. Peter Hill, he was the schoolteacher. Peter got time for the bank. When I ran into him, in Suffolk County Jail, he had a female lawyer, I'll never forget that, and he got probation and six months' jail time running concurrent for that bank. The other charges he got two to four."

"What other charges?"

"He had a lot of robberies. He robbed an HMC, the loan agency, and they shot him."

"Who shot him?"

"I wouldn't go with him on that one. He told me he was gonna do it, but I told him, 'I'm not going,' 'cause you had to go up a set of stairs. Sure enough, he went up those stairs, and they got him in a cross fire."

"Who did, Ronnie?"

"A security guard who was there. Peter was a sitting duck coming up those stairs. He got shot a couple of times. He got two to four. But for the bank, the judge wanted him to make restitution, and he couldn't, 'cause he woulda had to give me up."

"He didn't want to implicate you?"

"No, he was an all-right guy. Judge gave him six months' jail time and five years' probation after. I was never arrested, never indicted. It's ridiculous."

Ronnie DeFeo was a man caught permanently between unresolved guilt and righteous indignation. He seemed to resent every single person who had ever had a hand in *not* punishing him for wrongdoing. He was someone who had spent his entire youth trying to be as bad as possible in order to validate his father's opinion of him and then becoming angrier and angrier with those who failed to help him bear it out.

When he said it was ridiculous that he hadn't been arrested for robbing that bank, on the surface it might have sounded as though he was mocking the authorities for letting him get away. But I'd come to know him better than that. I knew by now that nothing gnawed at Ronnie's soul more than the idea that bad people got away with things all the time.

* * *

The New Orleans community is a separate world, happily detached. Like many other American ports, it was French first, then Spanish, and then French again, but its true fabric runs much deeper than that. The Louisiana Purchase opened the doors to everyone, and all manner of folks streamed in seemingly at once: French, Creole, Irish, German, Haitian. The first threads of a beautiful tapestry started to take form.

With it, the dark arts, practiced by many, took their place as well, and Louisiana Voodoo became a religion as important to some as the Catholicism that further separated the Big Easy from its Protestant cousins in the rest of the Bible Belt. Voodoo's practitioners weren't doing it as a lark. And they didn't appreciate outsiders.

The occultists, and the police who supported their privacy, didn't care how genuine Adam was in his interest. To them, he was nothing more than an outsider poking his nose around where it didn't belong. When they caught him for the second night in a row standing in the cemetery observing my rituals, they told him in no uncertain terms that he'd best make his way back to New York, where his curiosity could be put to better use. They even insisted on personally escorting him back to the campus, just to make sure he got back safely.

Adam came to see me a fourth time before he left. Perhaps the spirit had put this young man in my way, or me in his. In my head, I was already seeing the course Adam would take. His prying ways were going to benefit him later. He would not be a professional athlete. "I'll see you where my other foot lies, Chiefy," I told him. He looked at me curiously. And then he was gone.

It didn't matter. He was already well on his path, as I was already well on mine. And I knew those paths would cross again.

In the latter third of 2009, the gentle summer air was starting to take on an edge, and the leaves were beginning to turn. Ronnie DeFeo and I had been talking virtually every day for nearly six months now, but still I felt I couldn't take him back to the night of his undoing. Not yet. He had bottled the memory in a place deep inside that had remained locked for half a lifetime. The typical exercises I might use to return someone to an earlier event—immersion, forced recall, holding his face up to the mirror—weren't going to work here. The process was going to have to be slower. Like someone seeking catharsis but unsure how to take the first step, he would approach the topic of the murders himself but then abruptly step back. I could hear the pain begin to engulf him as he got close, the drug-induced haze of his youth replaced now by the stark, painful clarity of recollection. Inevitably, he would retreat.

I tried to come at it from different angles instead. "Do you want to talk about your siblings, Ronnie?"

"What is there to talk about? I loved them kids. Before all the shit happened, we had fun. In 1973, before Christmas, we had snow. I took them to Bethpage State Park, at nighttime."

"How old were they, Ronnie?"

"Let's see, Dawn was seventeen. Allison and Marc were about twelve and eleven. And John would have been around eight."

"Did you do stuff with them a lot?"

"Of course I did. Those were good kids. They never did nothing wrong. I said come on, put warm clothes on, gloves, hat—except me, I didn't even have gloves on—and we went. I took them tobogganing. And I told them, 'Listen, this is what you gotta do,' and I helped each one of them grab the cable. Because you try to walk up there, it's suicide, there's people coming down that hill like it's going out of style. You'll get run over. They're coming down on cardboard, garbage-can lids, sleds, skis, anything, all at the same time. So anyway, to make a long story short, each one of them I lifted up and told them to grab the cable; they thought that was funny. So they all did that; they went up the hill. I took the toboggan; I was the last one to go up. Everybody sat on, I told them, 'Listen, everybody gotta hold on.' I sat in the back; I was gonna steer. I said, 'If this thing hits the tree, or hits the road, oh my God.' Anyway, with all that weight on it, I'm telling you, we were doing at least fifty miles an hour. 'God,' I said, 'if we hit something now, I couldn't stop it'—we went across the road, we kept going, to the next lot. We finally stopped; every one of them was laughing. We went back up again. I had to go around a guy on skis. Then I took them somewhere, one of them ice-cream joints, Friendly's; there was one in Nassau County. I took them over there, bought them ice cream, then I went home. They were soaking wet and laughing."

"People have said you had to be the parent to your siblings, Ronnie. Is that true?"

"No, that ain't true. My mother took care of the kids. Drove them to school and picked them up in our station wagon. I wasn't their parent, but I loved them. Took them fishing all the time. I took them to Adventurous Inn on Route 110, the playland there. I took my little brother to the bar with me. I used to take them everywhere. I was in the process of buying them a motorcycle, but then this crap happened, and that was that. Tell you something about my two brothers. That show *Batman* was on TV, every night, five days a week. My mother hated when that show came on, because the two of them upstairs, Marc and John, they'd wait for me to come home, and when that came on, the music, the theme started, and boy oh boy, it was a free-for-all. The two of them got on chairs and just dove on me. I said, 'Aw, Jesus, here we go.'"

He had loved it. You could hear it in his voice as plain as day.

"Then the dog would get mad and start biting me. Candie. Hundred-ten-pound German shepherd. They'd wait for me to come home from Brooklyn, from work. 'Come on, we gotta watch TV!' Thank God that show was only half an hour. The two of them, jumping on me. Plus the dog hopping all over me, following me every-where, biting the crap out of me, every day. I go upstairs; I'm in the sitting room; they had a fifty-gallon fish tank in their room. No, bigger than fifty, it was on a wrought-iron stand my father had bought just for the tank, with expensive fish, exotic fish. They're beating the crap out of me as usual, and we stumble into the tank. As I'm breaking loose from them, I see the thing's coming down. I feel the water hit me, then *boom*—it smashes against the rug, water and fish everywhere. I said, 'Oh my God.' My mother comes up there, she says, 'What the hell?' We had to put that dog to sleep."

"Because it was wild?"

"No, because it was crippled. Bad hip."

"When was that?"

"A few years before all the shit happened with my family. The poor thing had a hip displacement. I carried her into the vet, and the vet put her down."

The sadness of the event was still there in Ronnie's voice. Or he was a very good actor. But I didn't think that was the case.

"Everyone in the house was crying. She was like a member of the family. I was real close with them kids."

"Did your father hit the other kids, too, or just you?"

"He and Dawn would get into it, but I was the only one he really went at. And my mother, she got abused all the time. If she woulda killed him, or did something, the whole thing wouldn't have happened. I mean, that's a fact. She had two boyfriends at least. At the same time. Look, why did she wear a red dress all the time? She gave a lot of people a certain impression of her. I mean, ain't that the devil's color?"

"Did your father know about her affairs?" I asked.

Ronnie said he did. "One time my father took me over to this guy's house; he took me there; we were casing his house. We were coming home from Brooklyn, got off at, I forget where, we got off the parkway, we were checking out his house in the daytime to see if she was there. We wanted to bust the fucking door down. I didn't ask him, but I was pretty sure he wanted to do away with the guy for good."

"What would she do, go over to his house?"

"She'd do it in her own bed. I don't know, I'm just saying. He admitted he had an affair with my mother out in the open. He was gonna get murdered. This was the hairstylist. We cased his house a few times. It was just waiting; because this guy had a family, it was gonna be hard to get him without his family. My father said we were gonna have to get ski masks. 'Ski masks?' I said. 'Listen, look at the size of you; ski masks ain't gonna do nothing. If they give a description, forget it.' He got mad and he cracked me. He said, 'Get him to come back to the house, and when he follows, we'll run him off the road and then shoot him. We'll put two in his head and then leave.' I said, 'Oh boy, this guy.' But he got the other guy. Brother Isaac."

"That's the one you mentioned before. You said he'd been your gym teacher at Saint Francis."

"Yeah, he was. I mean, the guy was a brother, for Christ's sake. There were two episodes. The first one, it was just a fight."

"Tell me what went down, Ronnie."

"We go to Sheepshead Bay, me and my father. He took me with him. I didn't know what was going on. He told me we're going to pay someone a visit, and he takes me to an apartment I never seen. He knocks on the door and tells me the guy's a brother. I said, 'What?' He said, 'Yeah, a guy from when you went to Saint Francis Prep.'"

"So he meant a priest."

"Yeah. They were all priests that ran that place. All of them were brothers. I went to Saint Francis Prep, and those were the brothers there. Them brothers would get on the bus every day with civilian clothes on. Not habits. And they were fooling around. Some of them had cars. Some of them took the bus; some of them took the train. They were fooling around with broads, I knew that for a fact. Like we saw one on a train with a broad. 'Cause I didn't get off where I was supposed to get off. And I'm gonna tell you something. Guy named Vito worked in our Buick dealership. One of his actual brothers was a brother in Saint Francis Prep. So I knew what he was doing. Vito used to advertise it. He had a broad on the side; he had a room somewhere. It's what they do. They were in there hiding, most of them."

"What happened after he knocked on the door?"

"I said to my father, 'So what are we doing?' I didn't see no brothers. 'This guy's not only a brother,' my father said, 'but guess what—he's screwing your mother.' I said, 'Come on, man.'"

"Did you think your mother was having an affair?"

"I knew my mother was sleeping around. She didn't do much to hide it."

"Were you afraid?"

"I never knew what to think with him. I don't know how, but my father had a key. There were two locks, and he had keys for both. He put the keys in the door and undid the locks. My father barges in, and there's Brother Isaac, the guy who used to be my gym teacher. He stands up. There was a couch in the living room and the TV; the apartment was just one big area. The only thing separate was the bathroom. My father rushes at him, and the next thing I know, they're throwing punches. I didn't know who was gonna win, I ain't gonna lie about it."

"He gave him a fight?"

"He gave him a fight. But my father prevailed, as always. He gave him a really bad beating. Threw him into the coffee table and just went to town on him. And Brother Isaac wasn't no small guy, he was just as big as my father, but more slender and muscular. He had to be a good two-fifty, and he was the same height, five-ten, maybe half an inch taller."

"Was he trying to kill him?"

"No. He knocked him out, but he didn't intend to kill the guy. I put one arm around him, my father put one arm around him, and we took him downstairs, where my father told me to look for a car—an old Buick, from the dealership. I guess he had it all planned. We threw his black coat over him; he was bleeding."

"Where did you take him?"

"Nowhere. We just left him in that car, behind the steering wheel, with the keys in the ignition."

"So it was a warning."

"I forget what he told him. 'Don't make me come back,' something like that. I don't know whose apartment it was. Might have been where he got together with my mom. Then there was the second episode. That was the next summer. And he made me watch the whole thing, with the goddamn heart. He made me participate, for Christ's sake. I had to watch, and then I had to bury the thing."

* * *

I'd been instructed by my elders as to the general purpose of my mission, but when I left Louisiana, I went not knowing quite what I was looking for or what guide to follow, other than my own inkling. The calls would come from clergy of all faiths, or, sometimes, from the families of the afflicted individuals themselves.

I learned there were people in need everywhere. Sometimes this need presented itself in the form of possession; other times, I was simply sent to visit the downtrodden and search their spirits.

I would do what I could to help right wrongs, fill the holes in doomed lives, or help provide deliverance to souls that had met their makers. Haiti, Peru, India. At first, I traveled alone. Arrangements would be made for me to meet up with a priest or a missionary group, and from there I'd find my way to the place where my cursed gift could be put to use. Canada, Rome, Sicily. I'd pass through towns and watch different souls interact. Each place like a new birth, like seeing with new eyes. A voice would become stronger and stronger, until I was standing next to one in need. Paris, Brazil, Mexico. I died a thousand deaths and passed a thousand souls from one side to the other. I was barely twenty.

"Do you want to talk about the second episode?"

Here Ronnie paused, which was so rare as to be completely disarming. After what seemed like an endless silence, he finally said, "It must have been September." His voice was uncharacteristically quiet—more like a frightened child than a grown man.

"When?"

"I remember it took a long time to get dark. Yeah, September. 1970. He took me back to the apartment again."

"The brother was still messing around with your mom?"

"He must have been. This time, when my father opened the door with the keys, Brother Isaac wasn't there. So we sat and waited for him. The guy was shocked when he came in that door and seen the two of us. He went to pull something out of his pocket."

"A gun?"

"My old man must have thought it was a gun, because he was on him immediately. The ironic thing is he did have a gun on him, but behind his back, in a holster. It was a Smith and Wesson revolver. It wasn't a Colt. When he put his hand in his pocket, he was just putting something in there, something balled up in his fist. That's all I seen, his hand going toward his pocket. When it was all over, that's when I found the gun on him. That gun never had a chance to come out."

"What's a man of the cloth doing carrying a gun?"

"I have no idea. As soon as he reached for that pocket, I never seen nothing like it, my father grabbed him by the throat and started throwing him into the wall. *Boom, bang.* He's throwing this guy around like a rag doll. And this guy wasn't a little guy, like I said. As big as my father.

But not fat. Muscular. My father was throwing him around like he was nothing. But this guy didn't want to die. He fought back. My father starts yelling, 'Butch, help me! Help me, fat boy!' He called me fat boy. I grabbed Brother Isaac's arm, and he threw me into the wall. He didn't wanna die. But my father just kept slamming him into that wall."

The pain in Ronnie's voice almost made me want to ask him to stop telling the story. It occurred to me that he sounded more confused and hurt by this event than when he made reference to the murders of his own family members. That memory seemed locked away. This one seemed enduringly fresh.

"I seen the guy's eyes rolling around in his head. When he got through throwing him around and the guy couldn't get up, he went over to him with a knife, a sheet knife. He cut his throat. And he was talking to him, 'You'll never screw my wife or anybody else's wife again.' That's what he said. When you cut somebody's throat, they don't necessarily die, so what he did, he started pulling his head. To separate it from the cut."

I was called savior and healer, but the truth was somewhere in between—a strange kind of liberator, maybe. I'm not sure if there's a name for it, and maybe there shouldn't be. Not everything should be captured and named. I would take in the spirits and become them, victim or destroyer, the one lost or the one searching. I absorbed them, housed them, released them. Across thousands of miles I communed with the dead or the dying, holding the spirits at bay until salvation could be, might be, had.

And out of all this death came life. A daughter. Joanne.

"When he knew the guy was dead, he ripped his shirt open, and he asked me, 'Where do you think his heart is?' What do you mean where do I think his heart is? His heart's in his chest—I'm not a doctor. Then, when he got the skin ripped off, he took a roofing knife—I was into roofing, construction, we used to cut the shingles with it—and man, he started cutting. He starts sawing up and down, up and down. For fifteen minutes he's cutting. I mean he cut his whole chest open. I thought we were in a funeral parlor the way he was going to work. I said, 'What the hell is this?' He puts a big *V* in Brother Isaac's chest with the box cutter, and then he went right down the middle. He also had a sheet knife with him, but he used the box cutters. Then, once he pulled the skin back and got in there, he tried to get at his heart. The heart ain't where everybody thinks it is."

"What do you mean, Ronnie?"

"It's just beside the breastbone. Closer to the middle than everyone thinks. But the box cutters weren't enough. He asks me, 'You got your tools in the trunk?' I said, 'Yeah, I got regular tools.' I had a brand-new axe in there, too, though I didn't mention that to him."

"What was the axe for?"

"I carried the axe because I couldn't carry a gun."

"So you went and got your tools for your father?"

"He asks me what kind of tools I got. I said, 'I don't know. I got some hammers, I think I got a chisel.' He said, 'You better get 'em.' Then when I was downstairs, I was thinking, I had a brand-new pair of bolt cutters, too. Them big ones."

Ronnie laughed. A sad, terrible laugh.

"I got back and I said, 'Those are ribs. You gonna go through ribs?' He said, 'I know what those are. What are you, a smart-ass?' So he tells me to go through the ribs, and I take the bolt cutters. Snap. 'Son of a bitch,' he said. 'You sure you never did this before?' I said, 'What the hell would I be doing some stupid shit like this before?' I just kept busting and busting those ribs open so he could eventually get his hand in there. I put a big hole in him. Those cutters are almost three feet long."

"Why do you think he wanted to involve you in this?"

Ronnie chose to ignore the question. I wasn't sure if he was caught up in the awful momentum of his own story or if, perhaps, there was simply no reasonable answer. "I snip the last rib with the bolt cutters, and finally he says, 'Oh look, his heart.' I swear to God it was still pumping. He tells me to stick my hand in."

"Why did he want you to take the guy's heart out?"

"How the hell do I know?"

"Sounds like he was testing you. Seeing what kind of a man you were. That's the sickest test I ever heard."

"I said, 'I'm not sticking my hand in there.' So he sticks his hand in instead, and he starts yanking. And he rips the goddamn guy's heart out. Right out. Tells me to

start cleaning the mess. There were two sinks. I'm washing the heart off in the sink. I found a bottle of fantastik
under the sink, that's what I'm using to clean all that shit
up. I just kept thinking to myself how thick a heart was.
I had to use a lot of paper towels—couple rolls' worth.
And I had to go get newspapers out of the garbage to
clean it up."

"What did you do with Brother Isaac?"

"We covered him with garbage bags. One bag on the
bottom of him and one on the top, then duct-taped both
ends together and sealed him up. Then we threw the
newspapers and all that shit I'd used to clean up the mess
into some other bags. We used four bags or six, I can't
remember."

"So you buried all that stuff with him?"

"No. The garbage didn't get buried with him. I know
that for a fact, because we forgot one of the fucking bags.
I didn't say nothing to my father. I didn't want to tell
him. So I took the bag and I looked for a Dumpster, you
know, one of them big Dumpsters in the street. I couldn't
find no Dumpster. I went everywhere looking. Where
they were knocking down buildings, everywhere. There
was a garbage company down the street, but I couldn't go
there with the bag. I mean, I was desperate. I couldn't
even find a garbage truck. So, I didn't have no choice, I
had to put it in one of them garbage cans on the street
corner. There was no air in the bag. The bag wasn't really
that big, but it was big enough."

"And the bolt cutters?"

"I washed them off and threw them back in the trunk.

I washed them in the sink in that apartment, with hot water at first, but then I said, 'What the hell am I doing? I need cold water. That's what you use to get rid of blood, not hot water."

This I knew. Hot water only sets the blood deeper.

"I used the sponge, had to get rid of that. I got rid of everything I touched. I was tired. I was disgusted. I wanted to get out of there. We carried Brother Isaac out—my father took one side; I took the other side—to the car. We had a black Riviera. Two-door. Put him in the back-seat. Wasn't dark yet, so we had to kill a couple hours. My father wanted to go and get something to eat. I said, 'I ain't really got an appetite.' He said, 'Ah, you're soft.' We went to one of them takeout joints, then buried him at Cypress Cemetery in a fresh grave, and went home."

I was twenty by then, a mother, older, wiser, stronger, more savvy about the ways of the world, but also exploring more obscure and dangerous places. My travels to help patch the wounds of injured souls had become well known to the voodoo community at home in New Orleans, and many within the inner sanctum were starting to worry. I was a priestess of my own spirituality, guided by my own group of elders, a creature whom the energies of the universe flowed through in singular ways. That may have made me unique, but it didn't make me invincible.

The community is powerful, but small. So when a brawny young man named Will Barrett was introduced to me as someone whom the elders thought would be a good candidate to accompany me on my journeys, I already knew his face.

I'd seen Will the first time while riding a streetcar in the Garden District. Voices had started talking and fingers pointing toward the back of the streetcar, and when I'd turned around, I'd seen a young man racing after the streetcar through the baking July heat. He caught up to the streetcar and got on beside me. As he reached for a strap to hold, his shirt opened a little, and I noticed, on his chest, a veve tattoo—a religious voodoo symbol. The god of the crossroads. The same as mine.

Over the next several years, I would see the young man during some of my trips home—hanging around the French Quarter, exploring the swamps and marshes—and learned that he, like I, had traveled back and forth frequently between New York and New Orleans.

"This young man is a drummer and ritual conductor," one of the elders told me. "He's strong and loyal and will be at your side through thick and thin." Will smiled his big kind smile. *This boy could crush me like an ant*, I thought. But off we went.

Will and I traveled and talked, talked and traveled. He became part of my secret society, helped me care for Joanne, delighted in watching her grow. At the same time, I learned that behind the soft smile there had been some dark passages. Like me, Will was familiar not only with the mysticism of voodoo but the practical matter of the law. He had been on both sides of the fence, he told me, but had straightened himself out in time to avoid landing irretrievably on the dark side of the path. He could play the trumpet, the piano, the drums, and the guitar, enchanting everyone around us. Then, just as quickly, he would retreat into the quieter part of his spirit and solemnly rehearse his ceremonial duties.

Will was fearless. With him at my side, I never felt scared or alone. He helped me care for Joanne while we traveled to far-flung places, never asking a single question other than, "How can I help?" He would have died for her, or me, without thinking twice. He made my mission his mission.

Joanne grew, and the three of us became an unbreakable team. We struck an odd collective image—people would often wonder who we were to each other. I would just smile and let them think what they wanted. I knew the truth: we'd been reunited from past lives. Anyone who is close to me in this life has been close to me in the past. When they return to me, I recognize them immediately. Titles mean nothing to me; loyalty, everything. Either I consider you my blood or you're no one to me.

If you got one of us, you got all three. If you were hungry, Will would give you his last dollar. If you crossed him, he would be the first to dig your hole. I would push you in. Joanne would pack the dirt.

"My mother and everybody was downstairs. My father went up to his bedroom, and he was carrying the heart. He had one of them big coats, big leather jackets, with the big side kangaroo pockets; he had the heart in there. And he put it under the blanket, on her side of the bed.

He came down and said, 'You won't have to worry about seeing your boyfriend no more. I brought him home for you; he's upstairs in your bed.' My mother ran upstairs and I heard her scream, 'Oh my god! Whose heart is this!' She was just screaming. 'Ask your son; he'll tell you.' So she asked me. I told her some guy that was a brother. Yeah, it must have been September. It took a long time to get dark."

I asked Ronnie what happened to the heart. He said he buried it in the backyard.

"Right there by the fence, there was a garden, and there was a retaining wall; that's where it's buried. It was a special stone wall, special blocks, then they had marble on top of that. We had a nice wall back there. Right up near the water. Right opposite the boathouse side door. There was three doors to get to the boathouse, one through the garage; then they had a side door on the outside to get in, then the big boathouse door. Directly across the garden and retaining wall, she had me dig a hole."

"Who did?"

"My mother. She asked me to bury the thing."

"And you did it?"

"I didn't care. I didn't care about any of it, because I'd just been drafted, and I figured I was going to be on my way to Vietnam, which was better than all the shit I was dealing with in my house. That's how I know it was the later part of 1970, because I got drafted, and they only gave me ten days to appear at Fort Hamilton, so it was in them ten days."

"You mean you actually went?"

"No, I got rejected. They did a spot check on everybody's arms, and mine were all marked up because of the shit I'd gotten into. I told the guy, 'Look, man, let it go. I wanna go, so just let it go.' He sent me to see a psychiatrist. He said, 'Once you see the psychiatrist, the choice is yours whether you wanna go or not, but you look high.' I said, 'No, I'm not high.' So I went in there and I start thinking, do I really wanna go? But I didn't get a choice in the matter. I should have went. My whole life would have been different. I should have went. Even if I didn't get killed over there, I could have just stayed and never have come back. Apparently, there are lots of pretty broads there."

I returned to the topic of Brother Isaac's sundered heart. "So you buried it?"

"Yeah, I buried it. She's asking me to go deeper and deeper. I said, 'Look, I'm getting tired of this digging. I'm digging for him, I'm digging for you—this is ridiculous. Maybe I oughta dig the hole a little bigger, four by six, for you.' Me and my mother were real close, we were real tight, till the day she died. But I couldn't get along with my father. You marry a pretty woman, you're gonna have problems. Before she gave me the heart, she took the newspaper from that day and wrapped it up. My father got angry because he couldn't find the newspaper."

"Are you serious?"

"She says, 'You gotta dig deeper, dig deeper.' I said, 'Listen, you're just like him. Maybe you should go help him at night, with the shit he does in the cemetery.' She told me, 'You gotta go down four feet.' I said, 'How would you know that?' She just looked at me, said, 'That's what you're supposed to do, when you bury a body in the cemetery. You gotta go at least four feet down, but they go six. That's because coyotes will come and dig up the bodies and eat them.' He cut that man's heart right out. It was like gutting an animal. To this day I can't eat meat. I can still smell it. I can still hear those ribs snapping."

"What were the kids doing when you guys came home with the heart and your mom started screaming?"

"I can't remember where the kids were. Maybe in the driveway playing, or in the pool. Yeah, probably in the pool. It was summer, and it wasn't that late, maybe eight thirty, nine o'clock. That first episode was the winter. This episode was in the summer. Yeah, I guess they were playing around in the pool."

Something else occurred to me now, a reason why this particular event in Ronnie DeFeo's life would produce such lasting pain, the pain that was so evident in his voice as he told it. It was that he had been merely an instrument for his father, a means, just as I'd been for my mother. And that what Ronnie had desperately wanted instead— like me—was simply to be loved. Maybe we weren't as different as I thought.

Will proposed to me for the first time after we'd been traveling together a year or so. I told him he should take the question back if he knew what was good for him.

"You need me," he said. "Joanne needs me. We're a family."

"I need space," I said. "My work is too demanding, and my schedule is too chaotic. Don't burden yourself."

He kept at it, asking me again at regular intervals. Each time I would say no. And each time Will would just smile his big sweet smile, a man more patient and devoted than anyone I'd ever known. We had grown to become best friends and mutual protectors, and I liked it that way. With him at my side, I felt I could harness my energies with absolute focus, never having to worry about what kind of place I was in or who might be over my shoulder. From every corner of the globe I was summoned by the living, the dead, and those in between. Will continued his practice as a psychic conductor, as committed as I was cursed. The more we roamed, the more strangely at home I felt. I didn't know if I'd ever put down roots, stay in one place. Then I got the phone call.

SEVEN

It was nearly Christmas 2009. My neighbors had strung their lights in swags across their rooftops and garage fronts. A dust-layer of snow covered the ground, though the experts on TV were promising more in time for Christmas morning, twenty-four hours away.

The night before, I'd slept little because of the fireplace. We'd had it installed only a few months before, one of those items you decide to splurge on because it has a transformative effect on the house and the salesperson convinces you that its efficiency will save a few hundred dollars over the course of ten years. It was brand-spanking new, wood-framed, glass-encased, gas-operated. Though it was only December, we'd already been using it regularly.

Around dinnertime, it had ignited with a loud *whoomp*, like the sound of a mast suddenly snapping open, making Will, Joanne, and I jump. A little puzzled, I got up and turned it off, then sat back down. A few minutes later it ignited again—*whoomp!*—and again I turned it off. After getting back up to turn it off three more times, I called the gas company.

The serviceman inspected the fireplace and told me he couldn't find anything wrong.

"What do you mean?" I said. "This is your company's fireplace. You need to tell me what's wrong and how to fix it. You're the expert."

"Sorry," he said, shrugging. "I've checked everything. No idea."

I called an independent company and asked if they thought they could figure out the problem. They assured me they could. But when their expert serviceman came to inspect it, he, too, was stumped, and left with the same apology as the first.

Six hundred dollars and five service calls later, I was ready to throw my hands up. My last call was to the company with the best reputation in the city for solving fireplace problems. True specialists. Nothing could get past them, they promised me. The owner of the company himself came to check on my temperamental fireplace. He flicked the switch on and off a few times, removed the glass casing, inspected the connections, moved the logs around. Then he told me there was nothing wrong.

"Nothing wrong?" I said. "This fireplace is turning on by itself. Wouldn't you say that counts as something wrong?"

"What I mean is *I* can't find anything wrong," he said.

"Well, can you look again?"

"I've looked," he said. "I've looked twice, three times. Like I said, I can't find anything."

"What do you suggest I do?" I asked.

He finished packing his toolbox, snapped the latches closed, and stood. "Sorry, lady," he said. "Maybe you got a ghost."

Sometimes I dream I'm back in New Orleans receiving the phone call again.

It was 1991. Joanne was nearing her eleventh birthday and I was nearing my thirtieth. Will had continued to ask me to marry him and I'd kept saying no, even though in my heart I knew our relationship was for eternity.

Father Vincent, the man called himself. He had a heavy Italian accent and an urgent, mysterious tone. There was little he could, or was willing to, tell me about himself, and he didn't provide any details on the phone. Only that I had to get to New York, immediately.

I started to question him the way I would try to get preliminary information out of anyone claiming to need help. "Just come as fast as you can," he said. "Too much information will put you in danger." I heard the truth in his voice. I didn't pack a bag. Will did, and also arranged for a neighbor to take care of Joanne.

On our way to the airport, we saw two different accidents on the highway, delaying us more than an hour. It felt as though something was trying to prevent us from getting out. The sky became slowly painted over with a dark, heavy blue.

When Will and I finally landed in New York, we headed straight for the destination Father Vincent had mentioned: the Surf Hotel, on Coney Island. Former playground for the rich and fabulous, now a fleapit. Will asked me if I wanted him to come in. I told him he should stay back. Almost as soon as I was through the splintered doorway, I heard the screams.

The door swings both ways, my mother used to tell me. For some of us, there's no lock on either side.

Despite my lack of sleep, there were things to get done on that Christmas Eve in 2009. Will was already off to the gym, Joanne already in the office. I heaved myself out of bed and walked groggily to the bathroom sink. When I lay my hands on the porcelain edge, they slipped off. I looked down and saw that they were red and sticky.

Blood covered not only the edges of the sink but the whole basin as well. It wasn't just spattered, like when you run to the bathroom trying to stop a nosebleed and a few drops escape. It was *covered*, like someone got their nose split open and then stood over the sink until it stopped. I grew up with brothers; I knew the difference. More red was visible than white. I turned to see Max, our bichon frise, looking up at me in the doorway. He locked eyes with me a moment, then turned and slowly ambled away. This was strange. Max usually stayed at my side for everything.

I called Joanne in from the office. She saw the blood and asked what had happened to me, if I had cracked my head. She remembered the incident with the bathtub.

"Nothing," I said. "I was going to ask if something happened to you." Joanne has her own bathroom. She never uses mine.

"No," she said.

I called Will on his cell and asked him the same question. Through the panting breaths of his lifting, he told me he was right as rain, nothing to worry about. Joanne and I looked at each other, said nothing, and set to cleaning the mess with bleach.

Not long after, Ronnie called, right on cue, midmorning. He sounded particularly worn, his voice drained. I asked him if everything was okay. Not bad, he said, except that he'd had a rough night. Nosebleed. A real gusher.

The devil gets into you physically and spiritually. For some weeks now, Ronnie had been complaining of a variety of bodily symptoms, and they were accelerating. But that was only half of it. Inside he was still poisoned as well, the deep hostility he still carried coming out often in our conversations. Whether it was directed toward me or someone else didn't matter. It was bile, and it was polluting his soul. The entity was seeping into him completely, filling him with darkness and anger and ruining his body in the process.

"I'm sick, Jackie," he said to me the evening after the nosebleed. We were speaking twice a day now. "I'm real sick. I had a hard time going to the clinic. I have a hard time talking to you right now. The phone is shaking a mile a minute."

The hardest people in the world suddenly become a lot less hard in the face of their own mortality. We had never spoken explicitly about death, but Ronnie had referred many times to the nagging symptoms of his own decline. He felt healthy on most days, but, like a victim worn down to the point of resignation by the relentlessness of Chinese water torture, he was almost ready, he said, to give up the fight.

"Listen to me," he said. "If this is going to be the end—if I die in my sleep, which I'm hoping I do, remember you gotta get my body and cremate it. No ceremony, no nothing. It's what I want done. There must be about five thousand in my account. It's only gonna cost twenty-five hundred, three thousand to get it done, if it's even that. I don't know how much longer I can go on like this. I'm getting old. I had to change hands with the phone. It's shaking too much."

In the world of Green Haven Correctional Facility, Ronnie DeFeo was both celebrity and outcast, admired by some, detested by others. On one side, he received letters from people in Japan, England, New Zealand, and all other points on the globe expressing sympathy, admiration, or both. He had sent me a letter he had recently received from the mother of a West Point graduate, requesting an autograph. On the other, there was just as large a camp of people out for his blood, those convinced he was every bit the monster he'd always been portrayed as and who wanted nothing better than to see him strung up. It was never clear to Ronnie from one moment to the next where he landed between these two factions, whether he'd be singled out for special treatment or ignored and left to wither away. But as he felt himself becoming weaker, it was starting to matter less and less.

"I'm gonna tell the priest you're gonna claim my body. I'm tired. If it happens by the end of the week, just get ready to claim my body. There's a lot of blood coming out. Just remember what I said. I don't wanna get put in no wooden box. I'm shaking like a leaf here. Gotta keep changing hands with the phone. They don't care about the mass in my lungs. I don't even want to talk about it. When you got fluid in your lungs, you do something about it. They don't wanna do nothing. They sent me for X-rays, sent 'em out. All the X-rays say is oh, yeah, it's getting better. It ain't getting better, it's worse."

The mass in his lungs had been diagnosed as fungal pneumonia.

"I'm urinating blood. It's coming out everywhere. When I throw up, when I cough, when I urinate, when I defecate. Doesn't matter. Anyway, I wanna talk about you. I know it's coming. Believe me when I tell you. Just remember what I said. Let's talk about you now. Did you get my card?"

"I did, Ronnie. Thank you."

Puss 'N' Boots, the tuxedo cat I'd had for twenty-two years, had taken sick a few weeks earlier, and we'd had to put him down. It was rough on all of us, especially Ray. Knowing one of your friends is passing into the next world and going to a better place doesn't make it easier saying good-bye. Ronnie and I had talked about it on the phone. His condolence card had arrived a few days later.

Four days after Ronnie's call about his bloody nose, Max, our beloved bichon, got sick, too, and died. Something was going on.

When you're a renowned killer, you are, in one way or another, a target, no matter where you are, no matter where you go. For better or worse, you are, and will always remain, in a macabre kind of spotlight. As Ronnie spoke of his growing illness and the desire to lie down and give up, I thought of the strange contrast between this person and the one who had bragged to me about taking on David Berkowitz, the Son of Sam, with a screwdriver.

It had been not long after his first incarceration, and also not the first time Ronnie said they had crossed paths.

"Me and Berkowitz met in the Cave, an underground discotheque in Southampton. Went to the Hamptons a lot back then, especially on the weekends. It was either 1970 or 1971. When I beat the draft, I went out and bought all new clothes and everything. In fact, my father took me. We went on a shopping spree; he spent hundreds of dollars on me. He felt bad, I don't know. I lost a bunch of weight. I bought leather clothes and everything. Leather suit. Pants, jacket. Tan. I bought a suede one and a leather one. Suede top and bottom. Powder-blue dungarees, designer jeans, with silver pins going all the way down the legs, and embroidered pockets. Now them jeans cost you probably a hundred and fifty dollars. Back then, they cost me forty, something like that. Not tan, beige.

Real nice color. Suede pants and the suede jacket. And then I had the smooth leather. I did it up."

By the time Ronnie DeFeo ended up behind bars with six consecutive life sentences hanging over him, he had become an entirely different sort of individual, someone forever infamous for a single extended moment. Berkowitz was, too. Of course, people who have little left to them but their notoriety will lay claim to that notoriety like a dog clings to a bone, and if someone else, willingly or not, encroaches on that territory, they will make a show of defending it. Nowhere else does this principle hold more powerfully than in prison.

"Saw him again in Clinton. I think this was 1981. He comes into my cell and sneaks up on me, just like that, out of the goddamn blue. I pull out a screwdriver and I say, 'One more step. You take one more step and you won't have to worry about doing this time. You don't sneak up on me like that.' 'Oh, I heard about you,' he says. I said, 'You heard about me? You don't remember me from the street?' He says, 'I don't want none of that.' Yeah, 1981. Clinton, APPU."

"What's APPU?"

"Assessment and Program Preparation Unit. As in substance abuse, mental-health issues, and so on. Support services. It's supposed to be a protection program, but it's a prison inside a prison. They got their own industry, they got programs better than population's got. They use the gym all the time. Population doesn't. It's ridiculous. It's a program they say that gets you ready for general population in another prison. If you can't go to population, that's where they put you, so you can eventually go back. Berkowitz went to court and got a federal judge to see things his way."

"To put him in APPU?"

"Yeah, to put him in APPU. Very few people they let loose in Clinton. A lot of guys ask to go in there. They had to go to their counselors; commissioner's gotta sign an order."

"Why were you in APPU?"

"Because I was notorious. Because of the nature of my crime and the spotlight I had that I didn't want."

"Sounds like protective custody."

"It was, in a way. Some people ask to get put in there for the fags."

"You mean for sex?"

"Yeah. And I'm not talking about three or four fags. I'm talking about a good twenty or better. Lot of these guys have breasts. You know how many cops they were busting?"

"You mean having sex with?"

"I knew one of them cops real good, I mean real good—he'd have done anything for me. He's down there having sex with one of them fags. I said, 'What the hell?'"

"You were talking about Berkowitz, Ronnie. What happened with him?"

"He comes in my cell; he's upset. I pull the screwdriver out as soon as I heard. 'One more step, this is going in you,' I told him. I didn't know who it was. Jealous over a fag. By the time I got to Sullivan, everybody, a lot of the cops, already knew the story. Two notorious guys, you know, they figured, showdown. The superintendent knew, deputy of security. But everybody liked me, so they made believe it didn't happen. Nothing did happen; it's what coulda happened. It just went to show I wasn't the guy with the contract to take him out. Families back then were paying people to try to get Berkowitz. It was in the newspaper, everything. I don't get down like that."

"You mean the families of his victims?"

"Yeah. They all wanted him taken out, for that terrible shit he did. Truthfully, I got a few offers through the mail. Two thousand, three thousand, five thousand."

"To take him out?"

"Right. I mean, these people must be nuts. I'm gonna finish this guy while I'm serving my own sentence? What do they think I am?"

"They think you're a killer, so you're happy to kill."

"They don't know what they don't know. They just want him punished, and they're looking to me for help? Come on."

"And now he's found God," I said. Joanne had done the homework for me. David Berkowitz had become born-again in prison and was now preaching the gospel of love and repentance to anyone who would listen. A lot of people had started listening.

"Oh, yeah, he went to the parole board talking God; they forgave him. He's got the federal judge in his pocket, I don't know. He's claiming he's with Jesus. And now he's the only inmate in the country with his own radio program. How does David Berkowitz get a radio program? You tell me."

"Was the incident with the screwdriver the last time you saw him?"

"I saw him again in Sullivan, back in 1991. Yeah, January third, 1991."

"How do you know it was January third?"

"Because that's when I got transferred to Disneyland. Eastern. We were in the yard, and he was going on about the dog giving him messages. I said, 'Oh Jesus, come on.' They were calling me back to the block, but I stayed in the yard, with him. I was going to Eastern, that's the sweetest joint in the state. He said, 'Ronnie, you almost stepped on Sam's foot.' I said, 'Oh, Dave, stop that crap.' He got mad, I said, 'What are you doing that shit for?' He was squatting, had about six hundred pounds on the bar, I said, 'Listen, man, what's the matter with you?' They called me again, so I had to go in from the yard. I told him good-bye. He said, 'Ronnie, take care of yourself, you're going to a better place.'"

"What did he mean, 'better place?'"

"Just what I said. Eastern. It wasn't just better; it was the best prison in the state. Big flags out front, looks like a big castle. They just told me to put my stuff in a bag, and they put me in a van. There's no wall around the jail. The wall is a phony. They got the wall in the back. If you came to visit me, I could shake your hand through the window. Then they transferred me out of there, and they didn't write down no reason." This set Ronnie off on another spiraling rant about prison administrators.

"Ronnie—Berkowitz," I said, trying to pull him back on track.

"All that shit about the dog, he made it all up. I was there one night when he did something in Sullivan. Somebody tried him, he picked up a baseball bat. The only reason why the guy ain't dead, I'm gonna tell you, is because me and a couple of other guys grabbed him and the bat. 'Cause he was gonna finish this dude. All over a softball game. No, Berkowitz could play. He could hit the ball and he could catch the ball; he was a catcher. Like I said, we were all together; we were hanging out together. I don't know about now, with this religion stuff. He's a minister. He's a little off. But he's the only prisoner in the United States that's got his own radio show. Every Sunday morning, he's on there, preaching. He's got a congregation."

At this Ronnie laughed his laugh, a distinct, childlike giggle that he always cut off almost as soon as it was out. It was always unexpected both to him and to me, and I got the sense that he felt it was an unfair sound coming out of his mouth. It reminded me of a small boy letting out a chuckle and then realizing quickly that there was an adult within earshot who was about to tell him to keep it in.

"I'll tell you something, he's gonna pull something. He refuses to go to the parole board; he went one time and now he refuses. Fired the lawyer. I know exactly what he's gonna pull. He's gonna give it a few more years, and then the people in his church are gonna go to the commissioner or the parole and get him out. The people that he killed, he's got their families on his side now. The mother wants to come up and visit him. Stacy Moskowitz or something."

He was almost right. Over the years, I'd become familiar with the Son of Sam murders, thanks to Joanne's research. Stacy Moskowitz had been the last of David Berkowitz's six victims in the blistering summer of 1977. Neysa Moskowitz, her mother, had forgiven the killer, the self-professed born-again Christian, and had even become his pen pal.

"She says oh, he's sorry for what he did; he's found God now. You watch—down the road, he's gonna get out of prison. Born-again. His own radio station. Jesus Christ."

"Have you talked to him since?"

"In 1994, he sent me a message. I'm telling you, he's a nut. I said, 'Oh my god, here we go.' I said, 'I don't need this; I don't need him contacting me.' You think I'm going to answer that guy? Look what he did to people. I mean, come on."

"I heard he and Charlie Manson are best friends."

"Of course they're best friends. The two of them wanted me to get together with them. I said, 'No, I'm not down with this shit; are you crazy?' Before Charlie came to prison, before that shit ever happened, one of the times I ran away, I was in Greenwich Village. There was this broad in a red convertible; she wanted me to go with her. Next thing I know, she's one of Manson's people. When that shit happened, I said, 'Oh my god, it's a good thing I didn't get in that car.' I ran away all the time."

"They seem different to me, Berkowitz and Manson."

"Berkowitz, I don't know, he's fooling everyone with his Jesus. Manson, he's out-and-out nuts. He poured lighter fluid all over a guy and burned him up in prison, started yelling 'Hare Krishna.' They did a routine cell search on the guy and found a goddamn cell phone."

"What?"

"Yeah, you heard me. He did that shit and more. And the person using the cell phone was sending out text messages."

"Are you messing with me, Ronnie?"

"Messing with you? That was everywhere, Jackie. This cell-phone shit is not private information."

Joanne, who was beside me, did a quick Google search of "Manson" and "cell phone." Multiple pages came up with a variation on the headline "Charles Manson Caught with Cell Phone in Prison." It was one of the few times in my life I felt naive.

"So now they're worrying about him being involved in criminal activities. He's in SHU now; they put him in solitary. I said, 'Oh my god, are you kidding me?' A phone in the man's cell? It was 1969 that happened. I mean, come on."

"What do you mean it was 1969?"

"I'm saying the case is over forty years old, and they're still terrified of this guy using a phone. Notifying his people. Remember, he never actually killed anybody. He just directed other people to kill. Public enemy number one, man. His name is a household word in Japan, for Christ's sake. I don't know how to send text messages out. I know how to use some cell phones. A guard showed me how to use his once."

"When?"

"I don't know, a few years ago. He got fired. Manson's

always cooking up something. I mean, he tried to kill Gerald Ford. With a .45. Something happened, the gun jammed or something. You remember that case? The man is insane. He told me in a letter if I ever had a problem to just let him know and he'd have someone in his posse carry out a subway special. A subway special is something you do with an ice pick. Before his time is up, he's gonna do something people are never gonna forget."

"How do you know that, Ronnie?"

"I don't know that; I believe that. I have an idea of who he's gonna do it to, so I'm gonna keep my mouth shut. I ain't even saying nothing because next thing you know, the Secret Service is gonna be in here on me. The guy sent me a message a while ago through some guy saying, 'Tell Butch I'm very upset with him because he won't write me back.' Wants me to be in the loop. Are you serious? Just because we're from around the same area and because what I'm in here for, these guys come up to me and say we could start our own cemetery. I said to myself, aw, geez, you wanna be down with these idiots?"

"Do you wonder why these people gravitate to you?"

"It's ridiculous. Manson is the most infamous criminal in the world. Berkowitz is number two. They're peas in a pod. They write to each other every week. I know that for a fact. You can't write another prisoner, so they do it from the outside. They get a third party to write the letter, then he forwards it. That's how they been doing it."

"It's like they want to bring you into the ring and have you acknowledge that you're on their level. They want to bring you close."

"I don't know, they all think I'm somebody. I told them you think this notoriety is nice? I'm paying a hell of a price. I never wrote Manson back. He and everyone else think I'm something I'm not. Amityville. Why do I gotta be Amityville? All because of the damn Lutzes. Anyway, I gotta go. I'm gonna drop this damn phone I'm shaking so bad."

Years before, prior to one of her trips to New York, my mother had told us she was heading there to buy a property on Sea Gate, Coney Island's westernmost neighborhood and proudly gated enclave. Coney Island itself was then far removed from its heyday as America's summer playground and had become more a place for drifters, tramps, and vagrants, but the exclusive areas still held their allure. She went there and purchased a mini mansion, and it wasn't long before the socialites and artists came flocking to Momma's door. They all wanted to be touched by her, read by her, imbued with the sense of power and light.

But the radiant side of life, the exultant side Mary Palermo lived by day, proved to be only her superficial existence. It was the darker side, the vague mysteries and faint transmissions, that became her cursed infatuation. The house at Sea Gate was her beginning; the Surf Hotel, her end.

By the time I arrived at the hotel, the exorcism had already been going on for several days. She'd been led to the hotel by a group of addicts, vagabonds, and whores and placed in a room where she was forced to confront the very demons she had spent most of her life freeing others from. She had chased the devil out of strangers countless times. Now it was from her own body that she needed to banish it.

I first saw her from the vantage point of a long hallway leading toward the room. It was her, but it wasn't. Her face and body had changed. The ceiling was covered with Latin and the walls spattered with blood. There were voices; there was movement. And my mother, now in the middle of the room surrounded by two priests and a nun, began slowly to rise toward the ceiling. On their faces, I saw horror and defeat.

"Remember me," a fiendish voice called out from my mother's body.

The demonic presence in her was resilient, I heard someone say. They told me they hadn't wanted to call me because they feared I would be as tempting a host as she was. The devil moves fast, they said, when he has a mission. Father Vincent felt different. He thought I might be the only one who could bring her back. But I could see that it was too late. Her eyes were vacant. She was already gone. Perhaps those leading the ritual weren't powerful enough. Perhaps they weren't united in their dedication to save her. Perhaps the dark spirit had simply settled too deeply, and she couldn't be won back.

"The drooling won't stop. This shit is pouring out of me."

"What are they doing for you?"

"I'm going to emergency sick hall."

"What time?"

"When I get there, I get there. I gotta fill out a paper, give it to the cop. Doesn't matter, it's not gonna do anything. I keep drooling; it won't stop. Doctors ain't gonna do nothing anyway. I called the nurse. I said if I didn't go down there complaining about my arm, they wouldn't even have done the CAT scan."

"Did you ask them about the HIV test?"

"Oh, yeah, I called the doctor. He's gonna give me a real hard time. This guy."

"A few nights ago, you could hardly breathe."

"Can't breathe now. Last night someone gave me a Christmas present. I don't fuck with that shit. I did last night. It wasn't drugs, either. Said it was 100 percent pure. Vodka. Real stuff. Didn't do anything to me. I'm too sick to get drunk. I did six shots back-to-back. Didn't do nothing. Now this shit is pouring out of me. All night I was coughing. Woke up soaking wet. Every day I gotta wash my sheets? They give me those blue sheets, like diapers, because of the prostate problem they think I got. They're trying to murder me now, I'm telling you straight out. And they're doing it because of who I am. Not who I wanna be. Now this shit is all over the floor, everywhere. That strip club may be the last one I ever see."

"What strip club?"

"They took me to a strip club."

"Who?"

"Them COs."

"COs?"

"Correctional officers."

"You mean guards? Guards took you to a strip club?"

"Yeah, last night. When they were supposed to take me to Fishkill. To the hospital there."

"Look, Ronnie, we've come a long way. You have to be straight with me. You can't put me on."

"I ain't putting you on. I guess maybe it was a Christmas present, even though they didn't say anything about that."

"Let me understand this. You're telling me that you went to Fishkill, to the prison, to get checked, and then the guards took you out to a strip club?"

"About midnight. I went to Fishkill and saw the specialist, Dr. Terry, pulmonary doctor. He told me the problem with my lungs, this and that, did the CAT scan, we left there, got all the paperwork, about quarter to twelve. They said, 'Look, we'd all go out and get something to eat and go to a strip club, but we ain't got enough money.' I said, 'Look, a fifty on the backseat, on the floor. Somebody must have left it here. It's mine now—possession is nine-tenths of the law, ha ha.'"

I started to ask myself the same question I usually asked myself when he launched into one of his stories: was this real or the product of a bored, creative mind needing to construct a retroactive life as different as possible from the one he actually had? Just like the tale of Officer Eddie of the Amityville police force helping Ronnie put up a ladder to have sex with a married woman down the street, I could either take this at face value or try to poke holes in it. The problem was, once Ronnie had momentum, he was difficult to stop.

"All right," one of 'em says, "come on, this is on you.' All the steel came off me, the shackles, everything. They told me, 'Look, I want your word you ain't going nowhere.' I said, 'Yeah, I ain't going nowhere.' I left my coat in the van, because it's a state coat. I forgot my shirt had my tag on it, too. We just went to the bar, sat down, two girls started dancing, you know, they got the metal poles up on the stage there."

"They bought you drinks?"

"Well, I bought us drinks, with the fifty. A drink is three dollars in this place. We got a couple of Heinekens and a shot of vodka. I wanted to drink it straight. Music stopped, and this girl came over. And, I don't know, she looked at me; I looked at her; I don't remember if my hair was tied up. Anyway, she said hello; I said hello back. She says, 'Correct me if I'm wrong; you're a prisoner.' I said, 'Yes, absolutely.' She said, 'What are you drinking, tequila?' I said, 'No, vodka.'"

"What were you drinking again?"

"Vodka."

"And what did she ask you if you were drinking? Whiskey?"

"Tequila. You trying to trip me up, Jackie? You think I'm not telling the truth? Come on. We're closer than that now, ain't we?"

I didn't say anything. It had been a poor attempt.

"I said, 'You want a drink?' I called the bartender over, and I said, 'Give her a drink.' She says, 'No, I gotta work.' So I said, 'While you're here, give me another.' That was my third. She started talking to me. She was saying how long you in there for, this and that, how long you been in there. I said I been in prison longer than you been on the face of this earth. She says, 'Get outta here.' I said I been in prison thirty-six years. 'Don't fuck up,' I said. 'You'll be in the women's joint. They only got two of them.' She says, 'Who's over there in Green Haven? Isn't that guy from Amityville in there?' Cops started laughing. I said, 'Yeah, he's in there, I know him real well—he's a real nice guy, nicer guy than I am. Unless you don't think I'm nice.'"

"And you're just sitting there, like a regular patron. No shackles, nothing."

"That's what I said, ain't it? 'No,' she says, 'I think you're real nice, or I woulda left by now. I'm not one to lead people on or get recreation out of it. You're a gentleman. I wish other guys were as nice as you.' Asks me when I'm getting out."

"Christ, Ronnie."

"I said, 'Look, there's something I need to tell you, and when I tell you you're probably gonna run out of here as fast as you can. I don't want to burst your bubble, don't get upset, but the guy you're talking about is me. Look at my shirt.' She says, 'That's his name!' I said, 'Of course it is. I'm him. Don't worry,' I said, 'I'm not gonna hurt you. I got railroaded.' She says, 'I assumed it was murder already, all that time you did.' 'Listen,' I said, 'you believe what you want, but I didn't commit that whole crime. I committed some of it, but I would never do nothing to my little brothers and sisters.'"

I tried to jump in fast. "Ronnie, maybe it's time we talked about—"

"She says, 'Oh, I saw that show on TV but I didn't get to see it all, 'cause I work late.' I said, 'Which one?' 'The one on Halloween.' So we start talking and talking. She says, 'I'm gonna tell you something, you're really a nice guy.' I told her, 'I don't know about all of that, but I try to be. What's an attractive young lady like yourself doing in a place like this? Is it the money?' She says, 'Yeah, it's the money. I get seventy an hour to dance.' I said, 'When you get a steady boyfriend or something, I don't know if he's gonna like what you're doing. I wouldn't like it. I'd work two jobs rather than see you up there.'"

"Do you remember the name of the place?"

"We went through the back, where they dump the garbage. It was between Fishkill and here. It was a big place. It wasn't small. Tom and Jerry's, something like that."

I imagined calling Green Haven and asking the two guards to confirm that they took Ronnie DeFeo to a strip club. As I chuckled to myself, Joanne angled her computer screen toward me. She'd done a quick search and found Tom and Jerry's, a dive bar in Fishkill, New York. But that was as much information as we were likely to get. The story of the strip club would have to join the numerous other stories that escaped Ronnie DeFeo's lips: ones that might be true or might not, but that, in the end, had little impact on whatever our strange journey together was to be.

"The bartender knew the COs. Both of them. Her boobs were in my face the whole time, girls swinging on the poles behind her. Then she came back with another girl, she wanted my autograph. I said, 'Oh Jesus Christ.'"

Then came the laugh again, suppressed as soon as it

had escaped, and in that laugh was both awareness of the absurdity that comes with being taken to a skin joint when you're a murderer and also the enduring pain of that absurdity, the resentment he felt toward anyone who gave him a break. He had been taught to deserve pain. The officers who never arrested him for stealing thirty-nine thousand dollars from a local bank. The COs who decided to treat him to the awkward pleasure of women peeling off their clothes. To Ronnie they were all part of the same group, people who didn't recognize that he was bad to the core and should keep suffering for all eternity. That was why he wanted to give himself over to the darkness finally. In his mind, it was simply the hand he'd been dealt.

It seemed since the beginning of my trip with Ronnie DeFeo that I could never reach that last stage of sleep, or that I wouldn't sleep at all. Two nights before he told me about the guards taking him to a strip club, I'd received a phone call in the middle of the afternoon. I was getting ready to see a client, and my landline rang. When I picked up the phone and said hello, a strange voice on the other end returned the greeting.

I'd been speaking with Ronnie twice a day for several months now, and I knew all of his voices and tones. The voice that said hello back to me sounded like Ronnie's voice, but distant, or muffled, the way a voice sounds when someone puts a rag over the mouthpiece. It sounded far away, but, in the way haunting voices can, unnervingly close.

This wouldn't have been unusual had the number been

an 845 area code, since the only number Ronnie was ever allowed to use was the one inside Green Haven Correctional Facility. He had to call collect and wasn't allowed on the phone until the person on the other line accepted. So it couldn't have been him.

After a pause, there was a click on the other end. I called the number back and was greeted by a female telemarketer who I could barely hear over the sound of other phones and voices behind her. I apologized, hung up, and turned around to see Joanne in the room. She asked me what was the matter. Nothing, I said.

"Wait," I said as she turned to leave. "You don't think it's possible Ronnie could get out, do you?"

"Nah," she said. "That's crazy. Right?"

"Right," I said. "Crazy."

But he had been out indeed, taken by guards to watch women remove their clothes after getting his lungs inspected, and then ignored. Normally Ronnie had to be taken everywhere separately from the other prisoners, always in shackles and at gunpoint, with multiple guards as his personal escort. He'd attained the dubious CMC status within the system—Central Monitoring Case—which meant he could only be transported according to certain guidelines.

"Oh, yeah. Shackles around my legs, a chain around my waist, handcuffs gotta go through that, black box gotta go on top of them. Because I'm the damn Amityville Horror."

He'd been out. And something wanted me to know it had been out with him.

* * *

It was worse than any crime scene I had witnessed—and by that time I had witnessed many. I looked around the room at faces I didn't know, all of them surrounding Mary. She now lay in a bed, her face drawn, her eyes not her own. I walked to the bedside and tried to find in this thing's features the face of my mother. I searched, but I couldn't find the person I had known. Hurt flared in me, hurt more than fear. I got down on my knees and tried to stare the demon straight in the eyes. Its eyes were mocking me, but I held my gaze and told myself not to back down despite the priest imploring me, "Do not speak to it; do not engage." I stared straight into those eyes, and as the storm inside me whipped up, I summoned the words so seldom spoken between us, the words that would get me slapped off my chair for weakness. "I love you, Mom. Come back."

For a moment I saw her face, like a flickering image trying to achieve resolution. She squeezed my hand, and her mouth tried to move but couldn't form words. I could see her fighting, pleading. My mother's eyes looked back at me with love as a tear slid down over her cheekbone.

Then she was gone.

As Ronnie's body continued to submit, his outward bravado continued to diminish. I knew this meant that, one way or another, things were coming to a head. The shadows around him were getting stronger as he was getting weaker. But his physical apathy was secondary. More important was that his spirit was slowly relinquishing. I'd heard plenty of people talk about the welcome relief of death before, but often these were people who were prone to melodrama. Ronnie DeFeo was a lot of things, but melodramatic wasn't one of them. In an odd way, he was understated. But our conversations had become infused with a single theme lately, and I believed I was beginning to hear in his voice a clear note of surrender.

"What are you talking about death for?" I said. "We're not talking about death. We're talking about life."

"I know that, I know that, but Jackie, it's getting real bad. I just had to go change my clothes, because the fluid's just running all over me. It's a constant flow; you can't control it. It comes out of the left side or right side a little; then it just starts pouring out."

"You feel it coming out?"

"If I'm up. I touch my beard and I say, what is this? It's white and it's real sticky and hard. It's nasty."

"Like spit?"

"Nah, it's fluid. You should see what it's doing to my clothes. Had to change my shirt again, it's covered. That's why I keep coughing, that's why my voice is like this. This ain't my voice. I'm just so tired. You don't know how tired I am."

"There is a different way to end this, Ronnie."

"I'm going to do what I'm going to do. I'm telling you right now I'm scared that I'm gonna do it. I'll do it real quick. We can win if I end it."

"Your spirit will be tormented."

"We're gonna meet up somewhere else, him and me, and I got something for him. It's the only way to end it."

"Ronnie, that's not true. I've seen worse cases than yours. In Haiti, in South Africa. I am telling you, there is no way you have to do yourself in. Because then he wins. All of this."

"No, he loses. He can't torture me no more."

"It's not going to be over, Ronnie. You don't just die and it's like sleeping without dreaming. It doesn't work that way."

"I woke up with two black eyes one day, and I still got them."

"Nobody knows the torment you've been living with all these years. I know that."

"Maybe that heart is still in the backyard. If that thing was to get dug up? Oh my god."

"Ronnie, all these things you've held on to for all these years, it gives him momentum."

"I gotta go. I gotta get ready."

"Ronnie, you're not going to go execute yourself because of your father."

"Tell Joanne I say good-bye."

"Come on, Ronnie. Tell me some good news."

"The good news is now you know how to stop it."

"No. That's not the way. We can dig up that area, where the heart is."

"Right outside the door of the boathouse. As far as you can go, to the fence."

"You can't kill yourself, Ronnie. You can't. You spent

all of your adulthood behind bars, and then you're going to just end your life? You're not a coward."

"Eighty years old. That's what the bastard would be. Tonight."

"You're a warrior."

"I ain't even gonna try to go to sleep."

"Ronnie, you can't beat him by joining him. It doesn't work that way. It would defeat everything. You can't beat it like this. When we first started talking, you hated everything and everyone. For the first time in your life, all of that disappears. You call me now and ask how everyone is, the cat, Joanne. You live, you feel."

"Well, that's because I love you."

It was the first time he had said it. I knew he had started to feel something like love, but hearing him say it meant something crucial: it meant the battle could still be swung, could still be, in the end, won. "And now you want to just turn around and end it? You can't. You're not *allowed* to."

"This is a game, don't you understand?"

"It doesn't matter who you're being haunted by. The only thing that matters is you have to have faith in yourself, and you have to have faith in me. You aren't a coward. Think of the places you've been and the things you've endured. You aren't a weak kid, you're a man. Am I right or wrong?"

"You're right, you're right. I mean, this is a maximum-security prison. Sixty percent of the population here is doing life. I met a kid yesterday, seventeen years old, seventy-five to life. That's his minimum. Has to live seventy-five more years before he can go to the parole board. They got another one with one-twenty-five to life. I'm not a tough guy, but when I first came to prison, I learned what I did and what I had to do."

"How many prisons have you been in, Ronnie? How many different places?"

I already knew how many prisons he'd been in. I was just trying to get him to talk about something else.

"Oh Christ. I've been in Sing Sing. I've been in Clinton twice. I've been to Auburn. I've been to Attica. Sullivan, Eastern. I spent the night at Comstock. They threw me out; the superintendent said he didn't want me in his facility."

"Why?"

"Same reason as always—they think I'm trouble because of this shit following me. The popular guy is always bad news. Superintendent, chubby guy, he had a suit on, no tie, he said, 'Mr. DeFeo, this is nothing personal toward you, but I don't want you in my facility. It's not that you cause problems, but the notoriety that follows you, I just don't want it. We don't need no celebrities here.' I said, 'Celebrities? I'm just trying to do my time, sir.' He said, 'Quick as the bus comes, you're leaving.' Took me back to Downstate. Bus driver said, 'You've been on and off this bus seven times this week. What the hell's going on with you? Nobody wants you. What the hell did you do?' I said, 'They don't want me. They think I'm trouble.'"

"So you were transferred right away?"

"I was only there about seven or eight hours." The giggle again, that disturbing childlike sound that choked itself off almost as soon as it had escaped. "I had to stay down in the basement until they got a new bus to take me outta there. It was eleven o'clock at night. Off to Sullivan. But it happened there, too. The priest this time. They hold services, you know, over at the church. They had an altar boy named Speedy, he was lighting the candles, but they kept blowing out. So I lit them back, and they went out again. And then suddenly it's, 'Maybe it's that Amityville Horror shit flying around here.' I had to stop going up to the church. The priest asked me not to come back. Anyway, it don't matter. This has all gotta come to an end."

"Don't start that again, Ronnie."

"The cell they put me in, the cell I'm in now, the guy was a friend of mine. He died. They got me in a dead man's cell. I mean, Jesus Christ. Most of the guys I know, they're dropping dead around here like it's going out of style. One more ain't gonna make much of a difference. They'll be happy to see me go. Anyway, you shouldn't be part of this no more. I don't wanna put you in harm's way."

"This is not an end," I told him. "You're talking about a fight for eternity. Who gets the crown?"

"I love you, Jackie."

"You can't use the words *love* and *suicide* in the same sentence. You can't love if you want to destroy."

"That guy named Robert Blake just died. His daughter had to sell the tow truck to get money to get the autopsy done and to bury him. Doctor showed her the picture— this is the cause of death. Both his lungs were full of mold. Fungal pneumonia. That was the cause of his death. Both lungs. And now who's got fungal pneumonia? There's something in this jail that I'm breathing, and that's how I got this. And the goddamn doctor is saying my immune system's so weak it won't fight it off. I said, 'Why is it weak? I don't have AIDS or HIV.' They're trying to cover it up. They take a big needle and put it in your back and try to get the fluid out. This might be my last night, Jackie. I love you. You know, I never loved nothing in my life. I think I loved my dog, the one I had to put to sleep. Candie. They had to put her to sleep."

"I know, Ronnie. We've talked about it."

"She needed a new hip."

"Ronnie, focus. Stop rambling. You need to stop talking like this."

"I'm real messed up, do you understand that? It's over. I'm tired. I'm tired of fighting with my father. I'm fighting a losing battle. I'm gonna go take a shower. I don't wanna be dirty when they come get me."

As Mary Palermo sank away and the devil re-emerged, the entire room began to shake. Signs and pictures fell off the wall and shattered on the floor. The thing occupying my mother laughed in a guttural voice. Its eyes darted back and forth and its breaths became a hiss. *You will be next*, it said. Behind me the priest spoke his ministrations, trying to keep his voice steady. The demon spoke to me again. *I remember you*, it said, and this time I slapped my hands over my ears and stumbled backward. The priest yelled to someone for holy water.

I sat in the corner of the room and held my knees to

my chest as the priest lay two sets of rosary beads across her body. He began to chant last rites. I struggled to my feet and raced for the door.

There was a large man guarding it, blocking my way. Or at least I thought at first that he was guarding the door, but then I realized I was wrong. He was coming in as I was running out. As I hurried past him, I noticed a badge clipped to his belt.

I thought I sensed someone else there, too, someone familiar, calling my name in entreaty. But as I staggered down the steps, pushing past the drug addicts and night crawlers, I processed little, my only goal to get away, as far away as possible from the terror extending its claws through the spirit of my dead mother and, it seemed, indefinitely toward me. I weaved around the tramps and vagabonds, my shoulders scuffing both sides of the narrow staircase. It seemed the whole building was being brought to its knees. The walls tremored and the floor buckled.

I felt as though something was running directly behind me, carrying with it the screams from inside, for as I ran I could still hear them as clearly as when I had been inside the room. I passed back through the broken entrance and breathed the outside air, though still it seemed a wicked hand was on my shoulder. Rain was coming down in sheets, and the fall air felt icy.

I kept running. I ran across the boardwalk, down across the empty beach, into the ocean until the water lapped at my knees. Above me seagulls circled and shrieked. The tears came hard and fast as I tried to process the fact that my mother had just passed away, during an exorcism, in a rat- and drug-infested hotel room. The tears turned to gasps, my throat seeming to close in on itself. I tried to snatch breath from the air, but it wouldn't come. All that air, but no breath.

I didn't want to turn and look back. But as I stood in the shallow water gasping for air, tears sliding off my chin and mixing with the rain and the ocean, I thought, *You know me, but I know you, too. And I'll be ready.*

Just then a wave curled high out of the water, swelling twice as large as the others, and slammed into me. It staggered me but didn't knock me down. A familiar voice registered in my head, a voice that soothed me amid the piercing anguish. Again it called, and I turned to see Will walking into the water toward me.

"Take my hand," he said.

I looked at him, tried to pull my soul up toward the reality of him—his face, his skin, his outstretched hand. "Please," he said. "Take it."

My first thought, when I had run from the hotel and across the boardwalk, was to keep walking into that ocean and never stop. I would let the water wash over me, I would float past the breakers, I would become one with the elements forever. Will's caring eyes held me and started to bring me back.

"Take it, Jackie."

As the flood of tears began to abate, I willed my hand to reach out toward his, to grab on and keep hold of this side. His palm, upturned, hovered there, the wrist still, the water below it forever in motion. A single, strong hand, the palm patterned with curves and arcs, a cool still-life against the dark energy roiling inside me. His fingers splayed, desperate in their appeal. I stared at the hand. It was my only anchor.

"Ronnie, listen to me. It can be beaten."

"I'm tired, Jackie. I mean, now I'm being sent anonymous obituaries."

"What?"

"I got obituaries in the mail. Four of them. I don't know who the hell sent them to me. Who's going to send me obituaries? What for? I had it checked out. The post office box and the zip code in New York that they came from doesn't exist. Four obituaries I got. The DA's obituary was a third of a page long. 'Amityville Horror Prosecutor Dies'—that's what it said. You don't think he had anything to do with that?"

"Who?"

"My father, that's who. Did you hear what I said? Not just 'Prosecutor Dies.' '*Amityville Horror* Prosecutor Dies.' *I'm* the Amityville Horror. It's ridiculous is what I'm trying to tell you. That was a story about the goddamn Lutzes. I ain't got nothing to do with it. He came to Clinton, George Lutz, offered me the money to go along with them. I said no."

"What?"

"I wouldn't go along with them."

"Just a second, Ronnie. Slow down. The Lutzes offered you money to go along with the Amityville story?"

"They started all this crap. And because of *The Ami-*

tyville Horror, I'm put in this position. But none of that is true. They wanted me to go along with them, because they knew that I knew. But nothing happened to them. Nothing. George Lutz walked into a house that he couldn't afford, and he had to try to find a way to get out of it. That's all that happened. The truth of the matter is he paid a hundred thousand for the house. Eighty through the bank, the rest cash. The man got into something over his head, and then he had to try to make the money back somewhere. Guy was a loony tune. He was in South Oaks."

Joanne did a quick search while I asked Ronnie some innocuous questions. She wrote something down on a piece of paper and handed it to me. It read, "South Oaks—mental institution—Sunrise Island."

"You're telling me George Lutz spent time in a mental facility, Ronnie?"

"I'm not sure of the year, but it was right before I came to prison, so I would assume 1973. His grandfather had died, and I assume he just lost it. He had more than a breakdown. I mean he snapped."

"How do you know this?"

"I saw the guy. Some of the people I was running around with, they were all older than me, they said, 'Come on, let's take a ride.' Three of them. We took turns driving. I don't know which car I had, to tell you the truth. It was all on the down-low, because one of the guys I took there was a big-time bookmaker. So the four of us went to South Oaks."

"And you had no idea why?"

"No, I just went because I went. I must have had my

father's car, or maybe my mother's, the new station wagon. I went, Duchek went, the bookmaker went, and his associate went. I said, 'What are we going to the nuthouse for?' The bookie says, 'We're gonna go see my friend George.' We go, and they introduce me to this guy. 'Butch, this is George Lutz.'"

I asked myself again how much of this story was truth and how much was invention. And again I came to the same vague conclusion: it seemed pretty detailed to be made up. Still, it didn't matter what I thought. Hospitals don't disclose patient records; therefore, this wasn't a claim we could verify or refute.

"After a couple of minutes I was asked to leave. I didn't know what they were talking about, but I figured George must have owed the bookie money or something. Whatever. Then I realized I already knew who he was."

Ronnie claimed he knew a circle of guys who used cocaine on the weekends and that he was their source. George Lutz, he told me, was part of that. "I didn't realize at first that it was the same guy."

"So you're saying George was doing cocaine at the time?"

"I don't know. I would assume so. I mean, this guy was in his own zone, man. Way out there."

"What did George have to do with booking?"

"How do I know? He might have been gambling. But something had to be going on for this guy, the guy I took there, to go see him personally. I gotta say, that man was out of his mind. If it was an act, it was a good one."

I'd been thinking the same thing.

"I mean, he belonged right where he was."

"Why would it be an act?"

"I don't know. I saw him after that, maybe a few months later, at a bar in town. I believe it was the Chatterbox, on Merrick Road. He came in there looking for somebody. He seen me and asked me if I saw so-and-so; I said no. Yeah, I believe that's where it was. Next thing I know, my family's all dead, I'm in jail, and this nut is making me an offer on the goddamn house."

"How did he get to that point?"

"The bank told me someone wants to buy it. But before anyone could buy it, I had to sign a release, since everything was mine. And when I inquired about who's buying the house, they told me someone named Lutz. I asked if his first name was George, and they said yeah. I told them he don't have that kind of money. They told me the bank's giving him eighty thousand. So I said, 'Screw that, let's make it a hundred.' I didn't care. I was happy to sit on the place. 'He better come up with twenty thousand,' I said. 'He better borrow it from somebody else, 'cause the bank ain't gonna give him the rest.' I don't know where he came up with the money, but he came up with it. Not through the bank, though."

"And that went right into the estate?"

"Not the twenty thousand; that went under the table. That went south. I got part of that in my pocket, so I didn't care. But the eighty. And as soon as he went in the house, he contacted Weber, my attorney, who came over to the house to see him, and his wife, and over plenty of wine, and they were also eating some cheese, they came up with the story. He took Weber's ideas—the red-eyed pig, the neighbor's cat, the marching band—they made all this nonsense up. They turned normal things into figments of imaginations."

"And he didn't want to come forward and say that he had ever met you before."

"Of course not. Nobody knew about that because I wouldn't feed into George Lutz and his nonsense. So he comes to Clinton, since Weber knew they were gonna have a hard time with me going along with this crap. George comes up to Clinton and offers me seven hundred and fifty thousand dollars—that was the first offer; the second offer was eight hundred and fifty—to go along with these shenanigans. None of it was true. A sixty-seven-piece marching band? Come on. The red-eyed pig, beds going up and down off the ground? Please."

"What happened when they left the house?"

"They went and got Jay Anson in California to write the book."

It was the first time Ronnie had directly referred to *The Amityville Horror*, the book that had started his macabre roller-coaster ride of fame, or to Jay Anson, the man the Lutzes had hired to write it. *A True Story*, the subtitle had read.

"Meantime, the Lutzes left all the furniture in the house and stuck me with the mortgage. They had to come to me. I had to get papers notarized, signed, before they could think about selling the house. The bank was screaming. Of course, I was incarcerated, so the bank wasn't about to get their money back from me. So it got sold again."

"Let's just be clear, here, Ronnie. You're telling me that the Lutzes offered you money to confirm the story."

"Seven hundred and fifty thousand. Then eight-fifty."

"If you want me to tell the world your story, this is part of it. So you're saying to me this is the rock-solid truth."

"Seven-fifty. I said no. Then eight-fifty. I told them to go screw themselves. But no matter what, I'm still the Amityville Horror."

I had taken Will's hand and gone back. "This is your mother," he'd said. "Your own mother. You can't be afraid. Something else may have taken her, but you have to bring her back home."

Her body was wrapped with the religious relics and removed from the hotel in the middle of the night. Along with the priests, I had blessed the room, which was then boarded up by a team led by the man with the badge I'd seen in the doorway. A burnt cross—the symbol of an exorcism—was smeared in ashes above the door, warning others never again to enter.

We took her remains to a secret location where curiosity seekers would hopefully leave to rest the mother I had loved and longed for and not disturb the demon that slept within, waiting to be reawakened. I was like a shattered piece of glass, in pieces but still strong, fractured but still dangerous.

After my mother passed, Will, Joanne, and I, along with Uncle Ray, stayed in Brooklyn. I was clinging to my mother's stolen spirit. I would go back home to New Orleans often to be with my father, but we seldom spoke during this long period. He would just sit, waiting—for what I couldn't tell. He was present but murky, one foot in this domain, the other already starting on the path back to my mother. In my memory it seems the only words we exchanged were with our eyes. The silences spoke volumes. Voices would have only provided false substance.

The greatest favor I felt I owed my father was to be genuine. He had both taught me life and allowed me to discover it through my own perception. At six, when I lost my first tooth, I sat on the edge of my bed holding it in my hand and wanting badly to believe that if I put it under my pillow, a magical fairy would come during the night, place it in her bag, and leave money in exchange. But by then I'd already seen too much. I threw the tooth out the window. My father never mentioned it.

He left the plantation and tucked himself away in the bayou, the comfortable heart of all he'd known. It was nothing more than a shack—the shack where my life had started. I'd watched my mother do her mojo there, watched her meticulously assemble her bag of charms, amulets, blood from medicine men, particles of bones, herbs from the Louisiana swamps. "Mojo can heal as well as take, Jackie," she would tell me. "The bag is an embodiment of strength and energy, its contents the physical infused with the spiritual. It is the essence of the person enhanced by the gifts of the practitioner. Respect the energy, and always remember, the same hand that rocks the cradle can dig the hole of death."

The mojo bags I most enjoyed watching her make were those commemorating a birth. She would sit alone, music playing, the music sometimes the newborn's cry from the next room. Her face would change as she went into full possession. "You are awakening the dead for their assistance, Jackie. Open up to them; let yourself be the conduit."

The bag would be placed on an altar to charge. Candles would be lit, and an offering would be given, something of worth, never to be touched again. When the bag was ready, it would be soaked in oils that had been handmade from a ritual book written in blood and passed down through my family for two hundred years.

Settled in Brooklyn, I developed a client base and a regular working pattern. Though letters would come in from all over the world from those experiencing paranormal phenomena and possession, I stayed put. Together Will and I continued to study our spirituality and enhance our psychic power. I welcomed the appeals from people wanting to be read or desiring help communicating with souls stuck in between. Our existence was becoming, at least in a relative sense, normal.

One morning, there was a knock at my door. I opened it to find a muscular man with a kind face. One I recognized.

"Hello, Chiefy," I said. "How did you find me?"

"I've got ways," Adam Quinn replied. "I'm a detective now. Of course, you knew that already."

I had seen the path he would take years before, back

in Nola, and now, as I invited him into my home, he talked about the individual steps that had taken him forward. After returning to New York, he had become a policeman in the Midtown South Precinct. Then a patrol sergeant. Followed by special ops lieutenant, detective squad commanding officer, and, eventually, captain of homicide.

"How did you come to be in New York?" he said.

"It's a long story."

"Then let me cut to the chase. I could use your help. Will you come to my office?"

I agreed, because I saw something in Adam I had seen the first time we'd met: sympathy across dimensions, a connection to both realms.

I accompanied him to his office in Brooklyn, a plain, low-slung gray building hidden in back of Gold Street behind the imposing courthouses with their columns and statues. Along the way I passed a number of people I figured were criminals, but Adam assured me that half of them were detectives working undercover. He was now in charge of overseeing all homicide cases in the city, and he had put away more killers than anyone previously in the role had done.

We walked into his office, and all I saw were boxes. Dozens of them, stacked on the floor, shoved up against the wall, piled on his desk.

"These are all unsolved cold cases," he said. "I wondered if you might be able to help."

"You never quit, do you?" I said.

"No," he replied. "I don't."

I was in his office the entire day and all evening. Most cases occupied multiple boxes, but it wasn't all that paperwork he wanted me to go through. He just wanted me to look at pictures.

His office was like a morgue, the boxes holding photos instead of bodies. It was like a bizarre twist on someone showing you his or her photo album, except Adam's album was of the dead or missing. He would place a picture in front of me and plead for information. *What am I missing? Give me a face, a name; give me something to go on.* He would pace around the office, nervous, angry, desperate. This went on for hours. I would tell him things, hand him pieces to try to complete the three hundred puzzles that filled his office.

The news was never good. This body has been burned and put in a drum, Adam. It was the boy's father, Adam. Abused him and then killed him. They used acid on this one. This one's bones were buried in different places. It was the uncle, Adam. Got the girl pregnant and then killed her and her mom. I'm sorry, Adam. I'm sorry.

He was devastated by each one of these cases. And I felt a growing duty to him, just as he felt a duty to those who had been forced out of this life and into the next. He had made it his mission to bring them to rest, and he wouldn't stop at anything until he could do them this one last favor.

"I need you, Jackie," he said. "I owe it to these families."

From then on, we began to work as partners, if not on paper, then in practice. Adam's was the gift of tenacity; mine was the gift of sight. He would review the cases and apply his unyielding logic to them; then, when that proved inadequate, he'd bring them to me, and I would try to see in my head what his cold reason hadn't been able to uncover. I would relive and re-enact. I would become. He became my advisor in the world of the practical, and I became his in the world of the spiritual. He respected my skills and understood when, and how, to apply them.

In the criminal underworld and in the homes of otherwise normal people, appalling things occur with awful frequency, and it's a sad truth that thousands of these crimes remain unsolved every year. Though I'd seen and experienced more than most in my life, I still wasn't prepared to see the cases that crossed Adam's desk every day. There was no end to these files, and each seemed to hold a story more terrible than the last.

Much more often than seemed possible, the stories involved young people. Most of us float through our lives with only the tiniest awareness of truly bad things happening. Most of us never see such things. Most of us don't come into even indirect contact with the people capable of doing them. For Adam, it was the opposite—his job was to be immersed in the depravity most of us never even glimpse.

It was the kind of job where you absorbed the pain of so many unhappy endings for the hope that one might turn out bright. Now and then, it happened. The cold cases would come in as an unending stream, from organizations, families, newsrooms, law enforcement. All of them arrived for the same reason. They hid something—something even seasoned detectives weren't able to find.

As Joanne got older, she became my assistant. She

would prioritize the cases, she told me, according to what she felt. I never questioned her. The order wasn't suggested by Adam. Different cases just pulled at Joanne more than others. I didn't ask why.

One evening we were having a birthday dinner at home for Joanne—just me, her, Will, and Ray, plus the pets. Suddenly Joanne said she needed to check the fax. One of us, I can't remember who, told her to take an evening off and stay at the table. It was her birthday, for God's sake. She ignored us.

A few minutes later, she returned, holding the single fax that had arrived: a flyer showing the face of a pretty young woman, accompanied by a note from her family. The young woman's name was Bonnie. Bonnie's twenty-first birthday had just passed, they said, and she was still missing, as she had been for several weeks. They feared the worst but couldn't bear to imagine it. The police had been of no help. They said they had no leads.

Joanne placed the fax, and Bonnie's picture, on the table in front of me. Almost immediately I felt a spiritual pitching, like a wave of nausea. An image slowly started to materialize. I tried to keep the surge at bay. Sometimes it crystallizes fast; sometimes you have to fight the psychic rush long enough to see all the way in.

"Call Adam," I said. Joanne got him on the phone, and he asked what she was doing working on her birthday. I took the receiver. "Adam, we have a missing person. Twenty-one years of age. Five-eight, one-sixty. Shoulder-length brown hair, dark blue eyes. Lives in the Valley."

"I'm at a family Christmas party," he said.

"She's still alive."

A short time later, Adam arrived at my house. The two of us, with Joanne, huddled. I told him what I felt: that the girl was in Florida.

"You said she was from the Valley," Adam said. "California."

"That's where she's *from*," I said. "But that's not where she *is*."

Adam looked at me oddly. I asked him what was up.

"I'm booked to go to Florida in two days," he said. "On a private case."

We contacted the girl's family and told them to book the earliest flight they could to a specific location in South Florida. I did the same.

Two weeks later, we found Bonnie. Adam had taken what I'd seen and used it to find out everything he could from Bonnie's family. My intuition and his common sense had then placed him in front of a particular hotel one sunny morning, and Bonnie had walked out the front door, her boyfriend beside her. He was no longer her boyfriend, however; he had become her husband.

Sometimes you get doubly lucky: not only do you find the missing person but that person also finds something in his or her heart that wasn't there before. That evening, sitting with Adam and me in our hotel room, Bonnie called home to her parents. They fell apart instantly, overwhelmed with relief that she was alive. Apologies and expressions of love were repeated back and forth through tears. She would come home, she told them. She'd come back home.

It was a special case. And, unfortunately, an exceptional one—that of a missing person who had chosen to leave her life behind and, eventually, saw reason to come back to it. Most of the crimes Adam and I investigated together had endings that were just as memorable but for the wrong reasons. He worked in homicide, after all.

We continued on, vowing to each other never to give up hope until the worst was confirmed. Most of the time, it was. But rare cases like Bonnie's kept us hopeful to the end, always. If we couldn't locate a person or reunite a family, we might at least provide the tragic answers as opposed to the ongoing nightmare of guessing.

Adam and I unfortunately never lacked for reasons to collaborate, but we tried to make what goodness we could out of often horrific situations. I was his secret weapon; he my spiritual kin. I made him a mojo bag for protection, which he still carries with him. He gave me a bulletproof vest.

In 2005, my father was in his eighties, but only his spirit had diminished. He still had a full, thick head of hair and the tender but calloused hands that had cradled me in childhood. And he still carried a rain stick and wore a medicine bag, ever the diviner inside a laborer's body.

He had started to resemble my grandfather—also named Andrew, though everyone had referred to him as the White Wolf. Though he had passed away when I was five, I remembered my grandfather well, a large, gentle medicine man and respected warrior chief and shaman.

It was only in adulthood that I realized how powerful he had been, and how he had recognized my gifts before anyone else had.

My grandfather died in old age, quietly, at home, and no one in my family said much about it. But afterward, I felt him coming to me often. If I felt sad, confused, or lost, there he would be, at my side, calming me, taking my hand, and making my spirit well again. He knew I could see past the flesh and feel his guiding touch. It was him, before anyone, who taught me how to part the trees of the physical world and see through the forest to the spiritual. He became my centering force.

During the 2005 trip, as on all my strange homecomings to New Orleans, I would walk the streets of the city I loved feeling on one hand as though I'd been gone forever and on the other as though I'd never left. I looked down as I walked, slowing down, taking in every step. There isn't a place in the world like New Orleans. Even the drunks are happy. The half-dressed dancers looking for the next dollar all knew me by name, and I would walk the French Quarter and be greeted by those who still regarded me as the voodoo queen, the fire walker. "Mornin', Miss Jackie," they would say, their lazy Creole accents wafting on the breeze like music, the smell of jasmine filling the air. The beads falling from decorated balconies. Crowds everywhere. They say New Orleans is 90 percent Catholic, 100 percent voodoo. I loved its spirit and vigor. I took it all in, feeling cocooned.

But a cocoon is temporary. It wraps around you from the outside; it can't prevent what happens inside. Soon my heart began to feel heavy with loss and regret, and I headed toward my favorite place in the world, and the only place I knew where I could find comfort: Bourbon Street. I walked it until nightfall. The music was loud; the party endless. Here you see the faces of the living in all their manifestations. Here the spirit roams free and is embraced by all. I was temporarily filled again. It would be short-lived, but I could at least drink it in for now. That one stretch of street, the celebration of life and spirit with no end. Amid all the raucousness, I had peace. I went back home and sat with my father, saying nothing, just breathing at his side, his connection to a fading conscious-ness. He sat in an old rocker with my mom's chair next to him, his aging hand holding one arm of her chair. He gazed out the window into the night. You couldn't tell whether he was the person or the spirit.

Finally, he turned to me, and for the first time, I saw a tear fall from his eyes. I took a tissue and wiped the tear from his cheek. I still carry that tissue in my mojo bag.

"The time has come," he said. "I'm going home to my maker. Go back to New York."

"No," I told him. "Not without you."

But he knew I remembered the fight, the one that meant he couldn't come to New York—not now, not ever. My father stood six foot six and was built like a bull. His physical constitution was matched by the firmness of his principles, which meant if he felt you were behaving badly, you were going to hear about it. This applied whether you were his daughter, his wife, or a professional boxer. So when he'd found Jake LaMotta flirting with my mother in a bar in Hell's Kitchen, he'd done the only thing that occurred to him: slugged the man. Or so went the story I'd always been told.

Jake LaMotta had come out of the Bronx slums to become middleweight champion. Before that, he'd been forced by his father into fighting other kids to entertain the adults in the neighborhood as they threw change into the ring, which his dad used to help pay the rent. Maybe that's what had helped him develop the legendary chin in the real ring, the one that allowed LaMotta to withstand astonishing punishment while remaining on his feet. He'd beaten Sugar Ray Robinson, thrown a fight to Billy Fox, won titles, testified to the Senate about the Mob's influence on boxing, then finally retired and bought bars, the place he felt most comfortable outside the ring. He'd also made and squandered millions, and needed the income.

And he'd taken a shine to Mary Palermo, according to the tale. Apparently, by the time my father first saw them together in that bar, it wasn't the first time she and LaMotta had met. Some say Mary came to New York looking for properties to turn into spiritual houses. Others say she came for a more basic reason: she couldn't resist the former boxer. The way it was always told to me, when Andrew Palermo entered the bar and witnessed the interaction, he didn't care whether LaMotta was a former champ or a palooka from the streets. When he was younger, my father had enjoyed bare-knuckle fighting in the local bars. He didn't need the cash; he just enjoyed the battle. He knew how to throw a punch, and how to take one. He just started swinging. And he connected.

Hard. The story I heard was LaMotta's jaw was broken. My father was tossed in jail.

I was told that they deported my father to Canada, back to Hamilton, an industrial port city nestled onto the west side of Lake Ontario's Golden Horseshoe. Don't bother returning to New York City, they told him. No one's going to let you in. Two weeks later, he was back in the bayou. Was the story true, or was it one of those family tales that become embellished over time—or perhaps changed to protect a child? I would never know. I'd never thought about the fact that it might not be true. In fact, I'd never thought about it much at all. Now, looking into my father's eyes, I thought about that and everything else I'd ever known, or thought I'd known, about him and my mother.

"I've seen the wolf," my father said to me. "My work is done, and I'm going home. But you still have work to do. Save yourself, and free the only woman I ever loved."

Upon returning to New York, I found I could do nothing but lie in bed. For five days I did little else other than poke occasionally at the food that Will placed in front of me. He made pleas to get me in motion, but I childishly refused. I wanted to be alone with my unrest.

On the sixth day, Hurricane Katrina hit.

I called everyone I knew. Many had died in the initial deluge. Others had become victims of gangs or looters. I went back as soon as it was possible. My dad was gone. He'd died in the shack, my mother's chair beside him.

EIGHT

When you're a child, owning up to a small lie is dif-
ficult. You took an extra cookie; you broke the TV remote.
Admitting to a larger transgression requires even more
strength and self-possession. You hit your sister. You
skipped the midterm. You and your friends were the ones
who vandalized that car. It's easier to bottle the truth if
it causes a bit of embarrassment or pain, but that truth,
as Edgar Allan Poe so eloquently showed us, will fester.
The bigger the truth, the more cancerous it will become
when kept inside.

Most buried lies stay that way until the perpetrator of
the lie decides to come clean. And in most cases, those
people ultimately will fess up, if for no other reason than
because it feels rotten to keep something nasty buried
inside forever. We're human, and we long to tell each
other our stories. They define us. Even a bad story is still
better than nothing at all.

Joanne had continued to plumb the Amityville files for me, and now I thought I was beginning to see the convergent sources of Ronnie DeFeo's conflict and anger. One of the by-products of his becoming a celebrity monster was the opportunity it presented to others. In the years since the murders, many individuals had come forth, or had been solicited, to examine the house and determine whether it was indeed haunted.

Among the most prominent of these opportunists was Hanz Holzer, a self-proclaimed paranormal specialist who had somehow wrangled his way into conducting an investigation of 112 Ocean Avenue a few years after the murders. In January 1977, he and another alleged spiritual medium, Ethel Meyers, entered the house, and the two of them claimed with fierce conviction that it had been built over an ancient Native American burial ground and that the angry spirit of a Shinnecock Indian chief named "Rolling Thunder" had possessed Ronald DeFeo Jr., driving him to murder his family.

The assertion was denied by the Amityville Historical Society, but Holzer wasn't concerned about the potential inaccuracy. Nor was his audience. He went on to write multiple books on the topic.

When I brought up Holzer's name, Ronnie reacted in a way he hadn't reacted to the mention of anyone else. Holzer had visited Ronnie, I learned, at Clinton, bringing with him William Weber. It was the first and last time Holzer came to see him, Ronnie said.

"What year was that?"

"Early eighties—1980 or 1981. He was gonna write a

book. He said, 'I believe you had sex with your sister Dawn, intercourse with her.' I jumped up and said, 'I'm gonna knock the shit outta you right here.' I threw my right and Weber jumped in the middle. I told Holzer if he said another word about that, I was gonna break him right there in the visiting room."

"Was that it? Did he leave then?"

"Oh, no, he wasn't done by a long shot. Then he tried to hypnotize me; that was the biggest joke in the—oh my god, what a joke—you ain't hypnotizing me. That was it, he was outta there; he left."

"Weber was your lawyer at the time."

"I figure he got screwed on *The Amityville Horror*, so now he wanted to cash in with Holzer. He says that crap about Dawn, and I went crazy. Guard came in and said, 'That's it, visit's over.' Weber said, 'Oh, it was just a mis-understanding. Ronnie, you're not gonna do nothing, are you?' Holzer tries to hypnotize me and I said, 'You can't hypnotize me. There's something inside me that won't let you; it's called a conscience.' Back then I was carrying about one-eighty-five, one-ninety, 'cause I was working in the wood yard, cutting and splitting wood all day with an axe. It's gotta be 1980 or 1981, because I left Clinton and went to Auburn in 1983."

"What did you think about the stuff Holzer said?"

"He said I had an Indian chief's spirit in my cell. I said, 'What are you, outta your mind?' He had the recorder going. What a load of nonsense. Weber said, 'You can't use none of that, Holzer.' Meanwhile, he was busy trying to make book and movie deals on the side."

Since we'd begun speaking, months before, I had thought constantly about the reasons Ronnie DeFeo and I had been thrown together. As the strange activity in my house continued, and he began to yield physically and spiritually, I had come to feel more and more uncertain about our ability to defeat the evil that had made itself known in various ways over the course of both our lives.

"Everybody wants a piece of this," he said. "They've all had their hands out, every one of them involved—Weber, the DA, the medical examiner, everyone wrote a goddamn book. My lawyer. The psychiatrist. The investigator. They all made deals."

"Are you upset that they made deals behind your back?"

"I'm upset because I want to tell the goddamn truth."

I paused a moment, thinking about Holzer, Ethel Meyers, and the parade of others who had passed in and out of the Amityville story over the decades. Was I becoming just another character in this bizarre saga? Had I become merely a sounding board for Ronnie DeFeo's flights of fancy?

"Ronnie, why trust me? I'm a medium, too. Aren't I the same as those others? How do you know I'm different?"

"Those others were spouting a bunch of nonsense. I know you, Jackie. I mean, you give a shit about me, right?"

There was one of those rare pauses at the other end of the phone. I'd often had the sense that Ronnie would have stayed on the line all day and all night with me, venting, spilling. I felt I hadn't even glimpsed the bottom of vitriol that he needed to get out. And nothing would come of this journey without the basic act of his washing himself clean of it all.

"Ronnie, you said to me once that everyone in that house was bad except the young kids. Do you still feel you're a bad person?"

"You gotta understand something," he said. "I'm sorry for what happened in my house. If I wasn't sorry, then you'd have had a real problem."

It was an opening. "What do you mean?"

More silence from the other end. The bluster retreating, as it always did when we approached the topic of what happened on November 13, 1974.

"I woulda done some damage."

"To what? To whom?"

"I was so angry. I'll let you in on a little secret. I had just went and bought a brand new carbine rifle. An M1. It fired .44 Magnum rounds. Some people thought when they saw it, 'Oh look at that .30-caliber carbine.' When I went to the store to buy it, the guy said, 'No, that's a .44.' I said, 'Like a pistol?' He says, 'Yeah.' I bought it. Hundred dollars, brand-new. Only problem was, I bought the big clip. They were twenty-round clips. I made the guy order some for me. I made him order twelve, plus the two that came with the gun. I was ready. Nothing coulda stopped me."

"Ready for what, Ronnie?"

"A .44 Magnum goes through an engine block. I gave it a lot of thought that afternoon. Plus I had two grenades.

Two hand grenades. In the boathouse under the floor. I know for a fact they found them. But I put it all on my father. I said, 'I don't own the house, he owns the house. He's dead now, but you ain't putting these grenades on me.' I coulda did some damage. But I'm not evil like that. I was gonna get a lot of them."

"Who? Who were you going to get?"

"Everything that had a blue shirt on, or a uniform, or a cop—I was gonna get 'em all. I ain't never met a cop that wasn't on the take. Ever."

"You wanted to go after cops?"

"I never even stopped for red lights. Never got a ticket in my life. A cop puts his red light on, there's two things I'm doing, either getting ready to pay him off or I'm gonna outrun him. Lost one in the cemetery once. That was my favorite spot. I knew all the cemeteries. You drive right through there like a maniac—they couldn't catch you. No lights on. I was good, believe me. My eyes at night are like an owl. Stealing all them motors at night, you gotta have eyes like an owl. I had my share, more than my share. Eight motors in one night once. It was about money. They never caught me. Never even a ticket."

He hadn't reconciled it yet. Ronnie still resented everyone in a position of authority or legal enforcement for not putting him away when they'd had the chance. He wanted the bad-seed label his father had convinced him he deserved. He was so bad, he was saying to me, how could they let him keep getting away with things? The longer they let him run, the more it reinforced Ronnie's—and his father's—picture of himself. If only they had picked him up for something. Running red lights. Stealing motors. Evading arrest.

If only they had got him for one of those things, he'd have been put away already. He would have been in jail, or in his mind, even better, killed. And if that were the case, he could not have committed the acts that he did on that fateful night.

"Ronnie, I want you to slow down for a minute and tell me about what happened on Novem—"

But Ronnie barreled ahead, talking about an incident that had happened two years previously, in 1972. He and his friends "threw some guy that had OD'd into the canal. We had to dump him in there, where all the swans are. It's real nice back there. We didn't want any trouble with this guy dying on our time. We just tossed him in."

I knew the area he was referring to. More than three and a half decades later, I had seen the swans, too. I had seen them while helping Adam and the NYPD scour the canal for evidence of seventeen-year-old Kieran McCaffrey's death. "Remember when I first wrote you, Ronnie? Remember I'd been on that police boat? A lot of disturbing stuff happened on that boat. No one who was on the shoot that day talks to each other now. People became violently ill. Bizarre things, Ronnie."

"I know what's in them waters that you were in. There's a lot of bodies. There's a lot of murder weapons. I know that for a fact. A lot of evidence that was dumped in them waters, so the police wouldn't find them. Great South Bay is my turf. For ten years I ran Great South Bay. The police could never get me. The Coast Guard could never get me.

One day a guy came out in a cabin cruiser, forty-foot. Really expensive boat. Stateroom, everything. He's on the boat. I'm on my speedboat with two of my friends—suddenly, *ba-BOOM!* That's all I hear, and I see a guy flying through the air like Superman. That boat exploded, right there in front of me. I had to pick him up out of the water. By the time the Coast Guard got there, the boat was gone to nothing; it went under. Let me tell you something about them waters," he continued. "You woulda never been able to find what you were looking for. The current in them waters is so strong, if you put something there now, in ten minutes it'll be gone. That's how strong that current is. That's the ocean on the other side."

I tried to get him back on topic, but he kept on bouncing from subject to subject, talking first about his old boat, then about the ease with which he'd been able to smuggle weapons into his cell when he was at Clinton, and even about how his favorite Christmas novelty song, "Grandma Got Run Over by a Reindeer," had been playing the night before.

I'd lost him. And when he spoke again a few moments later, the voice of the cocky delinquent had disappeared once more, replaced by the suddenly weary voice of the lifer.

"But then of course I couldn't sleep." His voice shrank to a pinch. "I'm afraid to go to sleep. I'm afraid I ain't gonna wake up. I think it's coming, I really do."

"What's coming? Your father?"

"I mean, I think you gonna have to call this Father Fernando and straighten some things out."

Father Fernando was Green Haven's chaplain, and, at least according to Ronnie, not a fan of the facility's most notorious inmate. Maybe he thought Ronnie was beyond redemption. Whatever the case, Ronnie claimed that Father Fernando saw him as bad news. He didn't exactly think of him as someone he might look to for salvation.

"I keep telling him, 'Look, I don't have no relatives left. Everybody's gone. If anything happens to me, something's gotta be done.' You need to tell him you got power of attorney, I wrote a letter and got it notarized. That should be enough. I mean, everybody in my family is dead. There's nobody left. Something happens to me, my body needs to be turned over to you. He said he wants a copy."

"Sure, Ronnie. I'll send it to him."

"I wish the guy would retire, but he ain't. He told me he ain't. He's been here seventeen years. Got his own little cemetery over there. It's bullshit."

I didn't think Ronnie was saying it was bullshit to have a cemetery for inmates who died and didn't have anyone else to claim them. I thought he was saying it was bullshit that he wouldn't be accepted there if he died, too. To Ronnie, Father Fernando was just another person who didn't want him.

"He's got a problem now, there's no inmates that work out there. They closed the annex, so the inmates can't bury nobody no more. They closed everything. There's a lot of them back there in that little cemetery. Holds a service in the church for them—that church is bigger than most churches in the state. Some gangster donated the money and they built it, thirty, forty years ago. Just like the one at Clinton. That's also a big church. He has a wooden box built, he puts the guy in it, he has the service, then he takes them outta here."

"What do you mean? For prisoners who die?"

"Yeah, for prisoners who die, that's what I'm trying to tell you. I don't want to go out like that."

I don't want to go out like that. I didn't think this had anything to do with Father Fernando, or the cemetery, or the church. I think Ronnie just hoped his remains could end up in the hands of someone who cared—at least a little—about him.

"I'll tell you truthfully, I don't think this is getting any better. The father said, 'Try to exercise this morning.' I said, 'Screw that. I got plenty of strength.' I'm having a hard time getting my beard even, I'll tell you that. I trim it three, four times a week, but I can't get the god-damn thing to look right."

"Ronnie, did you get test results back? Did they find something you aren't telling me about?"

"Look, I got a visit the other night, okay?"

"You got a visit from who?"

"I mean, that's why all the stuff's been happening in your house. He wants to see who I've been talking to. He wants to mess around with you now."

"Who?"

"It was 1990 he came to see me. No, excuse me, 2000—what am I saying, 1990? He came to see me in 2000."

"Who did, Ronnie? What are you talking about?"

"I was sleeping, and he woke me up. Kept tapping me

on the knee, I said, 'What the hell is this?' He had a long black coat and a black hat. I mean, he comes in different forms, right? It wasn't the face of an old man, it wasn't the face of a young man. It was in between. Clean-shaven, pure white face. Pure white."

"You mean—"

"Lucifer."

"Okay. What did he say to you?"

"I thought it was a ghost at first. I said, 'Oh my God.' Then he told me everything. Told me his name, said he was an apostle and Jesus threw him out. Said he was a real nice guy, threw him out. Said, 'They don't care about you or anybody else. They're up there having a good time.' I asked him if there's a heaven and a hell. He said, 'Well, it exists, but it's not the way you think it is.' He was in my cell for quite some time. Sat on the bed and he started talking to me. I got real nervous. Told me a lot of things. Said he was gonna help me, that it was gonna take time. The man knew what happened. He knew everything. He knew I didn't do them kids. He knew I got a bad deal. He respected that I wasn't a snitch, either."

"What else did he tell you?"

"Oh, this guy went on and on. Said Jesus screwed him over royally. His face was shining, it was so bright. I didn't need a light. A regular man, just like me. Like I said, he came with a black coat on and a black hat. It's the same man that came to your house that night."

"How did you know that?"

"He came to your house because of me. I've pulled you into this, and I'm sorry about that."

"That night you had a bloody nose, Ronnie—I didn't tell you, but there was blood in my bathroom sink. A lot of it."

"He's messing with you now. I got shit happening to my teeth, my arms. I had those two black eyes. I woke up that way, I had to tell them it was in the medication."

"Did he say anything about the church?"

"Said I was an altar boy when I was a kid, and I used to go to church, and I used to go to confession. Then he started bad-mouthing the priest, said the priests are a bunch of faggots; they love young boys. He says, 'You know you went the wrong way in life.' I said, 'Well, how am I supposed to know which way?' He says, 'You know, I can't believe it—I'm sitting here talking to you, and you're not afraid. I can tell if people are afraid or not.' I said, 'Why should I be afraid? You didn't do anything to me.' He said, 'Yet.' I said, 'All right, here we go.'"

"What did he mean he was going to help you?"

"He said somebody was gonna come eventually and help me. But it was gonna take time. I signed a contract."

"A contract?"

"He pulled out a pen and a piece of paper. But I couldn't read nothing on the paper. I don't know what it was written in."

"What did it look like?"

"A white piece of paper. It didn't have no lines on it or nothing, and it was in black ink, but the way it was written, I couldn't understand it. He said you're signing a contract, I carry your soul around. Well, I'm glad someone's interested in my soul, I said. I made a joke out of it.

He went on and on about the church and Jesus Christ, how they disowned him. I mean he went on and on. He said they don't care about you or anybody else. He went on about people praying to statues. He said you need to take all them statues and smash 'em up. Take the stone dust, put it back into a refinery, and make, whatever, bricks out of 'em, because it ain't doing anybody any good.

"There was ink on the paper, but it wasn't written in English, that's what I'm trying to tell you. Maybe it was Latin. That's their language, right? He says, 'How did it get that way, the life you lived?' He said, 'Twenty-three years old, and you did more than people did during their whole lives.' I said, 'Yeah, well.' He said, 'You had everything. Cars, boats. You had too many girlfriends. You're having sex with everybody. Your mother's friends.' Then he went on. 'This is between you and me,' he went on to say. 'You're lucky you didn't go all the way with your first cousin.' I come home real late at night, she was sleeping over, she was in my bed, naked. I mean, what the hell am I supposed to do?"

"Walk away?" I said. "That usually works."

"I asked him about my father. He didn't say a goddamn thing."

"Why did you ask him about that?"

"All he'd have to do is apologize."

"Who?"

"My father. Goddamn bastard. All he had to do is say he understood all the shit he did was bad, and he's sorry. But that bastard ain't sorry. I'm tired, Jackie."

While telling me the story, Ronnie's voice had become progressively weaker until it was no more than a wheeze. The shadow was beginning to envelop him fully. Each of our recent conversations had ended with Ronnie diving into a vigorous story and then quickly petering out. But it wasn't exactly petering out; it was more like being snuffed out.

"It's coming, Jackie. I'm sorry I pulled you into this. You tried to help, and I appreciate that."

I'd faced off against evil before, but maybe, all this time, over all these years, only indirectly. After my mother's spirit had been consigned to hell, after I'd seen her snatched from me, maybe I'd needed to stay close to death to try to cheat it myself. She was a prisoner for eternity, but I could beat the enemy by keeping it close. If I kept the darkness at my side, perhaps I could avoid becoming swayed by it. I could avoid becoming a medal on the devil's chest by confronting his handiwork everywhere I could. Jackie the secret weapon, Jackie the NYPD's covert helper. All those hideous acts: lost minds; dismembered bodies; murdered children. I kept it always in my view, dove willingly into every case, answered every plea for help after the disappearance of a missing loved one, took in every stray and cast-out drifter who wound up at my doorstep. If I embraced hell first, maybe I wouldn't be dragged there.

The piles of cases grew on my desk, as did my drive to help the lost and the grieving. My house began to look like a museum of death, with items belonging to murder victims and heartbroken families, their tears wrapped up in little boxes, the only thing left of the person they'd adored. Copies of coroners' reports, photos of autopsies, teddy bears no longer hugged but too painful for the families to keep.

Often while working a case, I'd feel I was challenging the demon on its own turf. While trying to close the wounds for families torn apart by grief, I'd felt the confrontation again and again. But I saw now that those had been individual battles, not the bigger war. The devil was strong. I had to be stronger. For better or worse, Ronnie DeFeo was a vessel. The demon had inhabited him in a cruel moment and started a domino tumble that would ultimately dictate the rest of his life. It had gone through his father, and, maybe, others in his family. It had lived at 112 Ocean Avenue for a long time. I knew that now.

But knowing wasn't enough, nor were our phone dialogues. I had to engage fully with the entity that haunted this man. Letters and phone calls could reveal plenty on their own, but in the end they were still at a remove. Ronnie was bottoming out. The dark spirit had its hooks in him and was close to pulling him down into the abyss forever. The obligation became clear to me. I needed to place myself directly in the path of the devil and invite him in. I needed to take the demon spirit out of Ronnie DeFeo and try to pass it back where it belonged. I would have to meet the man.

I called Joanne into the room. My daughter, my assistant, my kindred spirit. I didn't have to tell her anything.

"When do you want to go?" she said.

NINE

Before I could meet Ronnie DeFeo face to face, I needed his full trust and complete faith. And there was only one way to achieve that. The next day, when the reliable midmorning call came, I spoke first.

"It's time for us to talk about it, Ronnie."

He knew what I was referring to. We'd danced around it for close to a year. He heard in my voice that there was to be no more stalling. I knew that if I pressed too soon, I might upset him and never find out the truth. I also knew that waiting too long might lead to the same result. I'd resisted asking the question until now because I feared he might suddenly withdraw if I forced him to return to the night that had set the rest of his life in motion.

But now, he seemed ready to tell. He'd told me nearly everything else already, had curled back over his many stories again and again. We were both quiet, the moment hanging, and I think we both sensed this was the right time to finally broach the painful memory together.

"Dawn's was the extra room in the house," he began. "On the third floor. It was really the attic, but it was so big they made it a bedroom for her. And then she decides, that night, I mean, this whole thing was too obvious. I shoulda saw it coming, but I didn't. She had an electric typewriter they bought her, and everything that goes with it, all the accessories."

He was coming at the story from the side, but acknowledging to me that we had come far enough together, that he was ready—or at least that he might be willing to try.

"Who did she get along with best of the siblings?"

"At first, her and Allison shared a room."

I flipped through the file again and reviewed the DeFeo family tree. Next to Ronnie "Butch" DeFeo was Dawn, the eldest daughter in the family. She was eighteen at the time, and the next oldest sibling, Allison, was thirteen. Then came Marc, twelve; and John, nine.

"Then Dawn got some heart and decided she was gonna move in the extra room by herself."

"Was she nervous to do that?"

"Yeah, she was nervous. I don't know why. You're eighteen years old. She moved her stuff upstairs. But she still liked to come downstairs to sleep sometimes, to my room."

"On the second floor?"

"On the second floor. I had a TV in my room. She didn't have one. She liked to use my shower, too."

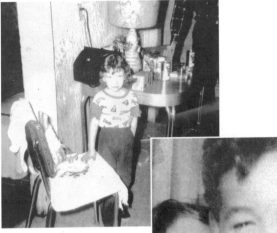

ABOVE: Me in 1967, age five. I had already started to conduct séances for my mother.

RIGHT: Me and my brother.
Jackie Barrett

Will and me.   *Joanne Agnelli*

The International Shrine of Saint Jude in New Orleans, where I go to pray for the dead and for my mother's soul.
Joanne Agnelli

LEFT: Will drumming during a ritual to call onto the spirits to protect us. RIGHT: Preparing for ritual. *Joanne Agnelli*

A ritual set up.   *Joanne Agnelli*

(Clockwise from top left) Will, Ray, me, and Joanne.
Joanne Agnelli

Ronald "Butch" DeFeo in police custody the day after the murders were discovered.

Suffolk County Police Department

ABOVE: The DeFeo kids (from left to right): John, Dawn, Allison, Marc, and Ronnie.
DeFeo family collection

RIGHT: The DeFeo family headstone, including Ronnie's paternal grandparents, Rocco and Antoinette.
Joanne Agnelli

Just for you Jackie

HOTEL

S
U
R
F

ROOMS

Somethings we never forget
right Jackie?

R. D.

Do you like it?
Lets think back
Remember NOW

peek a boo
I Remember You

TOP: The former 112 Ocean Avenue, today.
Joanne Agnelli

MIDDLE: Former site of the Surf Hotel, now an empty lot.
Jackie Barrett

LEFT: A drawing Ronnie sent me in September 2009. I'd never mentioned the Surf Hotel to him.
Jackie Barrett

A letter Ronnie wrote to me, signed in blood.
Jackie Barrett

ABOVE: Looking into the eyes of the devil.

RIGHT: Ronnie and me. The flowers on the walls were added for the A&E special to make the prison environment look nicer.
Courtesy of the Green Haven Correctional Facility

" Certificate of Authenticity "

To whom this may concern:

I Ronald "Butch" DeFeo 75-A-4053 who presently repose at
Green Haven Correctional, state the following;

That on November 7, 2011 the eve of my deceased mother's
birthday, for no apparent reason my front tooth broke off on
my gum line. This is not a hoax or a story, just the truth in
its entirely.

I believe the correct term is pay back for November 13,
1974 which later turned into "The Amityville Horror", and the
tooth is from my mouth.

"Wherefore" I state the above is true and correct.

Respectfully

Ronald DeFeo 75-A-4053
Ronald DeFeo 75-A-4053

Sworn to before me this
_10_ day of November 20 _11_.

_____
NOTARY PUBLIC

Jeffrey G. Cable
Notary, State of New York
Registration # 01CA6200119
Dutchess County, New York
Commission Expires January 26, 2013

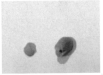

ABOVE: A letter from Ronnie, in
which he claimed that his tooth fell
out on the anniversary of his mother's
birthday.

RIGHT: The letter contained the tooth
itself. I almost threw up from the
smell.
Jackie Barrett

To Whom It May Concern,

I Ronald DeFeo Jr. have been communicating with Ms. Jackie Barrett for over two years. She is my confidant, advisor and has been for my failing health needs. She also holds the power of attorney and has my last will and testament. Jackie Barrett and myself are the only two people that know the truth about my life and the night leading up to the murders. She has hundreds of hours of audiotape along with other materials. It is a fact that Jackie Barrett is the only one person that knows every gruesome detail that took place in around what was formally 112 Ocean Avenue. This will be the first time I Ronald DeFeo Jr. have ever given anyone the true facts about my family's murder. Jackie Barrett knows the complete story and every shocking detail. There have been many books, movies and TV shows about me Ronald DeFeo Jr. non which were true about me just here say from people that were not in the house.

The world and public would be shocked, by the real story the true events. I planned on taking this to my grave with me! I opened up to Ms. Jackie Barrett I gave her permission in the power of attorney to put the truth out as gruesome as it may be. There is nothing that Ms. Barrett does not know and all of this comes from the source Mr. Ronald DeFeo Jr. never before was this done and never will it be done again. Ms. Jackie Barrett was granted full permission for books, TV shows and movies. What the world always wondered about Jackie Barrett has, Thank you in advance.

Very truly yours,

Ronald DeFeo Jr.
Ronald DeFeo Jr.

Sworn to before me this date
_1_, day of _March_ , 2011

Richard Ryan
Notary Public

RICHARD RYAN
Notary Public State of New York
ID # 01RY6050106
Qualified in Dutchess County
Commission Expires 10/30/__

ABOVE: Ronnie's way of telling the world about our association.

LEFT: Ronnie's gloves, watch, and a lock of his hair, which he sent me from Green Haven. *Jackie Barrett*

"Why do you think she liked to use your shower?"

"Dawn was not a slob, but Dawn's hygiene, Jesus. She didn't want to take showers. I told her, 'Use my bathroom; use my shower.' But she just didn't want to take showers. She would wash her hair in the sink. 'Why don't you just go in the shower and wash your whole body? I go in there twice a day,' I'd tell her. 'You're having sex with all these guys; you gotta clean yourself.' She got real tight. But she wasn't a slob. Her clothes were always clean and fresh. Her room was immaculate."

"Did she spend most of her time in Allison's room?"

"Yeah. Dawn was around before Allison. Allison was born in Amityville, Dawn and me were born in Brooklyn. So it was really Dawn's room. All the furniture in them, all that white furniture with gold trim—there's a name for it, it's very expensive furniture—that was all Dawn's. She was going upstairs, downstairs, upstairs, downstairs; it was getting like a yo-yo. She was upstairs; her clothes were downstairs. She didn't know whether she was coming or going. Hey, you don't sound good, Jackie. You okay?"

"I'm fine." I'd been trying to hide my coughing by covering the phone, but he'd heard it anyway. Will and Jo were looking at me with twin expressions of worry. I waved them off. "Keep talking, Ronnie. You need to tell me this. You need to say the words. I'm not a prosecutor or a judge. Remember that. I'm not asking you for a confession. But you need to tell me the story. I need to know. Others need to know."

There was silence on the other end.

"What happened, Ronnie? Take me back to that night. What happened?"

"All that bastard would have had to do was apologize for the things he did. Then we'd all be okay. Never even said sorry. All he had to do was say sorry."

"I know, Ronnie. What happened that night?"

"Last night I went and sat in the chair all night. I wrote you a letter. My hands were shaking. I'm tired, but I'm starting to feel lighter or something. I wanted to finish this shit once and for all. I'd even put the thing around my neck, but it broke. Just my luck."

He was trying to unnerve me. But this was a childish trick. First, no one in their sound mind would give him a length of rope to do anything with. Second, I didn't think he had the guts. "That's not funny, Ronnie. And I know you're lying."

"Then I tried again a few nights after. I thought maybe it'll work this time. I didn't do it, though. He came at me in my cell again that night. Came and sat on me and wrenched my legs right up. I tried to run at him, but I went right through instead. That goddamn guy. That was the same night you told me you and Jo heard music coming from somewhere in your house."

"That's right. We were talking, and then a sound like an old clock radio just came on. It sounded like it was everywhere. We checked all around the house and never found the source."

"Bastard was letting you know he was around."

"It was a bad night. Two of three bathroom toilets just

started running and flushing on their own. The lights in Uncle Ray's room were flashing on and off all night. Ray poured cold water on his face. But we made it through, Ronnie. We made it through that night like you've made it through all of the bad stuff. And now you and I have traveled this far together, and we need to take it the rest of the way."

Ronnie went back to his story, as if our digression had never occurred. "Two fucking boyfriends she had, at least. Two at one time, got one guy murdered, God knows how many more she had."

"Who, Dawn?"

"My mother. That's what I'm trying to tell you. Why did she have to pull that gun? She woulda never got shot. Three goddamn guys. The beautician, the priest, plus I think another guy. Fucking all of them. I mean, come on."

Ronnie had spent three and a half decades in prison for murdering six people in cold blood. No one on earth knew what had actually happened. I asked again: "Ronnie, what happened that night?"

"And the goddamn screaming. That would drive anybody crazy. I think it drove my parents crazy. Or it was the devil teaching them a lesson for all the wrongs they done. Him with the beatings, her with the boyfriends. I mean, Jesus Christ. I'm supposed to live under that roof like a normal guy?"

"Tell me about the screaming, Ronnie. Do you mean voices in your head?"

"In my head? No! In their room. Their bedroom. I ain't talking about in between my goddamn ears."

"You would hear screaming in their bedroom? You mean they fought?"

"It wasn't them. That's what I'm trying to tell you. There was a man's voice and a woman's voice, but not my mother and father, different voices. The woman's voice, Christ, it had a screw to it. Go right through you. And the man, it was like he was in pain, like he was being tortured. This would go on for an hour at a time. I couldn't stand it. It went on right up until the day they died."

"Up until the day they died? The day your whole family got killed?"

"Truthfully, I thought they were having sex, with all the screaming. Or somebody was killing them. Apparently the only one who heard what I heard was me. I asked Dawn if she heard it, and she said, 'What are you, what's the matter with you? Are you drunk again?' I said 'What are you talking about? I'm asking you a question.' She said 'No, I didn't hear nothing.' I asked every one of them kids, and every one of them said the same thing, 'We didn't hear nothing.' I asked them again. 'You didn't hear nothing, huh?' 'Nope, nothing.' That's what they said. That was the first time."

"There was more than one time?"

"The second time it was even worse. I said, 'What are they, going at it again?' This time I went to their bedroom to tell them to keep it down, and the door was open, a third of the way. I said, 'They don't even close the door? Jesus Christ.' But when I reached for it the door closed, hard. I heard something slide across the floor, like they were pushing something up against the door. I pushed against it from my side, but it wouldn't move. I don't know what they had behind that door, I assume it was the dresser. So I couldn't get in, no one could get in. I had my hand on the knob and my foot ready to kick the door in. It's locked. I couldn't get in there. Then I got worried, 'cause my mother and father wouldn't answer me, but that screaming was still going on. And I'm gonna tell you something, that screaming was not my mother and my father. Those voices were not coming from this world, they were some other thing. I ran downstairs and tried to look into their bedroom from outside. The curtain wasn't closed all the way. I did a lot of peeking, but I couldn't see anything other than a lot of candles lit. I said, 'Son of a bitch, what the hell's going on in there?' Not one candle, a lot."

"Did you think they were doing some kind of ritual?"

"Who knows what them nuts were doing? But I was worried. I didn't know what else to do, so I went downstairs to get a shotgun. Pump-action. Then I got the ladder from the boathouse and leaned it against the side of the house. I climbed up to my parents' window with one hand, I'm holding the shotgun in the other."

"What did you think you were going to find up there?"

"I wasn't thinking about that. I was just reacting. At first I thought maybe someone broke in or they were having sex, like I said."

"But you know the difference between somebody screaming if they're having sex or—"

"It wasn't sex. At that point I didn't know what it was.

I did a lot of peeking once I was up there, but I still ain't figured out what it was. I stood on the ladder there with the shotgun. Couldn't go back to sleep. It just kept going on. Crazy noises, Jesus Christ. Didn't sound right."

"Ronnie," I said again. "It's okay. Now tell me. What happened?"

For a long moment, he was silent. By now I was well familiar with Ronnie's remarkable memory. I knew it wasn't a matter of him trying to recall the details. He was simply pausing to consider.

"He came home early," Ronnie finally said.

Though I felt weak, I couldn't tolerate a dirty house. I had spent the evening cleaning all around our downstairs, then closed the laundry room and bathroom door to keep the cats out, locked everything up, came upstairs, and then went back down to get a stamp for a letter I'd written Ronnie. When I came down, all the doors were open.

I've got a firm rule about closing doors. I've let go of people who worked for me for leaving doors open. If you leave the laundry room door open, one of the cats could get between the wall and the stackable machines, and if they were to get stuck it would be lights out, because I can't move those damn machines, and even though Will can, he wouldn't necessarily be home then, or in time. If I couldn't get one of the cats out, it would start panicking. And I always worried about that, so I put a hook and eye on the door as a constant reminder.

After scrubbing the floors and the walls and the basin,

I'd locked everything down and come up. It was only minutes later I'd gone back down. The bathroom door stood wide open. Laundry room doors, the same. I'd closed them all. I'd locked them myself. There's no wind down there, no movement, nothing that could jolt open multiple doors at the same time. I closed all the doors again and went upstairs. In my office, one of the files I'd been working on having to do with Ronnie's case lay on the desk. On top of the pile had been a picture of Ronald DeFeo Sr. It was now on the floor, on the other side of the room.

"My grandfather would come two days a week to take care of the garden by the boathouse. He planted vegetables. That was a real nice picture to everyone else. Real nice."

"Listen, Ronnie. Let's continue."

When Ronald DeFeo Sr. returned home early from work that November afternoon, he encountered one of the most powerful and defiant forces known to man: a stubborn teenage daughter. Dawn DeFeo, a fresh high school graduate, had started attending secretarial school, but, according to Ronnie, she was more focused on moving to Florida to live with her boyfriend, a kid named William Davidge, who was a year younger than she.

Dawn was equal parts willful and reckless, and, like most teenage girls, she felt utterly misunderstood by her parents. Ronald was no sooner in the door than Dawn had launched into a familiar tirade: she was going to drop out of school and move south to be with her boyfriend. She'd had enough, she said. She wanted out, and no one was going to stop her.

"When my sister started that crap again that she's done with school and she's going to Florida, she's done with all of it, he started in with her, my mother started in with her. He went and put his hands on her, which was a mistake."

Kids who grow up in volatile households tend to go one of two ways. They either become quietly submissive, avoidant of confrontation at almost any cost, or they become as incurably hot-blooded and reactive as those who have served as their unfortunate role models. Dawn DeFeo had become the latter, and she wasn't about to back down from the man who, despite being her flesh and blood, she despised.

"She went and opened the kitchen drawer, nice and gently. She pulled out a blue steel knife with a wooden handle. Carving knife. That knife don't break. She got it and said, 'You fat motherfucker.' That's what she called him. I said, 'Oh my God, here we go.' This is about six thirty. She chased him into the dining room. Now he's running around the table, and I'm standing there, you know, laughing."

Ronnie himself had been virtually invisible for the previous three days, at home but holed up in his bedroom in self-imposed quarantine. He hadn't been dodging work or avoiding his family, he said. He'd simply been trying to kick a bad habit.

"I'd done too much heroin, and I knew if I went to work, I'd end up going straight to Harlem to buy more, right to One Hundred and Sixteenth. So I said, 'Nah, I gotta take a few days off.' I forgot I had a stash in my bedroom."

I asked him how high he'd gotten, or how long it had taken, or during what parts of the day he was stoned and which sober. Although he didn't know the answers to those questions, everything else apparently remained horrendously vivid.

"When all the shit started with her and him, I said, 'To hell with this crap, I can't deal with it.' So when things had finally calmed down a bit, I told her, 'Look, my car's in the garage, take it and go. That's what you should do.' That's what she did."

"She left for the night?"

"No, she came back about, I don't know, nine thirty, ten o'clock. I was in my bedroom. She came in, wearing her nightgown. I said, 'Look, I don't wanna be here no more than you do. I've had enough.' And she says, 'We gotta do something.'"

"That's all she said? Something?"

"I said, 'Look, I'm sick of them, too, but if we're gonna do it, this ain't the place, it's gotta be done in Brooklyn, make it look like the Mob.' She didn't want to wait. I said, 'I'm going to sleep.' She starts watching TV in my room. I said, 'See, you didn't want a TV, now you want to watch mine.' I had a brand-new Zenith, color, portable. Eighteen-inch screen. She didn't go to sleep."

* * *

We'd gone to the hardware store, Will and I, to look for bulbs for our inset lights in the living-room ceiling. While we were there, Will wandered over to another aisle and came out holding a long-handled axe. He walked toward me swinging it casually, mimicking a woodsman. I didn't like the look on his face. It wasn't Will's usual look.

"What are you doing?" I said.

He didn't say anything. Just kept walking slowly toward me, swinging the axe up and down. I thought about Ronnie's descriptions of splitting wood in the yard at Clinton.

"Will, are you crazy? What the fuck are you doing?"

"Don't worry," he said. "This is what I need to fix that house once and for all."

He said it with a grin I didn't know, a grin that wasn't part of his range of expressions. Quickly, I stepped toward him and grabbed the axe. He resisted for a moment. Tears were welling in his eyes.

"Will," I said, pulling on the axe. "Give it to me." I leaned in close so that my face was nearly touching his. "Will. Let it go. Let's go home." Finally he released his grip and reeled backward. He was trembling.

"Like I said, I'd heard my father talking with my grandfather about killing me. Yeah, my father and his own father talking about killing their son and grandson. I know how it sounds. I heard stuff all the time. I could see things, like you, Jackie. They thought I was nuts half the time. Put me in counseling, for Christ's sake. I didn't need counseling. They did."

"How old were you when you had counseling?"

"Eleven or twelve. They took me to Bay Ridge, Brooklyn, to see a guy named Qualler. Quavler. Quavlo. Starts with a Q. Psychologist. Psychiatrist. I went for about a year. Finally, he called my mother and father in. I was nosy. I was standing outside the door. I remember because there was an old man out there looking at me, I told him to mind his own business. Doctor Q told them they both needed counseling, like I just told you. They got very upset, stormed out of the place, grabbed me, let's go. They had a real bad attitude, like I was gonna get a beating again, which I did. 'What did you tell that man?' my mother said. I said I told him the truth. Well, that was that. I wasn't gonna see the inside of that guy's office again. He came to my trial and testified. The statement I just made to you, he made at my trial, he said, 'The DeFeos, Louise and Ronald, they both needed counseling. They needed to see somebody.' "

Whether the official court documents (currently sealed) support this statement is unknown. But whether Ronnie's memories of the trial are accurate nearly four decades later is, to me, largely irrelevant. When you don't have certified records to go by, all you have is your gut. My gut told me that something evil had run rampant through 112 Ocean Avenue, and it had made the DeFeos its prey.

"What did they tell you they were taking you for in the first place?"

"I don't know who put them up to it, they just decided I needed it. They said I wouldn't talk to people. And my school marks. He had a brick house, two floors, office was downstairs, in the basement. And I always went on a Saturday, because my mother and father both had to be there, and that's when my father was off, Saturdays. I had headaches all my life from the beatings that asshole gave me. Always kicking me and hitting me in the head. He didn't say they both needed counseling; actually, excuse me, he said they both needed help. That's what they needed, help."

"Ronnie—how long did you go for?"

"Age ten or eleven or twelve, all of a sudden I woke up, and my twenty-twenty vision was gone. Eye doctor said, 'What the hell is this?' We're playing catch, I'm a little kid, he's throwing the ball as hard as he can. It's a hardball—he throws the ball like you'd throw it to an adult, it hits the leather on the glove, glanced out and hit me in the eye. Looked like I had a plum on my eye for the next week. That's what he was all about."

"Competitive with you. Like he had to prove something."

"The day of my confirmation, they had it at my grandparents' house, so that means I wasn't living in Long Island yet. Everybody brought me money. There was, I don't know, two, three hundred dollars there. This was back in 1959 or 1960. He takes all the money, I was waving it around, takes all the money and rips it in half, then throws it on the ground and starts giggling. My grandfather had to pick up all the money."

It was a story he'd already told me two or three times before. "I know, Ronnie. We've talked about this. You have to get back to what you were talking abou—"

"It wasn't just me. He had the same reputation with everybody. No one wanted anything to do with him, including the cops. One day I saw my mom in trouble out on the road, a car speeding toward her car and trying to run her off the road, right in front of the house. I ran in as fast as I could—and I could run—I ran down the stairs. My father was sleeping on the new couch. I said, 'Out in the street, it's Mom.' He came out in his socks, no shoes. Ran out the back door as fast as he could. I thought a jet went by. The guy got out of the car by this time and was banging on my mother's window. My father grabs the guy. It was like these phony wrestling matches on TV; he had the guy up over his head, then slammed him on the ground and was on top of him. Amityville police cruiser drives by and keeps right on going. They wanted no part of him, I am telling you. There was two cars out there. The cops had to drive around those cars to get by. He's giving the guy a goddamn beat-down. The guy's wife came by a couple days later, apologized to my mother, said, 'Oh, sorry, he was drinking.' Drinking? Ain't supposed to be driving and drinking. One of the little Volkswagen station wagons. What a beating he gave him. My friends had been in the car with my mother, they'd jumped out. 'Oh, leave him alone,' she says to my father. 'Leave him alone—you're gonna kill him.' That's the only reason my father stopped. It was the Fourth of July. Maybe she was sleeping with him, too."

I was feeling light-headed. The room was starting to spin. "Look, Ronnie, none of that matters now."

"He didn't care about nobody. He used everybody. He had the police in his back pocket. A high-ranking PDA official was his goombah. I used to deliver the guy's car to upstate New York. I used to go there to pick up parts, I forget where. I didn't mind going. His wife was beautiful, she was from France, and his daughter was my age—she wanted to go out on a date with me. I said, 'Yeah, I'll pick you up.' He said, 'Forget it. I know you.' I had his car anyway. I didn't use my car; I took the brand-new car. He had a 1975 in the driveway, not a 1974. I'd come home from that or something else and get a beating for no reason. Headaches all the time, still. I take Tylenol."

"Speaking of Tylenol, I need one myself. Hold on, Ronnie."

He didn't.

"So my father and great-uncle are discussing me. All business with them. My father says, 'He's using drugs, he's using heroin, we can't trust him.' And Pete DeFeo says, 'Let's put a contract out.' They were gonna kill me. The Brooklyn DA's office had a wiretap, they listened to every word of this. Them people were gonna kill me. You know what the DA's office did? Nothing. They listened to the highest-ranking member of the Genovese crime family. They listened to Pete DeFeo talking to Mike Brigante about murdering me. Where was the law then?"

There was no evidence of this, of course. Ronnie was implicating not only his father in the murder scheme but also his grandfather and great-uncle. And even if there was evidence, we weren't going to get our hands on it. Like I said, when you don't have something on paper, you're left with your instincts—and my instincts said that, although Ronnie DeFeo may have been making up some of it, he wasn't making up all of it.

We all agreed we'd forgotten what it felt like to be a family. We were spending so much time battling sickness, pain, and unseen menace that we'd neglected to spend time with each other the way we'd always been accustomed to doing.

We decided to pull ourselves together, starting with the simple ritual of dinner. Everyone recognized how sick I was and told me to go to bed, but I insisted that we needed to show our strength and our unity against the forces gathering within our own walls, the spirits of a murdered family and the devil who had orchestrated their downfall.

We ordered takeout. Will and Uncle Ray came in with Chinese, and I came up from my office and sat at the table. Will, Joanne, and Ray looked at me the way you look at someone who looks awful—you aren't sure whether to say anything. They didn't have to. It was in their expressions.

Jo had set the table with candles and our good china, which had become dusty since the last time we'd used it. I wiped the dishes and thought about how long it had indeed been. A twinge of something came over me: through the pain and poison, the feeling of simple happiness that accompanies sitting down to a meal with those you care about most. I struggled to hang on to the sweet feeling this produced as we passed the containers back and forth and slid noodles, dumplings, and vegetables onto our plates.

I was jolted out of my state of easy joy when Jo knocked over one of the containers and jumped back from the table, screaming and pointing over my shoulder. Her finger was pointed at our large ballroom antique mirror. The mirror is from Paris and stands six by nine. The dining room table is jet-black with old-style New Orleans velvet chairs. I always felt the two items made for a dramatic contrast.

Will, Ray, and I sprung up, and in overlapping voices, we asked Jo what was wrong. Mutely, she kept pointing to the mirror, hand pressed against her mouth. I turned and saw what Jo was seeing. Looking out at us from inside the glass was Allison DeFeo, most of her face blown off.

Will and Ray, seeing Allison's face also, stood rooted to the floor. We were a silent tableau, unable to speak, united in our shock, until slowly Ronnie's younger sister and her shattered face began to fade. At the moment she finally disappeared, one of our seventy-pound wooden dining chairs flew across the room and smashed into the far wall, shattering. Jo ran out of the room crying.

Ray, Will, and I said nothing at first but started to clean up. Each of us was aware of the only thing that was important. We needed to stay strong, and we needed to stay together. *It destroys people and it destroys bonds, Jackie,* my mother would tell me. *It tries to get inside you, between*

*you and the people you love, but you can't let it. You have
to show you're stronger.*

Ray paused and looked up at me. "Jackie, I need to tell
you something," he said, breaking the silence. "I don't
know how much you remember about the hotel that day."

Will, who could barely form a scowl if you offered him
a hundred dollars, shot Ray a harsh look. "Shut up, Ray,"
he said. Will doesn't talk that way, to anybody. Ever. "She
doesn't need to know."

"I'm sorry, Will," Ray said, "but I can't keep it in any
longer. Jackie, I was at the Surf Hotel that day. Will called
me to tell me you were heading there. I just wanted to be
there to help. I saw everything."

"What?"

"I ran in after you and saw it all from the hallway.
When you ran out of the room, you went right by me. I
tried to stop you. I yelled your name."

I traveled back to that moment. Racing out of the room
after seeing my mother lost for good. Sprinting past the
man with the badge, weaving through the drifters, seeking nothing but to put distance between me and the dev-
ilish spirit that had claimed her.

But I had sensed a known figure, a familiar energy. I
thought I'd heard a voice calling my name. I'd wanted
only to reach the water and then to keep going. Will's
eyes had held me fast, maintaining my fragile grip in this
realm. It had been Uncle Ray I'd sensed.

"*Ray*," Will said. "She doesn't need to go back. Leave
it alone."

"But I was affected, too!" Ray said. I'd never seen him

look scared of Will, mostly because Will was as gentle to Ray as he was to anyone else. But the look in Ray's eyes now was one of fear. "I'm scared. I'm scared this thing is going to kill Jackie. I saw it. I saw it lift her mother off the bed. I saw it all." He was getting worked up.

"Calm down," Will said. "Just take it easy."

Ray was crying now, and his voice was rising. "No! It changed my life, too. I'm nothing now. You all take care of me. My mind went to fucking hell. Don't you tell me what to do."

Will was tensing up. My husband is soft on the inside, but on the outside he's a tightly packed statue of muscle, and every man has his breaking point. I quickly stepped between him and Ray. At the same time, Jo came running into the room.

"Stop it!" she yelled. "Just stop! We have to stay together. Don't you see that? This is exactly what it wants."

"Sorry—you're right, Jo," Ray said. "I'm sorry, Will. Jackie, I had to say something. I know Will wanted us to keep this a secret, but I can't keep it inside. I feel like I'm going to explode. This is getting out of hand, your involvement in all of it. I'm scared what it's going to do."

The devil can get to you directly or indirectly. It can snake its way inside you in a vulnerable moment and change the course of your life forever, as it had done to Ronnie DeFeo. Or it can draw you in and destroy your mind bit by bit. Ray had been there at the Surf Hotel. He had seen my mother descend through that eternal hole, just as I had. And he'd never been the same. His only solace had been the pets. Through them, he could escape to a simpler and more innocent existence. That's why he had so strongly linked his spirit to theirs. He wanted as little connection as possible to the world in which he'd seen a human soul forever stolen.

"Ray," I said. "Ray, it's okay. I'm so sorry for what happened and for what you saw. You were only there to help me. And look what it cost you. But your life isn't a waste, Ray. Far from it. You're a part of this family. As important a part as any of us. Always. Don't worry about me. I'll beat this. *We'll* beat this." I hugged Ray, and the last of the frightening tension that had been climbing moments before slipped away.

Ray looked at Will. "What do you say?"

But Will wasn't listening. He had turned toward the mirror again and caught sight of his own image, which I now saw, along with the others. The whites of his eyes weren't there. There was only black. My pillar of strength suddenly ran out of the room and locked himself in the basement, sobbing.

"I said, 'Look, if we're gonna do this, we're gonna do this,'" Ronnie told me. "She went back in her room, I didn't know why at first. Then she came back in wearing a pair of gloves, brown or black, and my gun, a Python, pistol, a .357 Magnum, which fired .38 specials. Stainless steel handles. Some people call 'em combat handles, hard black leather. Took the recall away from the gun, there was no recall from that gun, not for me, anyway. She had two hands on it. She knew how to fire it because I'd shown her how in the basement. I had a steel trap down there where I fired all the guns—rifles, everything, big steel trap, paper targets, silhouettes."

"Then what happened, Ronnie?"

"Next thing I know, it's five minutes to one. We went downstairs, in his room. She had gloves on, but I didn't pay her no mind. She didn't say nothing. She must have seen too many movies, that's what I'm saying to myself. I said, 'Wait a minute, close all the kids' doors, we don't need them waking up.' When she comes back, I said, 'You sure you wanna do this? I'm not a killer; I never killed nobody.' She says, 'What are you, scared?' I said, 'Listen, I'm not scared. You wanna do this?' She says, 'Yeah.' She got gloves on, but I only seen one glove, one hand. She had the pistol under her nightgown. A good minute went by, we were standing in the bedroom, looking at the both of them. All that was there was the votive candle under the statue. Just a little light, but enough. My mother and father's room wasn't that big, but the bed was real long. We were looking in the mirror at ourselves. I looked at her, shaking my head."

"What were you thinking about?"

"I don't know. I wasn't thinking straight, maybe. I started thinking about all the crap he'd pulled, that son of a bitch. There was already a round in the barrel. All I had to do was pull the hammer back. Pulled the hammer back, and I said, 'Here goes.' That's what I said, 'Here goes nothing.' He didn't move, nobody moved. 'You fat fuck,' I said. He heard that. He lifted his head up, but he was facing the other way when he was sleeping, so he's looking in the other direction and he sees me and Dawn in the mirror. He says, 'I'll kill you, you son of a bitch.' I said, 'That's what you think.' Now Dawn's yelling, 'Get him, get him!' I'll never forget that. I fired the gun. One round goes off. He's getting up now. I said, 'This is for all the shit you done to me, you fat fuck.'"

Jo had gone to a movie with a friend, and Will was working at the bar. I was sitting in my bedroom armchair, exhausted and ill but trying to read a book and pretend that life was normal, even if briefly. But it was hard to ignore the pain in my throat, the throb above my eyes, and the waves of dizziness that kept coming like an unremitting storm. When I sat, it felt as though I was falling through the floor. When I stood, it felt as though the room was shifting and twirling. The thermostat read sixty-two, but I'd have thought an electric blanket was attached to my back.

I heard Ray's door close downstairs and then his footsteps making their way up. I was glad for the company, since I'd tried to read the same paragraph several times without success.

"Hey, Ray," I said before seeing him. "Nice to see another face up here." My armchair is on the side of an oversized armoire with mirrored doors. I looked around the room and didn't see him, then caught sight of him in one of the mirrored doors, standing halfway in and halfway out of my bedroom doorway.

Both my ongoing delirium and the utter strangeness of the image made it hard for me to process what I was seeing. Only when Uncle Ray, dressed in an army jacket, raised the shotgun at me did I snap to reality. In such cases you always imagine you will react instantly and heroically, but when actually confronted with so bizarre a moment, it's hard to do anything but wonder what in God's name is going on. I was neither instant nor heroic. Instead, after a stunned second, I simply screamed, "*No!*"

Ray ran over to me, asking what was wrong. I shoved him out of the way and scrambled for my phone, repeating the words, "I saw it, I saw it," or something of the sort. I'd seen it all in the mirrors. The army jacket, his face, the shotgun. But none of it was there, of course. It was just Ray.

"Jackie," he said, "what are you talking about? I would never hurt you. Jackie, you're scaring me. I was coming in to tell you I needed to go for a walk. Look at me, Jackie. There's no gun. I'm not holding a gun. It's a watchband. It broke, and I was fixing it. You're imagining things."

I looked up and saw that he was telling the truth. He was holding the broken metal band from the wristwatch he wore every day.

"Why are you wearing an army jacket in this heat?" I asked him, still unsure. He just looked at me strangely.

"Jackie," he said, "you need to rest. You aren't well, and you're seeing things. I'm going to go for a walk. Do you need anything?"

I just stared at him, still more frightened than reassured. He smiled and then left the house.

I called Adam immediately and told him that if I were to die that night, it would be Uncle Ray who did it. I saw him wearing an old army jacket, I said, and holding a shotgun, which he'd pointed at me.

"Calm down, Jackie," Adam said. "You're talking faster than normal. Are you sure you saw what you think you saw? Are you alone now? Where is Ray? What did he say after you think he pointed a gun at you? I'll send a car to keep an eye on things. In the meantime, you just need to stay cool." I didn't know whether Adam was more shocked or upset. Fear in my voice was something new to him.

I called Joanne and told her to meet me at a late-night coffee shop instead of heading home. We then waited until 3:30 A.M., when Will would be closing up the bar, and called him to meet us so we could return to the house together.

We conferred with the driver of the car Adam had indeed sent, then went back in the house, Will first. Ray was seated in the same armchair I'd been in earlier. He was staring at the wall, looking vacant.

After looking him over to make sure he was holding no weapon, I sat down in the chair across from him. "Ray, I forgive you. We're here for you. We're all here, together. Talk to us."

Ray began to cry. "Jackie, I'm sorry. You've had such a hard life. If I could take it all away, I would. You've always taken care of me. You gave me the biggest gift a person can give: you made me feel part of something. A family."

"Of course we're a family, Ray. And you're a part of it."

He looked up. "I've never been the same since that day. I can't hold a job. I'm always depressed. I have real bad thoughts sometimes, Jackie. I hear voices. I hadn't heard them for a while, though, until earlier. I'm ashamed of what happened."

"What do you mean? I thought you said I imagined it."

"I thought I'd heard you telling Will it was time for me to go. Then I heard someone, a man's voice, say, *You're going to let her throw you out; you'll just be a bag man on the street; you have nothing. Kill her.*"

"Ray."

"Kill her tonight, when everyone is out."

"Ray, it's okay. We're strong. We're united."

It wasn't helping. He was spiraling again. "I felt the weirdest rage come over me out of nowhere. I went and looked around the garage for a weapon. But then a picture fell from the wall, and when it hit the ground, it kind of brought me back. It was a picture of you as a small kid. I fell to the ground yelling, 'I can't do it.' And something started to kick me. I couldn't see it, but something, kicking me over and over and yelling at me to do it. I'm sorry, Jackie. I'm so sorry."

TEN

"I got him right in the back, and he went down. But he wasn't finished. Now my mother's up and screaming, 'Oh my God, Ronnie!' They're looking at each other, she's coming over to his side. 'Oh my God, Ronnie!' I'm telling you he was getting up, he wasn't accepting this. Then my mother pulls out a pistol. It was one of them you clip on your ankles, real light, a .38."

In Ronnie's voice was again that peculiar dichotomy, the man who had been perfectly prepared to shoot his father but was still deeply pained at the thought that his mother might be willing to shoot him in return. Ronnie still spoke both like a man resigned to continue being punished for his sins and one who scoffed at those who'd allowed him to commit them.

"He's getting up; she's got the pistol out. I let the second round go. At the same time I hear shots from one of the other guns. I assume I'm hit; I said, 'Oh my God.'

I swing the gun around, hit the lever, put a second round in my mother. I didn't know she was shot till I seen the barrel flash. Then I look at Dawn, I said, 'Oh shit.' Dawn had two hands on that gun. I seen the front of the barrel come up, I seen a flash about two, three inches wide. I saw it all in the mirror, that's why I had to turn around. I thought I'd been shot. Now I'm looking back in the mirror. 'Oh shit,' I said. It was Dawn. I said, 'What the hell did you do?' 'I did you a favor,' she says. I picked up the pistol my mother had pulled out. The hammer was back."

"She was about to shoot you."

"Yeah, my mother was gonna shoot me right then and there. I quickly turned the ceiling light on, the chandelier. I said, 'Oh man, I thought I was shot.' Dawn said, 'I saved your ass. She was gonna shoot you.' 'Well, ain't nobody living through this,' I said. 'They're both dead. Did you see him? He was getting up.' 'Yeah, I seen him,' she said. 'He was gonna wrap that gun around your neck.' We're standing there looking at each other, and they're dead."

"Did you panic?"

"There was no time to panic. There were things I had to do now. I said to Dawn, 'There's things in this house that gotta go.'"

"You mean evidence?"

"I mean money. There was a file my father kept stashed away, with money in it. I told Dawn, 'We gotta clean the place out.' I found the file. I said, 'There's forty grand in here, you know about it, right?' She said, 'I know there's money.' I said, 'There's forty grand, four stacks of hundreds, ten thousand in each one.' Plus I had thirty-seven thousand and change of my own in the crawl space."

"Thirty-seven thousand dollars?"

"Yeah. I was pretty good with money."

Saying he was "good with money" was an interesting statement. From the stories I'd read, it seemed more that Ronald Sr. and Louise simply gave their son money whenever he needed it because they weren't sure what else to do.

"I said, 'There's an envelope, but let's leave that. The box on the floor, I don't think there's anything in there; the jewelry and everything's in a safety-deposit box.' We looked anyway. The envelope and the box are both lying there. We left the envelope, we looked in the box on the floor. We found the file with the forty thousand in a shoebox in the top of my mother's closet, hatbox, shoebox, whatever it was. Hatbox. We took the file."

"With the money in it."

"Yeah, with the money in it, of course with the money in it. Then I told her, 'Look, there's a million dollars in a duffel bag down in the basement.' "

"A million dollars?"

"Yeah. It was backup money that my father kept there. Dawn said, 'What are you, high?' I said, 'Yeah, I'm high, but that's irrelevant.' That money was hidden, it was just-in-case money. I know because I'm the one who put it there."

"You mean in case the business tanked?"

"Right. That money was my father's escape hatch. He had asked me to bury it, so I knew exactly where it was. No one else knew. Just me."

There were times Ronnie sounded nearly proud to have been his father's son. And it was just as pitiful to me as when he was describing his father using him as his personal whipping boy.

"I told her, 'You stay right here. Let's make sure the police ain't on their way.' We wiped everything down. I said, 'You had gloves on. I didn't have no gloves on, there's paraffin all over my hands. I hope the police don't come in here.' Anyway, I decided I'll deal with that later."

"Where were the guns?"

"They were still in the bedroom. But I wasn't thinking about that. I was thinking about what I had to get out of that house to somewhere else. I told Dawn to stay upstairs, then I went down to the cellar, to get the duffel bag. Dawn is goddamn stubborn, of course."

Dawn is stubborn. He was talking about her in the present tense. In his mind it was still happening. How many times had he replayed this tape? How often had he tried to convince himself it never happened?

"She didn't stay upstairs. She came down."

The fact that my bichon, Max, was an old dog didn't make saying good-bye any easier. He'd been my best friend. To those who have never owned dogs or cats, the statements made by pet owners read like so much fluff. He was more than a pet. He was a member of the family. He knew my moods and made me feel okay when nothing and nobody else could. All of these things are true, and were true of Max. I would say things that are stronger yet. Max had soulful eyes. He felt love deeply and gave love deeply, too. We all cried together as he was put down. Out of this life, into the next.

The next morning, the phone rang. The caller ID said "Unknown Number." When I picked up, it was Ronnie, in his other voice, laughing. Every other time he'd called, the number for Green Haven had come up on the display.

"Hey," he said, "if I showed up at your door late at night with a puppy, would you take care of it?"

Ronnie relished speaking in code.

"I know what you're doing," I said.

"Come on," Ronnie said. "He was old."

I hadn't told him about Max's passing. I hadn't told him a thing.

"I had gasoline down there. A big cherry jug, for the boat—more than five gallons. I said, 'We'll use it to burn the house down.' But there wasn't enough gas. So I said, 'Let's just burn their room up.' 'No,' Dawn said, 'don't be starting no fire.' I said, 'All right, fine, you're right,' and I told her again to go back upstairs. She said no."

"She didn't have any idea about the million?"

"No one knew about that but me. I'm the one my father had asked to hide the goddamn thing. When I finally got it out, Dawn said, 'Let me see, let me see,' like she'd never seen money before. All the money was wrapped—clear bags, then black garbage bags, then the duffel bag. I said, 'Look, you see, all hundred-dollar bills, a million dollars. There, okay? A million, right there, right in front of your face.' She said, 'We have to keep this money.' I said, 'No way are we keeping this money.' "

"Did you ever think of keeping it?"

"I didn't want no cops finding a million bucks there after what happened in that house. I told her, 'I'm taking it to Brooklyn right now, 'cause we can't call the police with the money in the house. God knows what'll happen. We can't call the lawyer, 'cause we'll look guilty.' "

"What was in Brooklyn?"

"My grandparents."

"You mean your dad's parents?"

"Yeah. I told Dawn, 'Don't do nothing. I'm taking this money where it belongs.' I said, 'I'll be back in an hour and a half, maybe two, tops. Don't do nothing. We got time.' "

The laundry had piled up. I could barely see over my own clothes as I carried the basket to the basement. I was focusing on each individual step so that my fatigue wouldn't produce a catastrophic stumble.

"Okay, you're right. They want me out."

It was Uncle Ray, gazing ahead at something I couldn't see. Talking to someone invisible.

"I'll do it."

"Ray?" I spun toward him. A trail of mist, like a thick cloud, swept past my face, obscuring my sight and making me feel faint. I swayed back and forth. "Ray," I said, trying to stay conscious. "Ray, who are you talking to?"

"No one," he said, still looking straight ahead.

"Ray."

He kept staring ahead. I was about to black out. I didn't know what to do other than speak directly to whatever was speaking through him.

"Look, you get any fucking ideas, I will have him in jail in a heartbeat."

Uncle Ray only stared.

The problem was our neighbors," Ronnie claimed. "The Colemans, Olivia and Jimmy. The wife and husband. Dawn and I went back upstairs to the bedroom and could see them standing on their back porch. They were just standing there. I couldn't see that good, 'cause the window had an air conditioner in it, so I could only see through the top. But I saw something. I didn't know at first if it was the police or what, then I saw it was them. I went into Allison's room and told Dawn to be quiet. We both went to the window, the second window, and I know the Colemans had to see me, because I had to lift up the window from the inside. And we had glass storm windows, I didn't bother lifting that one up, 'cause then they woulda seen me for sure. But I lifted that first one, I had the rifle in my hand. I wasn't gonna shoot them. I don't know what they thought I was gonna do. They just stood there."

"What were you thinking?"

"I was thinking about what to think. I thought about maybe going in that house and wiping them out, but I didn't know how many people were in there, and I didn't know how many bullets I had left. So that idea was out."

"But you just said you weren't going to shoot them."

"I'm saying I wasn't thinking of shooting them at first. Then I was, then I wasn't again. I'm trying to tell you everything happened fast. You can't sit there and think about it forever, you just have to move. One way or another I had to go. I took off for Brooklyn."

"What were you thinking you'd do if the Colemans did see you?"

"I wasn't considering that. I figured I'd deal with all this other shit later. I just knew I had to get going. When I left the house, Jimmy's pickup truck was there, and he was sitting in the goddamn thing, in the back of their driveway. He watched me come out of that house. Them two were right there watching me come out the door. And I know they seen Dawn, because Dawn came down with me, she was standing there at the storm door, the front of the house lit up like a Christmas tree. They were standing on that back stoop, that back hump there. But they never said anything. They dummied up good."

According to Joanne's research, if the Colemans had indeed seen Ronnie or Dawn DeFeo that night, they'd never said a word about it, at least not as far as the public record was concerned. Maybe it had all been a figment of Ronnie's drugged mind. Or maybe, like he'd said, Olivia and Jimmy Coleman had just "dummied up." Either way, there was nothing to corroborate his story.

"I've seen pictures of the house. The front door was actually at the side, right?"

"Right."

"So your neighbors would have had a full view anytime someone came out of the house."

"Yeah. I remember Dawn said, 'Why don't you take a picture—it lasts longer.' Real loud. I just shook my head and got in the car and left. I went to Brooklyn with the money, I took the .357, I had that on me, five rounds in it, one round was fired. I took the rest of my guns, too. I got in that car. The gun's right there, with the hammer back. I'm gonna tell you exactly when I got there. Couple of minutes before three A.M. I had the radio on. I wasn't feeling good, my mind was messed up. I was high, I never did nothing like that before. I said, 'What the fuck am I gonna tell this man?'"

"You mean Rocky?" His paternal grandfather.

"Yeah. I got to their house and rang the doorbell. Then I start banging on the bottom of the door, they had a stainless-steel front door. Fourteen Twenty-Three East Twenty-Ninth Street. I start banging on the door with the butt of my gun. The lights across the street come on. I knew all them people, I used to sleep over at the house all the time. They woke up. Somebody was sitting in an unmarked car. I know police cars. It was an old fire chief's car—faded red four-door Plymouth. Somebody was in there, I could see his head. Looking at me. Down the street, on the opposite side. It's a one-way, very narrow. I said, 'What the hell?' I was all paranoid and wired. I'm saying, 'It's me, Butch.' The whole neighborhood's waking up now."

I was down in the garage cleaning up when I came across the axe. Red, long-handled. It was the one Will had been swinging in the store. Puzzled, I touched it. He would have to have gone back to the store. He'd have to have done it without me, behind my back.

When he got home that night from his shift at the bar, I didn't say anything. I just held out the axe. Will isn't a great actor. He doesn't have to be, because everything he does is done with sincerity. So when an expression of shock came over his face, I knew the look was genuine. I asked him to explain himself anyway.

"I don't know," he said. "I didn't buy the damn thing. I never went back to the store. I didn't." I must have looked skeptical, because Will walked out of the house.

I drove over to Adam's and handed him the axe. "Hold this for me," I said. "Better yet, keep it."

Adam studied my face. "What the hell is going on, Jackie?" he said. "You don't look right. You need to see a doctor. Is something threatening you?" Adam and I have worked on more high-profile murder cases than I can remember, he in the forefront, me in the background. He thought maybe someone got to me, or wanted to.

I shut the door, then turned to Adam. "It's coming," I said.

He said nothing for a minute, then took the axe from me. "Yeah. I figured someday it might."

"The two of them come down, my grandfather and grandmother. I said, 'Something bad happened in the house. Something real bad. You gotta take this money.' I said, 'The police are gonna come, and when they come, what am I gonna do with this?' He says, 'What are you, drunk, high?' I say, 'Look, don't worry about that. This is your money. You don't understand—something happened to my father and mother.' He asks me what happened. I said, 'Use your imagination.' He said, 'What are you, a smart-ass now?' He pushed me out the door. He didn't want that bag."

Once again, if this was true, there wasn't any evidence of it in the public record. Ronnie's grandfather certainly hadn't come forward to say that his grandson had come to see him that night. But given the circumstances and their relationship, that wasn't so surprising. "Why didn't he want it?"

"It was all messed up. Him and me are getting all crazy with each other, yelling, screaming. Eventually I left. I pulled outta there burning rubber. That car was three-hundred-seventy horsepower, a big engine back then. I hit the gas; I was upset. I went all the way back home, money was in the trunk. I still had the pistol on me. I released the hammer."

"You went back home?"

"I went right back home. The Colemans were still sitting out there when I got back."

"At three in the morning?"

"That's right. And I can hear goddamn music from outside the house. I go upstairs, I said, 'What the hell?' I look in Allison's room. I see blood all over that pink-and-white chair. 'Cause her bed was right there in the doorway. Allison's dead, and the room is soaked in blood. I walked in the boys' room, oh my God."

So there it was. The bombshell we'd been heading toward all these months. Ronnie was absolving himself of any responsibility for the deaths of his three youngest siblings. I thought to ask him whether he really understood the magnitude of what he was now telling me, whether he could swear it was true. But in the end, this was a question that mattered as little to him as it did to me, because Ronnie DeFeo knew me well enough by now to know that I would give less weight to his swearing on his words than I would to my own instincts. It wasn't whether he believed what he was saying; it was whether I believed it.

"So you find Allison dead, then both boys. What happened next, Ronnie?"

"The music's still playing, loud, Eddie Kendricks, "Keep On Truckin'." I went upstairs to my room, the lamp is on. Then I find Dawn in her room, the lamp and the ceiling light are on, she's fucking dancing around. She looked weird, there was something off about her. Her eyes looked real dark, and her teeth looked different. I had the pistol. I didn't even think about it. The pistol fell on the floor. I said to her, 'Dawn, what the hell?' She said 'Butch, what are you doing here?' "

"She acted surprised?"

"Surprised? She was shocked. I said, 'What am *I* doing here? What happened to them kids?' I ran into my parents' room to get the rifle, the Marlin. The same gun that was the goddamn murder weapon. But it wasn't there. Dawn had run and picked it up out of the boys' room. I start chasing her, and next thing I know she's holding the thing up with the fucking barrel right in my face. I slapped it out of her hands. The rifle hits the ground. Me and her are wrestling. The gun falls onto the floor, thank God the hammer wasn't back—if it was, that would have been the end of that. She gives me a kick, right in the shoulder. I'm fighting with her. I throw her down on the bed. That gave her a crack, and it jolted the rifle out of her hands. Before I knew it I'd grabbed it and hit the lever, and a live round jumped out. I hit the goddamn lever twice. I thought I'd shot her in the neck. But it was in the head. I got her right in the face. I didn't even know it."

"The same rifle you'd shot your dad with."

"Yeah," he said. "The Marlin. The .35. Same one."

Ronnie had been speaking in his fevered voice during the entire call. As he had relived it all, he'd spiraled upward. Now, suddenly, his voice dropped. Fevered became sad, quiet.

"Everything happened so fast. It was just a big clusterfuck."

"Ronnie, six people lost their lives that night. You've just told me that you were responsible for only two of them. That you intended only one, your father. That you weren't even in the house for the deaths of Allison, Marc, and John. That's what you're telling me. Right?"

"That's what I'm telling you." His voice wasn't wavering. I've interrogated lots of people without them knowing it was interrogation. Adam has taught me all the verbal cues to look for when someone is lying. I detected none.

"Do you think Dawn was high?"

"Of course she was high. All Dawn did was smoke that reefer and smoke the dust."

Joanne hadn't found any evidence pointing to Dawn's having been high that night. But this was Ronnie's version.

"Every time she smoked one, she smoked the other. This was on a regular basis. The dust was made from ice, not formaldehyde. I smelled it as soon as I came in."

"What made you do it, Ronnie? What made you shoot your sister?" He had to take responsibility; he had to own it completely, or we were done.

"I just lost my mind when I seen them kids. I went off. I didn't even realize I was wearing the .357. I'd put it in the shoulder holster on the way back from Brooklyn. It was only missing one round, the round she shot my mother with. I didn't even realize I had it on me. I seen them young kids, and I just snapped. They didn't do nothing wrong. They didn't do nothing."

"You saw your little brothers and sisters killed in cold blood."

"I couldn't handle it."

"All this time, you've been sitting in jail with the world thinking you offed your entire family. That must have eaten at you every day."

"All that bastard had to do was say sorry. Just be a normal fucking father. And her, with the affairs. It led to all this shit. All of it."

"It led to six murders."

"Yeah."

"Only two of which you committed. Your father, and

then Dawn, after she'd killed both your mother and the other kids."

"Unless he helped her."

"Who?"

"Moretti. I spotted him in my room after I came out of Dawn's. Goddamn son of a bitch. I had no idea he was there with her."

Carl Moretti was, like Ronnie, a known dope fiend. He was also a highly connected, very dangerous character. Ronnie had mentioned him before, but I'd never made anything of it. Now he was claiming Moretti had been there, in the house. "Ronnie, you're saying Carl was in your bedroom? Right there in your room when you came home?"

"I come outta Dawn's room, the stairs up there, they went straight, there was a landing, and then it went down. He takes off. I come outta Dawn's room, and he's already down those stairs, making the turn. I'm thinking, 'You son of a bitch.' He didn't have no gun on him, or I'd a been dead. I had the rifle in my hand. I ran after him. Out the front door and down the stoop, around the car, now he's on the Colemans' front lawn. 'You son of a bitch.' I kept saying it over and over. I hit the lever, figured a round went in there. All that came out was empty shell cases. But I didn't know that, I hit the hammer. Click. I hit it again. Click. 'Motherfucker,' I said—he's still running. I had to pick up the shell casing that was out there on the driveway. He got away. I don't know where he had his car parked, it musta been on South Island Place."

"Hold on a second, Ronnie. Why would you leave the

house? If Dawn is in the house with Moretti, why would he stay there, take the chance of the cops rolling up with Dawn alive and everybody dead, including the kids. Why would he take that chance?"

"I don't know. I wasn't there."

"You're smart, Ronnie. You mull things over. If I'm Moretti hanging out with Dawn in the house, everyone's dead and you're gone, why would I sit around with Dawn, where she could turn the gun on me, or she could say I did it, or one of the neighbors could say I heard a shot and I'm gonna send the cops?"

"All I know is I'm thankful he found my stash, fifty drums of heroin, because if he didn't, I would probably be dead. We wouldn't be having this conversation. It wasn't hidden anyway, it was in the drawer, and the drawer was open."

"I get what you're saying, but I want you to get what I'm saying."

"The police did find the spoon."

"Say you and I were in the house. Everybody's wiped out . . ."

"I understand what you're saying. I don't know what happened, I wasn't there. You're asking me to believe a theory."

"It's not a theory, it's common sense. Why would Moretti hang out with Dawn?"

"I don't know, maybe because he wanted some money. The forty grand was missing, so. Four stacks with a band on 'em, each one with ten grand in it. It was gone, nowhere to be found."

During our hundreds of conversations, a lot of what Ronnie DeFeo had told me carried a ring of truth. For most of it, there was no concrete evidence and never would be. All I had to go on was the sincere anger I sensed in Ronnie's voice whenever he spoke about Dawn. Maybe he'd invented it in his mind to put it all on her, to make himself feel better. Maybe not.

But I was getting a different feeling about this story—about Carl Moretti lingering in the house with Dawn and then taking off when Ronnie arrived. Something seemed odd. Ronnie's stories were, if nothing else, always consistent and, in their strange way, airtight. This one seemed more an imaginative ramble. "What were you wearing that day, Ronnie?"

"My army jacket."

"What was Moretti wearing when you saw him?"

"An army jacket."

The devil has many tricks. It can make you see things so clearly you believe in them as strongly as you believe your own hand in front of your face.

"Ronnie, did anyone else see Moretti running out of the house?"

"No, I was the only one. That son of a bitch."

"In the public records, it says your neighbors didn't see anyone but you running out of the house. They heard you shouting threats."

"Yeah, I was waving that shotgun around saying, 'I'll blow your back out, you son of a bitch.'"

"Ronnie, you were high. You weren't thinking or seeing clearly."

"I know what I saw."

I suspected Ronnie DeFeo had not been chasing Carl Moretti but an image of himself. The devil throws up one illusion after another until you don't know what is real and what isn't.

I was starting to feel unsteady. But we had to get through this. "Let's forget about that for now. What did you do next, Ronnie?"

"I went back in and cleaned everything up in the house; then I changed my clothes. They were all bloody. I threw the clothes in a pillowcase and grabbed the pistol from the floor. The gun that shot my mother."

The gun that shot my mother.

"Ronnie, a gun didn't shoot your mother," I said. "Dawn did. Your sister Dawn shot and killed your mother, Louise DeFeo." I didn't know whether Dawn had truly shot Louise DeFeo, or whether Ronnie had and was mentally blocking it out, but I wanted him to start admitting that it really had happened. The version he believed mattered less than the importance of his bringing it all the way to the surface, no matter how painful.

"I was going to drive to Brooklyn, but I had to get the goddamn rifle. I went back and got it, trying not to look at Dawn. I mean, I'd gotten her right in the head. I ran to the side of the dock and threw the rifle in the water."

"And that's where they found it."

"Yeah. When I was being held in the county jail, that's when they went down there and found the damn thing. Instead of throwing it off the end of the dock, the big dock, big water, where the current woulda taken it, I threw it on the side, where there was only a couple of feet of water."

"Why did you throw it there?"

"'Cause I was going fast and not thinking right. All I had to do was walk to the end of the dock and just wing it. Even if somebody seen me, they still woulda never found that gun. As strong as that current is, hell no. The width of that canal, gotta be half a mile. I watched an outboard motor fall off the back of the boat once. Everybody jumped in to try to get it, the motor was already moving from the current. That's where I shoulda thrown it, but that was a mistake I made."

"What did you do after you threw the gun in the canal?"

"I drove to Brooklyn with the money in the trunk and the thirty-seven thousand I had. Right up to the last minute before the jury went out, the Suffolk County police were going everywhere trying to find that pistol. They found the shoulder holster in the house there, but they never got the pistol. They kept going to the Nanowitzes' house, our housekeepers, hassling them, 'Where is this gun? Did you see him with this gun? Where is it?' They shoulda put her on the stand, the housekeeper. They shoulda treated her as a hostile witness, but they didn't. She seen it all. She seen me getting beat all the time. Seen my mother getting beat. She had all the information. It's bullshit."

"Who else did they ask about the gun, Ronnie?"

"Oh, they went to everybody. 'Where's this gun?' And everybody said the same thing: 'We don't know where it is.' Because I had the gun that shot my mother. The bullet went right through the floor. Right through the body, through the mattresses, and into the floor. I mean, it was a Magnum. They couldn't identify it because one bullet didn't have enough characteristics to say it came out of the Marlin, but the judge let them lie and say it came out of the Marlin. One bullet couldn't be identified."

"Why didn't you take the rifle with you, too, instead of throwing it in the water?"

"Because I had to move fast, so I wasn't thinking too straight. I just had to get things done. The forty thousand was missing. I went to get it, but it was gone. I'd told Dawn to hold on to it, so I figured she must have took it up to her room. I also had that file. I didn't want to put the file in the duffel bag, 'cause if they found one, they woulda found the other. I wanted to put it in a goddamn garbage can."

"But you didn't. You held on to it."

"Yeah, I held on to it. Plus I turned the heat way up before I left so that things would go faster, you know, the bodies, and they wouldn't be able to figure the real time of death."

"You mean decomposition."

"Yeah, right. That's right."

"You said you were in panic mode. How did you know to turn the heat up to make the bodies decompose faster?"

"I don't know how I knew. Something just told me to do it. I was trying to think of anything I could do to throw them off, I guess. They always say 3:15 was the time of death. It was actually 1:15. I admit I was laughing in the back of the cruiser as those cops poured into the house. It was like a steam bath in there. But none of them noticed."

Joanne dove into the files, looking for corroboration of any sort. There was none. But then, I supposed there wouldn't be if no one had noticed.

"Ronnie, this is the first time you've ever said this."

"I know that."

"Why haven't you ever mentioned it before?"

"What good was it gonna do me?"

"What good is it going to do you now?"

"I ain't telling you this because it's going to do me any good. I ain't telling you any of this because of that. I'm telling it to you because I want it out of me. That's all."

As it was with so many of Ronnie's claims, I had no reason to believe him. I also had no reason not to. "Did you just leave the house, or did you shower first?"

"I didn't take no shower. Like I said, I changed my clothes, because I couldn't go to work all filthy and with blood on my clothes, but forget about taking a shower. There was only time to change. How could I go back to work with the same clothes that I had on? It just wouldn't look right. Them clothes were dirty and smelly from sweating, and then there's the blood. Plus I was too shocked to take a shower."

"How long did you stay in the house?"

"I had to find the file, the second set of books. I had to find them, because the police woulda came in and found them. My father had it taped with a folder, underneath one of the drawers. I had to take all the drawers out. So I took them out, and I found it. It was in a plastic bag, taped with duct tape. And I took it. Son of a bitch hadn't been paying taxes on a dime of it. I still had the rest of my guns in the car so I could get rid of them. I didn't want the cops finding any guns at all in that god-damn house."

"What did you do with the bloody clothes?"

"I drove to Brooklyn and threw the pillowcase down a storm drain in Seaview, in the suburbs, by the ham-burger joint, Gary's Hamburger. Charcoal burger place. Right by Rockaway Parkway."

"And the pistol that Dawn had—?"

"I drove to Charlie's house. Charlie Brooks. That was my best friend. The black guy that testified at my trial. Member of the Black Panthers—they called him the Bear. Charlie would do whatever for me, we liked each other. I hid the pistol in the basement of his apartment building, behind a set of pipes. He had no idea what it had been used for, but he figured it had been used for something. Otherwise, why would I be so concerned about hiding the thing? He saw the gun had been fired, he knew it had been used for something."

"What about your other guns?"

Ronnie listed all the guns he owned, which he remem-bered in great detail. "Every gun that I owned went to Charlie's house. The only ones I couldn't get out were the ones on the gun rack. I had a gun rack in my room. I couldn't rip it off the wall. It had two guns. A single-barrel shotgun that my mother signed for in Ithaca and a .22 Marlin, semiautomatic, like an M1. I couldn't get that rack off the wall, so those guns stayed. But I took a 30-06 Remington DGL. That was a three-hundred-dollar gun. I took a 12-gauge pump Mossberg. I took a 12-gauge Ithaca Deerslayer. I took a brand-new .44 Magnum. That'll shoot through an engine block. It had two fourteen-shot clips. I took the .357. I took a .25 automatic. And I took all the ammunition. Boxes. I'm gonna tell you, I had, no exaggeration, two hundred, maybe three hundred rounds of ammo." He added, pragmatically, "They were on sale."

"Did Charlie bust your chops about the fact that you're asking to stash all these guns at his place?"

"I woke him up. I gave him some of the money in exchange for this favor. I'm trying to think how much money I gave him. I think three thousand. I said, 'Here, this is for you and your wife.' I said, 'Make sure you tell Angie I gave you some money.' He said, 'You messing with my wife?' She was a pretty black girl. I said, 'No, I ain't messing with your wife.' He told me he was only kidding. I said, 'Make sure you take care of the kids, buy them all stuff.' Yeah, that's what it was, two thousand at first, then I gave him another thousand and told him to take care of Angie and the kids. Three thousand dollars. That was out of my own money, out of the thirty-seven thousand. We hid all the guns down in the boiler room, in the basement, with the pistol. Then we locked the room and left."

I looked at the file. Charlie Brooks had taken the stand, but unlike most of the witnesses called, he built Ronnie DeFeo up rather than tearing him down.

"Charlie testified at your trial."

"On my behalf, not theirs. He didn't tell them I was at his house or that I had the guns or any of it. He just stood up for my character, said, 'That man did not kill his family. Butch's father was very violent, but Butch wouldn't have done this.' Charlie used to take me down to the black neighborhoods where white people can't normally go. He'd say, 'This is Butch Brigante.' He figured if he dropped the name Brigante it would give me more cred. 'Do not fuck with him. If anything happens to him, you're gonna have to deal with me.' We'd go from place to place. Charlie and his friends would say, 'Buy Butch a drink,' and they'd do it. They liked me down there. I met this black girl there from the Marcy Avenue Projects. She was a fox. You have to be out of your mind to go in there white. I was going in there picking her up."

"Did Charlie know about the extent of your troubles with your father?"

"Of course. He knew how abused I was. Charlie had nothing but trouble with my father, too. The whole time he worked for him." I wondered if Charlie Brooks had stuck up for Ronnie not because he believed Ronnie was innocent but because he knew what a punching bag Ronnie had been for his father; maybe he'd figured Ronnie's actions were, on some level, justified.

"Is Charlie still alive?"

"No, he's dead now. He was forty-three at the time."

"A forty-three-year-old man was a twenty-three-year-old kid's best friend?"

"Why not?"

I decided to leave it alone. I'd seen stranger matchups.

"He would have been more than eighty years old now. Do you ever think about that?"

"Sure. I think about Charlie all the time. He told me right from the get-go, 'You have any problems in prison, you let me know immediately.' I said, 'No, it's all right, I know all the black guys. Except they're all junkies.'"

"Ronnie, did anyone ever find that Magnum? The pistol?"

"No, never. Charlie told me he wasn't getting rid of it. I said, 'Charlie, the gun was just used in a murder.' He told me not to worry, said he could do something to the barrel, maybe take the twist out. I said, 'Sure, whatever.' They had six kids. He cleaned the gun, scratched off the serial number, and had someone sell it on the street. That gun is gone."

"Where did you go after Charlie's?"

"I went back to Long Island, back to work. I spent the day at the dealership. Although I went to the luncheonette once it opened, you know, to get some more people to see me."

"Ronnie, when Dawn was still alive and you were looking to dump the money—at that point you're out of the house, the kids are dead—did you ever think she's blasting music, the neighbors saw you with the rifle in the window, what would happen if the cops walked in at that point and the kids are all dead and she's prancing around?"

"I don't know. I don't know what she woulda did. Ain't too much you can do."

"How stoned was she?"

"Every month I would buy a 35-millimeter vial of angel dust from a local guy for her. This was the real good stuff, the stuff made with ether. Smelled like spearmint. I tried it, it was good. And the reefer was always excellent."

"You bought the stuff for her?"

"Yeah."

"Why?"

"So she wouldn't have to go out and get it by herself. You meet some dangerous people in that world. I didn't want her going to see those kinds of people alone."

"Where did you go after work, Ronnie?"

"I left work early. Early afternoon. And I came back in the direction of the house. I kept driving by it. I ran into Duchek, right outside my house. He asks where was I last night. I said where were you last night. He drove off, and I drove off. That was the conversation. They kept bringing that up at my trial."

"But you didn't go in?"

"I didn't want to go in the house during the daytime. Kept driving right by it but didn't go in. Duchek has the audacity, right in the middle of the street, to ask me where was I. See, we'd had a falling out, a big thing, on September 26, about the fact that he was stealing checks from my family, from the dealership. Our relationship had stopped after that. Him and them checks, man. He was robbing our dealership so he could support his habit."

"Is that true? Can you prove it?"

"What do you want me to prove? It's fact."

Most of what Ronnie told me he also claimed as fact. That didn't mean it was. The public record included the information that Ronnie had run into Duchek during the day following the murders. The rest of the details, as usual, couldn't be backed up.

"I told him, 'You don't have to rob nothing; your family has money, plus you work.' He was a stonemason for his father's business. I told him, 'Look, whether you show up or not, you got a paycheck.' His father did just fine. What does Duchek need to go stealing for?"

"Where did you end up after you saw Duchek?"

"I went to Mindy's house."

I looked at the file. Mindy Weiss was a girl in the neighborhood who Ronnie spent time with. His girl-friend, if such a term could be applied.

"I think I took her shopping, I can't remember where, could have been Massapequa; then we wound up at her house. She wanted to fool around, but I didn't really have it in me. We started in a bit, but I didn't have no sex. I told her I wasn't in the mood. That shit was all going through my mind; I was trying to get rid of it. I was drinking, but the booze didn't do nothing. I called my house while I was there, so she'd see me do it. My mother would have been home that time of day, so that's when I called. And Marc had a broken leg from playing football. There was a lot of animosity about that. My father, of course, blamed me for him getting his leg broken. Now how do you explain that it's my fault my brother broke his leg? It was during a goddamn football game. I went to the hospital with him, but I was drunk, in the emergency room. My father started a fight with me about that. That goddamn guy."

"How long did you shack up at Mindy's?"

"I was with her for a couple of hours, then I told her I gotta go."

"Did you give her a reason?"

"Nah. I just said, 'Look, I gotta get going.' She asked me if I'd be coming over that night. I said, 'Hey, you remember when I got caught in your house and your father and mother started screaming and I had to run out of the house getting dressed? Well, we ain't gonna go through that again. I had to send your mother a dozen roses to get back on her good side.' Mindy had two different apartments. Guess who was paying the rent on them? Yeah, me. The second one had a bathroom but no shower. It had a fireplace, a bar, everything else, but no shower. I said, 'What good is this? I come over here and have sex—I gotta go home stinking. I gotta walk by your father and hear his mouth. It's a joke.'"

"If it was her apartment, why would you see her dad there?"

"Because parents come by to see their kids. Parents do that."

This was just one of the times I thought I'd caught an inconsistency in one of Ronnie's stories and had tried to call him on it. He'd have an answer ready every time. Were they the answers of a great actor quick on his feet? Maybe I was wrong, but I didn't think so.

"So she gave that up and went back home with her parents. That's how I got caught having sex with her in her room. Then we started having sex in the den downstairs, so we could hear if anybody was coming. That broad, I ain't gonna lie to you, she was experienced, she knew more than I knew. She said she'd had a good teacher. Then I had to get even, you know, the masculinity comes out, she said, 'Oh, whoa, you gotta stop, I can't take no more.' That girl, I'll tell you, I ain't gonna lie, that girl knew more about sex than any broad I ever been with. I was with a lot of married women then, and she still knew more."

"Did she have any idea what was going on?"

"No, I didn't say nothing about it. After I left her place, I stopped in at Henry's Bar, the one at the corner of Ocean and Merrick, just to scope it out and see who was hanging out there."

"Did you have a drink?"

"Yeah. And I didn't drink no vodka and 7UP. I was a scotch drinker. Dewar's on the rocks. But I couldn't get drunk that night even if I tried. I called the house in front of everyone, so they'd see me. I was letting everyone know I was pretty worried 'cause I'd been calling the house all day and no one was answering. I also told them I didn't have my front door keys and had no way to get in."

"Did you have a plan in mind?"

"My mind was going crazy with the shit that had happened. I didn't have no plan. I was just doing one thing and then the next thing. I was figuring it out as I went. I decided to leave the bar. I went to Janet and Andy McCormack's house and got high. They lived in a small apartment in Amityville. That broad was a big dope fiend, big heroin addict. We had sex once. I bought a lot of dope from her that night, before I called the police. That was a mistake, boy. A hundred dollars on donk dope."

Joanne placed the file on the desk in front of me, with a particular page sticking out. It was the page referring to Janet McCormack, who had indeed testified at the trial. Butch DeFeo had come to her apartment that evening and gotten high, Janet had said. She'd also noted that Butch was regularly violent and had rage issues. And then she had stepped down.

"So you bought the dope from Janet . . ."

"I gave her fifty and said, 'I'll give you the other fifty in a little while.' I was stoned outta my face when the police finally got to the house. I was stoned when they had me in the precinct."

"Ronnie, when you went to get high, did you ever think, 'Maybe I should just turn myself in?'"

"I didn't know what to think or what to say to who. I just knew I didn't want to go back to that house."

"Why not?"

"I couldn't deal with it. I wanted to make believe it didn't happen."

"Do you think that's why you stayed away from the house for so long after? You waited seventeen hours to report the crime."

"It's very possible. I don't know. I guess, maybe."

In all our conversations, Ronnie DeFeo had never said this. He had never come out and told me, until now, that he had spent all those hours simply wanting to put the act out of his mind, and by doing so, hopefully erasing the fact that it had ever happened. He'd tried to visit his common haunts or be with those who represented his normal life—his workplace, his girlfriend's, his fellow junkies—to make it seem as though this was just another day. We all do it sometimes, even in the face of small mistakes. But sooner or later, we know we have to face our deeds.

There was another question that I'd wanted to ask Ronnie for a long time but that I'd kept inside because I figured I already knew the answer. I wanted to know if his answer would be the same. "Ronnie, why didn't you just run? Before all this, I mean. Why not just go? You had money, you had access to the cars, you had some skills. Why didn't you just take off and leave all the crap behind?"

"Look," he finally said, "as bad as my mother and father were, when there was a problem, they were the first ones there. I mean, regardless of the beatings, I actually thought my father was my friend until I found out the man had ordered a contract on me. I mean, come on."

I actually thought my father was my friend. I was as saddened as I was shocked to hear these words. So it was the same answer I'd had in my head. When you're a dog and your owner kicks you over and over, you don't run away. You keep slinking back, because you hold out hope that, one of these times, instead of a kick, you're going to get a pat on the head. It never happens, but you keep going back anyway. At the same time, you convince yourself of the virtues of the person kicking you, since they're providing you food and shelter between the kicks. Maybe later, much later, you decide it was their fault. But at the time you occupy yourself mostly trying to figure out what you must be doing to deserve it.

"People giving funny looks to me weeks before this happened. Then the fun starts. The bastard."

"When did you finally go home, Ronnie?"

"After Janet's, I drove back to the bar."

"Henry's."

"Yeah. I ran in real upset and yelled to everyone, 'I think something bad happened to my family.' Everyone looked up. Joey Yeswit, the bartender, drove with me back to the house, with a couple of other guys."

I thumbed quickly through the file again. Joey Yeswit had driven. Ronnie had been a passenger, along with Duchek and, possibly, others from Henry's. I quickly glanced through the transcript of the 911 call that had been received by the Suffolk County emergency switchboard from 112 Ocean Avenue at six thirty-five that evening.

"This is Suffolk County Police. May I help you?"

"We have a shooting here. Uh, DeFeo."

"Sir, what is your name?"

"Joey Yeswit."

"Can you spell that?"

"Yeah. Y-E-S-W-I-T."

"Y-E-S . . ."

"Y-E-S-W-I-T."

". . . W-I-T. Your phone number?"

"I don't even know if it's here. There's, uh, I don't have a phone number here."

"Okay, where you calling from?"

"It's in Amityville. Call up the Amityville Police, and it's right off, uh . . . Ocean Avenue in Amityville."

"Austin?"

"Ocean Avenue. What the . . . ?"

"Ocean . . . Avenue? Off of where?"

"It's right off Merrick Road. Ocean Avenue."

"Merrick Road. What's . . . what's the problem, sir?"

"It's a shooting!"

"There's a shooting. Anybody hurt?"

"Hah?"

"Anybody hurt?"

"Yeah, it's uh, uh—everybody's dead."

"What do you mean, everybody's dead?"

"I went into the house after they did. Had to go through the window to get in. I walked upstairs. I was so messed up, I forgot what had happened. Forgot everybody was dead. I had one of them blackouts. I seen it all in the mirror. I was using that mirror to do all the shooting. Looking in the mirror, not at them."

Ronnie would come back to this description often. I got the feeling that he repeated it so frequently because it was a way, still, after years of serving time for this act, of trying to believe it had happened in another dimension, not in this, his actual life. It was something that had occurred in the mirror.

"They knew the blood on the clothes was mine."

This, too, happened often: Ronnie suddenly, seemingly out of nowhere, bringing to the surface individual elements of the crime and then refuting them. I didn't think it was out of nowhere at all. I believed, no matter what he claimed, that the details of his family's deaths replayed itself on a constant loop in his head and that the anger, guilt, and confusion boiling inside him were still just as fresh as they'd been in the immediate hours after the act.

The element he was referring to now was the blood found on his clothes. Not the clothes he'd put in a bag and tossed down a drainpipe in Brooklyn—the clothes he was wearing when the police came to 112 Ocean Avenue and found the DeFeos murdered. They'd determined that the blood was Allison's and that Ronnie had picked up a shell casing from the floor where her blood had pooled, then wiped it on his pants.

"It wasn't enough the old man beat me up. The cops wanted to get in on the act, too."

"What are you saying, Ronnie?"

"That wasn't my blood. It was from the cops beating me up. Not once—over and over. They wanted a confession, and I wouldn't sign one, so here we go. That's what they did till I said I did it, I did it. If they'd tested the clothes, then they'd have a problem. But of course they missed that little piece of information."

I looked at the file. No, there hadn't been any DNA testing on the clothes—it wasn't a possibility at the time. It was his word against that of the Suffolk County police.

"Why would the cops beat you up, Ronnie?"

"That's what I'm trying to tell you—to get me to confess. I wouldn't. They knew the blood wasn't Allison's, so they had to beat the confession out of me; then they'd be in the clear. They wanted me to be their guy."

It was, again, a case of Ronnie DeFeo making claims that could no longer be corroborated. He might as well be speaking in a vacuum. "I just want to say this one more time to be clear, Ronnie. You're saying the blood on the clothes was your blood. Not Allison's blood, yours. The cops beat you up enough to make you bleed and to get you to confess."

"They knew what they needed out of me. They wanted me to be the guy. I mean, that's all they had, my confession and Allison's blood on my clothes, according to them. 'Oh, her blood on his clothes, that proves it, that shows he's a liar.' But where are your witnesses? There were no witnesses. That's *my* blood."

That's my blood. Present tense again. He was there in the house, reliving it.

> *"I don't know what happened. Kid come running in the bar. He says everybody in the family was killed, and we came down here."*
>
> *"Hold on a second, sir. What's your name?"*
>
> *"My name is Joe Yeswit."*
>
> *"George Edwards?"*
>
> *"Joe Yeswit."*
>
> *"How do you spell it?"*
>
> *"What? I just . . . how many times do I have to tell you? Y-E-S-W-I-T."*
>
> *"Where are you at?"*
>
> *"I'm on Ocean Avenue."*

"What number?"

"I don't have a number here. There's no number on the phone."

"What number on the house?"

"I don't even know that."

"Where are you at? Ocean Avenue and what?"

"In Amityville. Call up the Amityville Police and have someone come down here. They know the family."

"Amityville."

"Yeah, Amityville."

"Okay. Now, tell me what's wrong."

"I don't know. Guy come running in the bar. Guy come running in the bar and said there—his mother and father are shot. We ran down to his house and everybody in the house is shot. I don't know how long, you know. So, uh . . ."

"Uh, what's the add . . . what's the address of the house?"

"Uh, hold on. Let me go look up the number. All right. Hold on. One-twelve Ocean Avenue, Amityville."

"I didn't kill them kids. I loved them kids."

"Is that Amityville or North Amityville?"

"Amityville. Right on . . . south of Merrick Road."

"Is it right in the village limits?"

"It's in the village limits, yeah."

"Eh, okay, what's your phone number?"

"I don't even have one. There's no number on the phone."

"All right, where're you calling from? Public phone?"

"No, I'm calling right from the house, because I don't see a number on the phone."

"You're at the house itself?"

"Yeah."

"How many bodies are there?"

"I think, uh, I don't know—uh, I think they said four."

"There's four?"

"Yeah."

"All right, you stay right there at the house, and I'll call the Amityville Village P.D., and they'll come down."

"So in your mind there was no blood of Allison's on your clothing."

"In my mind? No, not in my mind. I'm telling you what the facts are. That's what I'm saying, they made the whole thing up."

"Ronnie—"

"It was either him or me, for Christ's sake." His voice was spiraling upward again.

"I know that, Ronnie—"

"I mean, I was doing my mother a favor! And how about her? Two damn boyfriends, right out in the open in front of everybody's face! The hairstylist and Brother Isaac. At least. I mean, come on!"

He was close to losing it. I had to bring him back down but keep him within the story. "Ronnie—what do you believe Dawn had been thinking?"

I could feel him coming back to me, just a little. Retreating from the house, again. It was his awful spiritual magnet and always would be. He might escape it for a minute at a time, or an hour, but not forever.

"I believe Dawn was gonna tell the police I came home drunk and stoned like always and then I killed everybody. I guess she never expected me to come back to the house. I had to come back; I had to get all the guns, get everything out of the house. My concern was getting all the money and all the stuff outta there."

"Just a few hours before, you thought she was trying to save you. Now she's picking up a gun and pointing it at you. That must have messed you up."

"'Butch, what are you doing here?' she says. No shit, what am I doing here. My sister saves my life, and then she puts a gun in my face and gets herself killed. All I was gonna do when I seen her was kick her ass for killing the kids. But she had to grab the gun."

"Say it panned out differently. Say—"

"She saves my life in the bedroom because my mother's gonna shoot me, then she goes and gets herself shot. I thought I was shot, but Dawn got her before she got me. The hammer was back on the pistol when I picked it up."

"Ronnie, say you came back and saw the kids were killed and Dawn didn't pick up the gun, so you didn't have to do her. Would you have turned her in for killing the kids?"

"No. We woulda both wound up in prison."

"Could you have gotten away with it?"

"Yeah, we coulda got away with it. Nobody saw nothing, nobody could place anybody at the scene of the crime.

Those two idiot neighbors that were standing there, they had their chance when they heard the gunshots."

"Who? The Colemans?"

"Yeah, the Colemans. They dummied up good. I mean, what did they think? They heard shots. Why didn't they call the police? Then the stupid kid next door, the one who said he heard Shaggy barking. He didn't hear Shaggy barking, it was a dog in the neighborhood."

"What kid, Ronnie?"

"Some kid who was home from school the next day because he was sick. He said he heard the dog barking."

Others had said the same. My file, and the public record, was full of nameless, faceless people claiming to have heard the dog barking throughout the daylight hours of November 13, 1974.

"Shaggy was the dog you got after Candie?"

"Yeah. It was a few years before that we put Candie down. 1971. Yeah, I was twenty. My father decided to get Shaggy a month after that. That crazy thing was, that dog barked at everything, night and day, except when that shit happened with my family. That whole time, the dog was quiet. I put him in the car with me when I left for Brooklyn."

"The dog was with you in the car?"

"Yeah, I untied him and took him in the car with me."

"Why?"

"Why what?"

"Why did you decide to take the dog with you? You're in the middle of this crazy situation, and you stop to untie the dog and put him in the car?"

"Yeah."

"Why?"

"I just didn't want to leave him alone."

"Dawn was there, and the kids were there."

"That's true."

"So?"

"So I don't know what. In that moment I didn't want to leave him alone."

Ronnie didn't like when I pressed him, maybe because it made his memory seem less certain. I already knew the dog had been in his car. Joanne had read me the report: the police had taken Shaggy out of the car and delivered her to the pound, where she'd been picked up by an aunt on Ronnie's mom's side.

"Back to the Colemans, Ronnie. Why do you still seem so angry with them? They didn't commit any crime, did they?" I was pushing on purpose. As always, Ronnie remained deeply resentful toward anyone and everyone who had played a part in not seeing him punished for his sins.

"Maybe they didn't commit a crime, but they just sat back and did nothing, which is just as bad. What did they think was going on in there? I mean, Dawn had her agenda."

Dawn hadn't gotten him in the end, and neither had his mother. Of everyone in the house, only he had survived. But at an enormous cost.

"Ronnie, have you ever thought about why you went back to the house? You had money. You could have just taken off. Why go back?"

"Because somebody had to report it. I couldn't leave 'em in there no longer. It was really bothering me."

"You had a lot of money."

"Yeah. I coulda done a lot of things. I coulda left and never came back. I coulda called my lawyer and told him what happened. And he woulda told the police, 'Listen, you can't talk to him without me.' That's what I shoulda did, but then they woulda said, 'Oh, this is the one that did it.'"

"You could have gone lots of places. Brazil."

"I had a million in cash in the duffel bag in my trunk. Plus the thirty-seven thousand of my own. I coulda got on a jet and never came back. I coulda went anywhere in the world."

"You could have disappeared. It happens."

"I guess I ain't like that. Especially when it came to my family. That's why I didn't run. I was gonna burn that place down and then make like the wind. I was scheming and conniving all day long, I said I still got plenty of time to do it. I had ten gallons of gas. Sunoco 240, high-test. I was gonna burn that place to the ground."

"But you went back to the bar."

"I went back to the bar. To make it look good."

"You could have hopped a jet, and that would have been it. But you went to the bar."

"My friends called the police. The cop who went into the house looked terrified. He didn't know how many bodies there were. They'd only discovered my mother and father at that point. He went in there with his gun drawn. I wanted to laugh, but, you know. It was showtime. They found the kids and everything; oh boy, now it really starts. They talked to me in the kitchen, they told me they gotta take me to the precinct. Me along with everyone else. Oh, yeah, they just started grabbing everybody. They grabbed Duchek, they grabbed Janet and Andy. Not Mindy, though. When she got to the house, she said to the cops, 'You ain't taking me to no prison. I'll call my father, and his lawyer will be right here.' Her father was a doctor who owned half of fucking Hempstead Turnpike. He owned the Nathan's and the steakhouse. The cops didn't touch her."

There was a very long silence—the longest one in any of our conversations, going back to the very first. He was finally spent. Exhausted. He had released it.

"Ronnie?"

"Yeah."

"That must have taken a lot."

More silence. His tank was empty.

"But it was important that you did it. How do you feel?"

"Tired."

ELEVEN

Green Haven Correctional Facility, originally a federal prison, sits discreetly in the town of Beekman in Dutchess County in the state of New York, though the address is listed as Route 216 in Stormville. In the mid- to late 1970s, during a brief period when the state upheld the death penalty, Green Haven was famous for housing New York's death row. A notorious electric chair, "Old Sparky," was moved from Sing Sing to Green Haven, though never used. Capital punishment was reinstated in New York in 1995, fulfilling then-governor George Pataki's campaign pledge, but in 2004 was once again struck down as unconstitutional by the New York Court of Appeals.

Removal of the death penalty did not mean an absence of death, of course. Two correction officers had died in the line of duty while at Green Haven. One had disappeared while working only to be discovered later in a garbage dump twenty miles away, sexually violated and strangled to death. Another had been found lifeless in a watchtower with a gunshot wound to the head. That death was deemed a suicide.

Authorities of the state, of course, always hold out hope that the instinct for death can be changed to the instinct for life. In 1975, the Alternatives to Violence Project was conceived and implemented at Green Haven to help develop inmates' abilities to resolve conflicts without resorting to manipulation, coercion, or violence. The prison also participates in the Bard Prison Initiative, a college-sponsored program enabling inmates to work toward a liberal-arts degree while incarcerated.

Yet it is the darker impulses of the individuals behind these bars that fascinate people on the other side. Most people don't want to know whether these criminals are recovering; we want to know the details of what they did to get put in such a place. We recognize in them some of our own dark urges, the ones we fight every day to control, and so we are strangely gripped by those who have allowed those urges, even for a moment, to take over.

Certain inmates at Green Haven have carried with them some notoriety. There was bank robber James McBratney, aka "Jimmy from Queens," who kidnapped Manny Gambino, related to the Gambino Mob family, and who was later killed in a bar on Staten Island by John Gotti and others in a Mob execution.

There was Robert Golub, convicted for the murder of his thirteen-year-old neighbor, Kelly Anne Tinyes, who lived five doors away.

There was Leroy Antonio "Nicky" Barnes, former drug

lord and crime boss, and leader of The Council, the group of black gangsters who controlled the heroin trade in Harlem during the 1970s, later turned government informant.

There was twenty-seven-year-old John Giuca, former student at John Jay College of Criminal Justice, convicted in the slaying of Fairfield University student Mark Fisher, despite Giuca's mother's desperate public efforts to have the decision overturned.

And there was Ronald DeFeo Jr., tried and convicted of killing his parents and four siblings at their home in Amityville in the middle of the night, for reasons still uncertain, amid circumstances still unknown.

Joanne scheduled my visit to Green Haven Correctional Facility for a Wednesday morning. I remember that detail well because at Green Haven, Wednesdays are referred to as Wedding Wednesdays, the day when inmates get married. Though it was a chilly morning, the sun shone almost blindingly, making it hard for me to see the road as Will prepared to pull out of the driveway. From other parts of New York, different members of the A&E film crew—the same ones who had filmed me finding the coin Ronnie had buried when he was nineteen—were also getting ready to leave. They'd filmed me in the forest; now they wanted to film me at the penitentiary.

I was in the passenger seat, Joanne in the back. Jo had complained of dizziness the evening before but this morning said she felt good enough to join us. Turning around to look at her now, I thought different, and told her so.

"I'm fine," she said. "Let's go."

At home, Joanne was my daughter; on cases, she was my assistant, accompanying me everywhere. But not today. "You have a fever, Jo," I said. "Go on inside and we'll debrief later."

The only thing that could stop my headstrong daughter from arguing would be an actual fever, so the fact that she relented confirmed my suspicion. Though not happy about it, she went back in the house and lay down, though first turning around to tell me to be careful. It was the first time since she'd started working alongside me that she wouldn't be accompanying me on a case.

Will turned the key in the ignition, and we heard only a series of wheezing chugs. Again he tried, and again came the chugs, diminishing this time to a series of clicks. He waited a minute, tried again, and again failed. It was only after soliciting the help of our neighbor and his jumper cables that we were finally able to get on the road.

Once the car was running, I entered the address for Green Haven into our Global Positioning System device. It defaulted instead to the address of our own house. I entered it again, but the address kept getting rejected. The GPS, it seemed, wasn't interested in helping us make our way to Green Haven. I went inside and printed out the directions instead.

On the way, Will started to complain of the same dizziness that had persuaded me to force Joanne to stay home. I wasn't feeling great, either. And Will looked washed out.

When we neared Green Haven, our intended two-hour trip now having taken almost four hours, the air took on a chill; by the time we pulled into the parking lot, dark clouds covered the sky. The members of the film crew, having encountered their own car troubles, had arrived only minutes before.

A large, black-haired man in a Texas-style suit with an oversize silver belt buckle approached the car as we parked. He was surrounded by a posse of uniformed, armed guards who walked in a *V*, him at the front. The man walked slowly and deliberately. I was used to this kind of walk; it was a walk that said this was his turf. The walk of a big fish demonstrating that every ass in this small pond belonged to him.

The man leaned toward the window. He had sharp eyes, a chiseled jaw, and a tough look that had no doubt turned more than one hardened criminal to instant jelly. It doesn't usually take long for me to detect weaknesses or cracks in a person's character. Sometimes it's in the movements of the eye or the look of the mouth. Sometimes it's just a feeling. In the first few moments of our interaction, I searched this man for cracks in the armor. I detected none.

He looked at Will, then at me. Arching an eyebrow, he introduced himself as William Lee, Green Haven's warden. I imagined someone who ran a maximum-security prison didn't appreciate people showing up two hours late to interview inmates.

I was right.

"Can't do it today," he said, in a tone suggesting that his lack of appreciation ran even deeper than I'd assumed.

I apologized, explaining about my daughter's illness and the troubles we'd run into trying to get there. Warden Lee softened a little at this, but he was nevertheless unrelenting. A prison warden at his softest is still harder than most others. He repeated that we couldn't do it today and would have to return first thing in the morning.

We called home to Joanne, who found all of us a nearby bed-and-breakfast called Le Chambord, five minutes down the country road in Hopewell Junction. The house was a beautiful old southern-looking mansion that seemed like it had been lifted directly from the set of *Gone with the Wind*. Will and I checked in, along with the rest of the crew; went out to grab a burger at a drive-through; then went back and settled in for the evening.

When I awoke at five the next morning, my eyes ached—or, more accurately, the area below my eyes. Will looked at me and asked me what had happened. I looked in the mirror to see the beginnings of twin red welts under each eye. Will went down the hall and got some ice, which he then wrapped in a towel and handed to me.

As I stood in front of the mirror holding the towel against my face, I rewound the events of the night, which I'd convinced myself were part of a dream. The feeling of being pinned down in bed. Small hands touching my ankles. The anguished voices of children. Multiple phone calls—how many I couldn't say—and a threatening male voice telling me to go back home.

You might say my work requires being an open book for as long as possible, because when the pages get filled up, they get filled up fast. What I mean is that, when a client comes to me—or, more accurately, contacts Joanne, who then sets up an appointment—I allow no predisposition and make no advance judgments. I can offer true help only if I go in blank. Whether helping Adam fill in the gaps on a homicide case or helping individuals answer questions that are tormenting them, my process is the same. Erase myself as completely as possible so that the client's spirit can enter and illuminate.

As a result, I feel a certain kind of nothing when preparing to speak to a client for the first time. I don't ask the person's name. I don't ask about his or her background. I ask only for a client's picture, if he or she is comfortable sending one, through Jo. My discovery is through seeing and feeling the person and the spirit around him or her.

But I never forget a face. So when a woman contacted Jo saying she'd had readings from me before, and Jo handed me her picture, I felt uneasy—for I would have staked my reputation on the fact that I had never seen this woman before. When Jo asked her name, she answered simply "Mary." Jo said the woman had only one question: *When will I feel complete again?* The question itself is not so odd for a medium to hear. Sometimes folks just want validation about life. But the woman continued to insist to Jo that this wasn't her first encounter with me. Against my better reasoning, I advised Jo to book the appointment.

Mary called that night at eight sharp. I was holding her picture in my hand when she called. I realize voices don't always seem to match faces, but the voice I was listening to clashed against the picture I was looking at in an irrefutable way. As I placed the picture facedown on my desk, my mind began to race. Her hollow voice had sent a chill through me. But there was now silence on the other end, and I needed to say something. I began to explain the process I use: the client simply begins speaking about something pedestrian, anything at all, perhaps what he or she did that day, and soon I will begin to see. I may disappear briefly and then return. I may write things in another hand writing through me and then see what I've written only after the possession is complete and the spirit has withdrawn.

Though I'd explained my process a thousand times before, this time I was finding it hard to stay focused on the simple task of conversation. This woman's voice was like a shudder, and I felt she was aging by the second, as though a thickness was seeping into her voice. She began to slur. Her words began to run over one another until she was making no sense at all. It was already happening, and, for the first time, I couldn't stop a spirit from entering before I was ready. It was only after her spirit had finally lifted and I'd returned to myself that Jo explained to me what had happened. On the pad at my desk, I had begun immediately to draw roads leading up to and away from a door. I'd scrawled different versions of this same image many times over. The voice on the other end of the phone would giggle in a sinister fashion, then change into that of a lost child, then would sob. I have instructed Joanne many times not to interfere with the process even if it is distressing in the moment. It is a trancelike state, numb on the outside yet frenzied on the inside. As I continued drawing and writing and the paper ran out, she continued to slide fresh pages in front of me.

My eyes darted around the room, searching for something or someone. In a shaky voice I had said, "Mary, are you there?" Even in the midst of transformation I would normally have resisted uttering such desperate words. *Let it bait you and you're done, Jackie. Don't let yourself be taunted. Don't let it get into your head.*

A demonic laugh had come out of the phone. "I tricked you," said the voice posing as Mary. It had giggled, then roared. And our room in Brooklyn had begun to shake. Joanne tried to keep her footing as the voice said, "Why did you let me die? Why?" I had dropped the phone, but from where it lay on the floor, Joanne had heard the voice continue: "You coward. Your mother never loved you."

The room had continued to quake, sending items in every direction. A book on photography I keep on the side of my desk flew across the room and struck me in the nose. Blood started coming out. Joanne, though shaken, had torn off a wad of paper towels and pressed them against my nose until the flow subsided.

Then everything had ceased, and there was silence. I knew two things for certain. First, it was back. Second, it knew I wasn't going down without a fight. I'd often felt alone, as though trying to fight my way out of a shadowy maze. Every part of my life an open book to the devil. Blue-black thoughts dripping into my mind. The dread and panic came frequently, and most of the time I could repulse them. But when I came back quickly, like now, they rushed in with overwhelming force. I shook my head back and forth, as though if I did it hard enough, the wickedness would fly out of me. All these years fighting for someone else. I'd never stopped to think about who was going to save me.

I was sweating and seemed dizzy, Joanne said. I'd fallen backward into my chair and, as a click came from the other end of the phone, had come back into myself. Joanne had witnessed the flight and the return, and I now saw two things in her eyes you never want to see from your child. Fear is one. The other is sympathy.

That was the point when my conscious awareness had resumed. I'd looked down at the papers and all my scribbles, then at the picture of the woman. Across her face, I had written, in a different hand, two words.

Remember me.

After our night in the B and B, Will and I arrived again at Green Haven with the rest of the production crew. It was the break of dawn, but the sky was still the color of a dark bruise. On cue, Warden Lee walked out, his armed entourage in their perfect *V* flanking him again, and greeted us. I returned his greeting and asked if there was always a dark cloud over Green Haven.

The warden didn't respond to the question, but replied only, "He knows you're here," then turned, followed by his posse.

It's hard to really get an idea of the height of a prison's walls until you walk past them. As I followed Warden Lee and stared upward, the thought occurred to me that, when you're surrounded everyday by four vertical cement slabs that seem to rise forever, you must truly feel cut off from the world, which is exactly how they want you to feel. The warden saw me looking up at the towering walls and said,

"Think you can scale that?" It was a joke, but I could imagine him saying it to an inmate in a much graver tone.

I'd been inside detention facilities before—Rikers Island, Bellevue—as well as state prisons in California and New Mexico. None had seemed so foreboding. Set periodically along the walls at Green Haven were gun towers, anonymous faces behind the guns whose only duty was to keep bad people scared twenty-four hours a day. A sense of menace pervaded the space, chilling me.

But as we went deeper into the prison, my feeling of dread began to change into a dreamlike, nearly fantastical state. This was more like a movie set than reality. I had to remind myself that, for everyone on the inside of these walls, reality was of a type those of us on the outside couldn't even begin to comprehend.

We passed though a gray entryway into the large main cellblock, a massive, walled enclosure. This was the administrative engine of the prison—offices for the warden and deputy, a staff room, the library—that hid the hub of the complex, a network of eight-by-twelve-foot cells laid out in long rows and stacked five high, each separated from the next by two-foot-thick stone walls to prevent inmate communication. Better the prisoners should have as much time as possible to focus individually on the consequences of evil. A man wearing a clerical collar came by and introduced himself as Father Fernando. It was obvious to me right away that his happening by was no coincidence. I sensed a callous spirit.

Will was told he had to stay behind, where he would be overseen by a few members of Warden Lee's band. The production crew was asked to stay behind, too. Warden Lee informed me that Ronnie had requested I go in alone before any cameras were on him.

The warden asked for my wallet and jewelry so they could be scanned and inspected. My wallet was opened first. Credit cards, subway card, health-insurance certificate—nothing special. "Wait," I said, remembering another item that I'd forgotten to remove before leaving the house: a skeleton lock pick that I carry on homicide cases. The warden started laughing and asked me to remove my jewelry next.

I had two rings, five gold bangles, a solid-gold Mardi Gras bead necklace from the 1920s that had been restored, a chain with antique amulets, and my mojo bag, which I'd worn around my neck for this trip. Sometimes the mojo bag hangs from one of the loops on the side of my pants, but today I'd wanted it in a more prominent place. The contents of the mojo bag are more precious and more powerful than any gem. In the bag were the charms and talismans of my native ancestors, ashes and bones from powerful medicine men—the spiritual items that, after all is said and done, protect me.

I don't allow anyone else to touch the bag. In voodoo, this is referred to as the bag being fixed to its owner—as in, you don't want someone else's energy disturbing the spiritual balance represented inside. I looked at Warden Lee and asked if I could wear my mojo bag inside. He paused, considered the bag, arched his eyebrow again, and said no. Though I felt like I was being sent into battle without a weapon, I saw there was no point in arguing.

Warden Lee escorted me through a series of heavy steel

doors and iron gates. An unseen voice over a loudspeaker would instruct me to step forward toward a door, which would then buzz open and, after I walked through, slam down behind me. I felt I was being guided through a disorienting maze, each passageway becoming narrower. The towering cinderblock walls loomed constantly in my mind. Even inside the depths of the prison, you could constantly sense the futility of trying to escape.

After passing through several of these checkpoints, I finally came to a dark room fronted by twin iron gates. To my left, a correctional officer seated at a high counter instructed me to place my left hand through the bars between him and me. I did so. The top of my hand was stamped. When I pulled it back I noticed only a number on it, fluorescent in the black light. An electronic scanner passed over my body, head to toe, back to front, then over again. The warden kept a close watch on me.

I was instructed to move straight ahead. I did, and came to a large metal door with a small slit on the side. I was instructed to put my hand through. I did. Over the loudspeaker I heard a voice say *There's no turning back for you now.* I didn't bother to ask whether anyone else had heard it. The heavy door swung open, and several correctional officers stood waiting. One of them, a woman, gestured for me to walk forward.

I found myself in a plain visiting room whose simple classroom desks might have made it feel like a school were it not for the armed guards standing in every corner and the four-inch steel bars and barbed wire covering the windows. I was guided to a desk at the far side of the room, as far away from the large metal door as possible. I looked down at a piece of old gum that had become part of the cement floor and had the thought that this place felt as much a tomb as it did a prison. How many different feet had stepped on that piece of gum? How many had been imprinted on it, the essence of how many misguided souls? I stepped over it. I didn't want to leave any part of me behind.

Walking toward the desk, I scanned my surroundings, the same exercise I conduct when called to a crime scene. Adam had taught me to assess the most important elements of any environment quickly. I detected the smell of a musty mop that had probably been sloshed along this floor days ago. That meant it was unlikely anyone had occupied the room since.

Everything began to slow down. I turned and looked at the clock on the wall. Each of its ticks sounded in my ears like a gong. This is how it happens sometimes: all the elements around me become a collective slow-motion montage, and at the same time, individual sights and sounds become amplified. It's one of the signs that the spirit is preparing to detach itself for a period. We call it becoming separated.

I looked at the young guard who stood in the corner nearest to me. Beads of sweat had formed on his forehead, and now he swallowed. I smiled and said, "Good morning, Kevin." He nodded; then, with a start, he looked down at his own name tag, which bore only his last name.

"How did you know my name?" he said.

"Your dad told me."

His face started to become blotchy and red. "My dad is dead," he whispered.

"I know," I whispered back. "By the way, don't get too worked up. You're holding a gun, remember." Kevin turned toward the window and didn't look at me again. *He's got a lot of heart*, I thought, *but he doesn't belong here. He should go back to the family farm.* I pulled out the small chair from the desk and sat down.

Warden Lee walked over to me and said, "I'll keep a close eye on DeFeo. Don't show any fear."

I looked him in the eye. "Mr. Lee," I replied, "do I look like I'm scared?"

Warden Lee walked toward the opposite wall and positioned himself behind a desk resting on a slightly raised platform, so that it sat a couple of feet above the other desks, including the one at which I sat. The warden's posse fanned out around the room. Two bookended his desk. One took a spot to my right, another to my left, and a third behind me. The warden sat, so that he was now facing me, along with the empty desk immediately in front of mine. I could see that this was a psychological move. Ronnie's back would be to the warden the entire time.

In my line of work I've seen just about everything. I'd looked the warden straight in the eye and assured him I wasn't scared. But I confess I was unnerved when, over the loudspeaker, I heard the name Ronald DeFeo called.

A slim man in an olive jumpsuit entered the room, his hands cuffed in front of his thighs. As he approached me from the doorway, I took immediate notice of his perfect skin, shiny hair, striking dark eyes, and straight white teeth. Then, as he came nearer, that image diminished and the real man was revealed: boyish features now hidden by a weathered, sickly mug and a frail figure. I stood up from my desk and asked the warden to remove Ronnie's handcuffs. Warden Lee arched that eyebrow again, saying nothing. I repeated the request. The warden nodded at one of the COs, who walked slowly over to Ronnie and, with two other guards at his side, removed the cuffs. They backed away quickly.

Ronnie DeFeo walked up to me, the only thing between us a small school desk, and smiled. It was a regular smile, neither sweet nor calculating. Then he gestured with his eyes toward the white circular clock on the wall, the one whose ticks had become gongs in my ears. It showed that the time was 7:46 A.M. As I looked up, the clock issued one thunderous tick, then stopped. Ronnie was still smiling. I couldn't tell whether I was imagining that the clock had stopped the moment he'd looked up at it, but his smile had turned to a smirk. I sat down. He sat down across from me.

Apart from the fact that I was a psychic medium and he a convicted mass murderer, there was also between us the fundamental strangeness of knowing someone well without ever having actually met him or her in person, like longtime Facebook friends meeting for the first time. We had shared secrets and talked about pivotal moments in our lives but had never stood in the same room or looked at each other's faces. Now here I was, sitting across from him, and his face reflected what I'd heard in his voice during all these conversations: the expression of a man who had seen—and done—too much, wishing to be no more than an innocent boy starting with a clean slate. He knew, of course, that he could never be that, would never be that. He hated his father and mother. He hated his lawyer. He hated his old friends. He hated his grandparents. He hated Hanz Holzer and all the other opportunists. Mostly, he hated himself.

Ronnie leaned across the desk and turned his palms up. "I'm dying, Jackie," he said. "Please help me. I want to die knowing I'm human. Let me feel what's inside of you, even if it's just for a minute."

I reached out and took his hands. The guards clutched their guns a little tighter.

"Ronnie," I said, "I'm going to let your spirit come into me and mine into you. But you need to let yourself go."

He squeezed. I closed my eyes and immediately felt a jolt, as though my body had been plugged into a battery. I surged with a foreign energy as my spirit flew away, allowing room for something else.

I felt a sensation of intense heat from my feet upward, like running across hot sand. It skimmed through me like a broken current, flaring one moment, dying the next, but eventually spreading its way across the entire circuitry. Psychic energy is like water following a sluice. It will fill the channel it can find. The strength with which it rushes in depends on both the size of the opening and the degree to which it was pinched before.

Voices came into my head, low at first and then wild, like the sound of a siren starting at a distance but quickly becoming a bone-rattling wail. I couldn't tell how many voices there were. They shouted over each other, livid, feral. My insides started to throb with the effort to contain this ferocity, but I held it. The spirit thrashed inside me, an animalistic force let loose. The voices climbed.

There were moments when the energy abated, breaks in the current, before it would course through me again. One wave would burst forth, the voices delirious, the heat intense, and then, like a wave exploding against the shore, pause briefly before the next one followed. I held on, calling upon all of my strength to give it temporary shelter.

And then Ronnie and I were standing together at the front door of 112 Ocean Avenue. From inside the house I heard growls. Before my eyes, grisly images swirled, forming an appalling mosaic. Eyes appeared as dark pools. Teeth, blackened and stained. The ground opened and we fell, plummeting down a hole with no bottom. My father's words rang in my ears, echoing the warden's: *Don't show fear, Jackie. Strength will always be in your heart.* I grabbed Ronnie's hand and held it tightly as we endlessly fell. Voices screamed, six or seven of them at once. In Green Haven, my eyes opened and fixed on the cross dangling from Ronnie's solid gold necklace. In possession, this cross plunged from the sky on a silver chain. Then, in reality, the cross rose above the chain, as though lifted by an unseen hand, and detached itself violently, tumbling downward and landing on the desk with a sound as loud as a car crash.

Ronnie was a conduit with no memory; he was merely a hapless channel. If the spirit wants more, it will continue to use the conduit like a parasite hungrily attached to its host.

I came back, him alongside me. We were still in the

strangely prosaic visiting room of a maximum-security prison, separated by the two-foot length of a school desk. I let go of his hands. Ever so slightly, the guards relaxed the grips on their guns. Ronnie looked terrified. He said to me, "I'm so sorry. Jackie, if I die right here and now, I'll die knowing I'm human. I know I'm still inside somewhere. Thank you." Later, he would tell me that he'd seen my face change. "I'm scared I'll lose this feeling," he said. "I saw hate in your eyes. My hate. What happened? Did we trade places?"

"It's a common feeling," I told him. "You feel like you're falling backward. Try not to worry. It's going to be fine. We're on a mission, Ronnie," I said. I knew now what had to be done. He begged me to help him be free of what was inside him. He'd had visions of someone who looked like me, he said. He told me I held the keys to hell. Well, I said, I suppose you're right.

I'd felt the chaos in Ronnie, and I had shared with him the peace inside me—peace, or, by another name, *amity*—so he could feel it, hold on to it while I pulled from him, and temporarily housed, the sinister essence.

His eyes welled up, and he begged me again to free him of the dark weight holding him prisoner. I had him sign the release form allowing the cameras to start rolling. But the crew wanted to film Ronnie in his cell. I began to stand up from the desk, but as I did, Ronnie said, "You know, Jackie, if I ever get out, the first thing I'm going to get is a big-screen TV."

It was no longer his voice. It was a more sinister one, coming through from a different place.

"And then I'm going to get a French red-leather couch,

plus a bear rug with all of the claws still intact. Don't you think that would be nice?"

I stood silent. He was describing my living room. I'd never sent Ronnie any pictures of my house or my things. I'd kept that part of my life completely off-limits to him. Or so I'd thought. The devil, with his shiny hair and black eyes, was grinning at me now through Ronnie, turning his face back into the one I'd seen for an instant when he'd first walked into the room.

I turned away quickly and nodded toward Warden Lee. The guards cuffed Ronnie's hands again and led him across the room toward the steel doors. As he walked toward the door and out of the room, I could hear a song coming out of him in a soft whistle: "I Remember You." The song my mother used to sing to me.

I wasn't allowed to leave until Ronnie was secured again in his cell. As I waited, the air in the room became thick, and a smell of rotting meat emerged. Bile rose in my mouth as the smell of old blood and decaying bodies saturated the space. The guards twisted up their noses, as did the warden. The stench of decay can quickly transform the toughest of people into shrinking children. I didn't know whether Ronnie had been secured in his cell or not, but Warden Lee abruptly gave authorization to release me.

I was directed through another mini maze of passageways and steel doors and placed in a holding cell with steel blue walls, which felt more like a cage than a room. I looked up at the clock, which read 11:15 A.M. One guard after another passed by, paying me no attention. I felt anxious and claustrophobic. The toxic spirit had entered me. It was seeking channels to fill. From this moment on, time would be vital.

I looked up and saw, peering through the window of a door, staring at me, Father Fernando. His hands were resting on a black pushcart, and his collar was hanging unevenly from his habit. As I caught his gaze, he looked away, fixed his collar, and cleared his throat. He was then buzzed into a different cell. Different guards passed back and forth in front of the cell and whispered to each other while sneaking glances at me.

Forty-five minutes later, the door opened, and the warden came to escort me, along with the crew, out of Green Haven. I would learn later that the camera batteries, which should have been good for ten to fourteen hours, had kept running out of juice, so they'd stopped and started multiple times. It was reminiscent of the way Adam's air tank had depleted itself so quickly on the canal.

But before leaving, the crew wanted to take some shots of me and Ronnie together. I was taken back in, and Ronnie and I were photographed in a room using a backdrop of flowers for the special. It would give things a slightly less menacing feel, the crew said. Those were the only flowers Ronnie had seen since being sent to prison. Other than the inmates, there's nothing alive in prison. Even using the term *alive* for some of them isn't quite right. Many are more like the walking dead.

Ronnie had repeated his story of the murders for the cameras just as he'd told it to me a few days before. When the special aired a few months later, some people would see a sixty-year-old man finally coming clean about his

sins after years of fabrication. Others would see a permanently stunted sociopath continuing to twist the story at
his whim. I would see what I'd seen from the beginning:
a man whose soul was still in the grips of evil.

I went back through the broader maze the way I'd come
in, the enclosures and entryways this time widening with
each individual passage until I emerged into the normal
world again, Will and his gentle strength holding me up. As
we walked outside, a swarm of bees, to which I'm allergic,
surrounded me. Will and the crew members were trying to
swat them away while hurrying me to the van for safety.
Though the day was warm, I was freezing inside. They found
sweaters and blankets to cover me with. I knew the real
Jackie was inside somewhere, but for now she was missing.
You have to pass through the darkness to reach the light.

There was one more thing we had to do for the special,
my producers told me. They had to film me going through
the house at 112 Ocean Avenue—or at least a comparable-
looking imitation, since it was unlikely we'd get permission to shoot inside—and reporting on what I felt or saw.
I agreed, though to be honest, I wasn't sure what I'd
gotten myself into.

The four-thousand-square-foot Dutch Colonial at 112
Ocean Avenue in Amityville had, like any house, experienced
its own history. The land had once been owned by the Coleman family (ancestors of the ones who'd lived next door to
the DeFeos), and in 1924, that family had sold the quarter
acre to John and Catherine Moynahan, who built the house

at 112 the following year. When John and Catherine died, their daughter Eileen had moved in with her family and lived there until October 1960, when another John—Riley— purchased the house with his wife, Mary. Ronald DeFeo Sr. had purchased it in July of 1964 from the Rileys.

After the Lutzes had moved in, and then back out, the house had changed hands numerous times. First they'd handed it back to Columbia Savings and Loan without ever making a mortgage payment. In March 1977, it was purchased from the bank by Jim and Barbara Cromarty, who changed the address to 108 to dissuade the constant hordes of tourists.

On August 17, 1987, Peter and Jeanne O'Neil purchased the house from the Cromartys. During their stay, they changed the famed eyeshaped windows to square ones and filled in the pool. Peter died on 9/11. In 1997, a man named Brian Wilson—not the Beach Boy—bought the house for just over $300,000 and renovated it. Thirteen years after that, the infamous property on Ocean Avenue was put on the market for $1.15 million and sold a few months later for just under asking.

As suspected, we didn't get permission to film inside the house, but outside would be fair game. The crew decided it would be best to shoot whatever parts we could manage on the outside property and then find a decent replica to reenact the inside elements for the A&E special.

As I approached the house, I remembered a conversation I'd had with Ronnie a few months earlier. He'd just been released from the prison's medical ward after undergoing biopsies on his lungs. He was having trouble breathing again—but that wasn't what sounded different about him. There was something brewing in his voice. I asked him what was going on.

"Nothing," he said.

I told him not to lie to me. I'd spot the lie before it even exited his mouth. He told me he was indeed cooking something up. He was on borrowed time, he told me, and it was time to put an end to it all. This time, he wasn't talking about himself. He was talking about this house.

"I can run fast even in shackles, you know," he said. I asked him what the hell he was talking about. And he told me. Ronnie DeFeo always rode the prison bus alone. He was never allowed to travel with other inmates. He would be chained to the back of the bus with a handful of armed guards watching over him. But he could do it, he said. Take them all out, get control of the bus, and then run the thing right into his former house. Evil lived in those walls, he said, and they shouldn't continue to stand. His plan wasn't to run for freedom; it was merely to end the nights of torture and fear. He was resigned to his place in hell, he said. They might as well all go together.

I had talked him out of it then, but as I walked toward the house now, I again felt the anger and sadness that had pushed through the phone that day rippling around me. And as I looked up at the windows, there was Ronnie, in his army jacket, staring down at me. In the other window was my mother, slashes across her face, waving me back. She was yelling something I couldn't hear, but I could see frost coming from her mouth, coating the window glass.

Scott, the lead cameraman, was halfway up the driveway in his jeep. Suddenly he slammed on the brakes, yanked his hands off the wheel, and shouted something none of us could understand. I ran over to him, asking what had happened.

"I hit a kid!" he yelled. "I hit a kid!"

I rushed around to the front of the jeep. There was no one there. I looked underneath. Nothing.

"What are you talking about? There's no kid there. You didn't hit anything."

Scott jumped out of the jeep and looked in the same spots I had. "But . . . I saw him. A little kid. A boy."

A moment later, one of the other crew members, who had approached the side entrance of the house, burst across the lawn, looking as pale as a ghost. He collapsed onto the curb mumbling words that didn't make sense. Within a few minutes, we calmed him and asked what was wrong. While he'd been scouting around the perimeter for camera angles, he said, a high-pitched, bloodcurdling shriek had startled him, and after that, all his senses had seemed to cave in, like he was in a black hole. He didn't know where the scream had come from, but it was as though it had suddenly sealed him off from himself. He started to feel disoriented, then dizzy, and that's when he had simply run. That's what we do when faced with energies we don't recognize or understand, isn't it? We run.

We told him everything was going to be okay. He wasn't having it. He asked to leave, stumbling as he tried to get up from the curb and make his way back to the truck.

Most of the others were refusing to enter the grounds of 112 at this point, but a few were still keen. One of them, Alicia, was telling the rest of us we were nuts, and that we needed to just do the job at hand and then get going. She stayed firm in this opinion until she stood on a spot near the doorstep, because that was the moment she felt the spirit of her uncle, who had passed years before, sweeping through her. To say she freaked would be understating the fact. I don't think a million dollars would have persuaded her out of the truck after that.

Being in the environment of a house like that is like standing at the edge of a volcano that erupted long ago but continues to smolder: the toxic stuff continues to leak. As people continued seeing and hearing things that spooked them and equipment began to break down, including cell phones dying—not losing reception, dying—we all looked at each other and said it with our eyes: screw it. We bolted.

The following week, the producers found a lookalike house in the Hamptons. It had been built according to the same model as 112. They agreed to pay the few thousand to rent it for a day, and that's where we filmed me at the Amityville house. I didn't have a problem with that. None of us wanted to cross the threshold any more than the next person did. The spirit still stirred. One of the crew voiced concerns that, if we faked this part of the documentary, it might call into question the other parts we taped. I understood his concern, but I didn't want to subject anyone to the spirit living inside that house. Plus, I had a feeling I'd be returning to it.

Days later, the post-production supervisor for the special, a hearty soul named Emyr Graciano, called me. You could put Emyr in the middle of a graveyard and he'd yawn.

He's respectful of people like me but doesn't buy any of it. While working on the tapes, he said, he'd repeatedly encountered a certain technical problem that he couldn't fix. He wouldn't tell me what it was—only that his efforts to solve it were coming up short, and he was annoyed, because usually there weren't any glitches he couldn't resolve. He'd called Jude Weng, the producer, and said, tentatively, "Maybe Jackie can help out." It was his way of acknowledging what he didn't want to acknowledge.

I called Emyr. "You're going to laugh at this or think it's crazy," I told him, "but you need to take a photo of me and put it beside whatever machine is breaking down. Then get a big black candle, not a white one, and light it. Don't blow it out. Let it burn all the way down."

He laughed, as I expected him to. But he went and did it. He texted Jude an image of my photo taped next to a machine called the unity—it's the machine that holds all the footage—and a black candle burning beside it.

I called him later that evening. He said the problem had been rectified but only temporarily. I was surprised. I asked what had happened.

"After I did what you told me to," Emyr said, "the unit was working fine again." He sounded nervous.

"So?"

"Then this assistant editor was heading out to lunch, and he blew out the candle. The fucking thing crashed again."

TWELVE

The feeling of holding a wicked spirit inside you isn't that different from having the flu. It comes down to a battle between your own internal resources and an alien entity that has found its way in. There are, in most cases, two important similarities between the flu bug and the spirit of the devil. First, both go blindly, and constantly, in search of a host. They hunt again and again for targets, infiltrating any candidate who displays the right degree of weakness. Second, both enter their hosts uninvited and unknown. With a flu, the person afflicted only realizes it once his or her symptoms appear. With the spirit of the demon, most never realize it at all.

Since early in my life, I had held spirits inside me, passed them from one side to the other, communed with the dead and the cursed. I had stood by my mother's side as her special conduit, the child who stood out not by throwing a ball the farthest or looking the prettiest in a dress but because of her ability to liaise with both sides of the spiritual world. Sometimes I had contained them for seconds, sometimes minutes. They passed through me like lava: slow, powerful rivers of fire that surged and bubbled, cramming the space available to them and settling temporarily until melting away into a different place.

Most of the time, I had opened myself by design, admitting the spirits willingly. I was doing right by someone, helping people connect to something lost or to understand something never understood. Once helped, they were gone from my life, and I was gone from theirs. And the spirits, having passed through, would retreat, vanishing again to the mysterious realm they occupied.

This time, I had invited a spirit more hostile than any to which I'd ever offered a temporary home before. I had taken from Ronnie the poison within him, welcomed it fully. Now it was in me. Some people are more susceptible than others to venomous spirits. I had spent my life oddly impervious, a way station that showed the countless marks of its visitors but that still stood strong. Now the inner wall I had built up over the years started showing cracks. I was a fortress holding something in while at the same time holding it back. If I didn't do something about it, the walls would soon crumble.

Following the visit to Green Haven, my calls with Ronnie resumed as normal. They were occupied mostly by his rambling agitatedly and my trying to interject with questions that would keep him more or less on track. His stories were like nonlinear films that jump back and forth, repeating certain scenes, providing one important bit of information here and then, much later, another bit that you eventually figure out is related to the first. It had gone this way for months, the enigma revealing itself slowly and erratically, until the true mission became clear to me. There was only one path toward closing the circle, and it involved two acts. One would have to be done by Ronnie, the other by me.

But before that, I had to put something in its proper place. It was midmorning when Ronnie called, as predictably as the sun. And for the first time, I stopped the conversation before it even had a chance to start, telling him he'd have to call back later in the day. At first he was stunned; then, following a pause, he asked me why.

"There's something I have to do," I told him.

Ronald DeFeo Sr.'s grave, part of the family plot Ronnie spoke of, sits in Saint Charles Cemetery, an unassuming burial ground just north of Amityville. Will drove me there on a warm day at the beginning of September. I'd woken up in a cold sweat the night before, the result of a memory I'd tried to forget pushing its way to the surface: my mother standing at her altar, Christ on one side, Lucifer on the other, a line drawn down the middle and covered with coins. The give-and-take. I was sweating, as I had been since leaving Green Haven, and coughing great heaving coughs.

I pulled the small velvet pouch from my pocket and stared at the headstone. Without taking my gaze from the name Ronald DeFeo Sr., I reached into the pouch and pulled out the Indian-head coin a demented father had given to his untamed son nearly four decades before.

Say less and do more, Jackie, my mother would tell me. *Communicate with your actions.*

This wasn't a peace offering, nor was it an attempt to soothe. Quite the opposite. The Indian-head coin was a symbol. Returning it to Ronald DeFeo on behalf of his ill-fated namesake was a statement, the first strike in what I hoped would be the final showdown. Ronald DeFeo couldn't be brought back to this world to be dealt with by his son, but perhaps the dark spirit that had ruled his soul could be incited. I was provoking the bully deliberately. I was trying to fling open the gate and have at it.

It roiled inside me as the headstone doubled and tripled in my vision. My head throbbed and my muscles cried, but I stood, as stalwart as I could be. Rocks were piled on top of Ronald's grave, along with those of the other DeFeos. In some religions, rocks are meant to keep the spirit at peace; in others, to hold them down.

I noticed, along the top of Ronald's headstone, someone had lined up six pennies: three heads up, three heads down, the eternal balance simply expressed. Will stood nearby, watching me closely. He would tell me later that I had not in fact been as steady as I thought. I had been swaying, he would say. He spent the entire time worrying that I was going to faint and preparing to catch me and take me home. As far as he was concerned, it would be fine to just put me in bed and keep me there until I got better. My sweet, practical Will.

As we'd approached the cemetery, something had

forced me to get out of the car while it was still moving. Will had slowed down driving along the inner roads, and the car was going at a crawl, but in motion nonetheless. The darkness inside me, concentrated already, was intensifying, making me feel like a prisoner in the seat, as though the windows and doors were being sealed. Before either Will or I were aware of the fact, I had opened the door and walked out, somehow without falling or getting injured. Will had yelled after me while driving with one hand and leaning over to close the open door with the other. I had ignored him, walking forward. Though I had never visited the DeFeo family plot, I knew I was heading directly for it.

Now I knelt at Ronald DeFeo's tombstone and removed the rocks and pennies piled atop it. Our interaction needed to be clean. The entity was black inside me, ink seeping through the ocean of my soul. I began chanting an old ritual of protection, but I could feel myself flying away and couldn't stop it. Dim images started to make their collective assault. Joanne, that day on the canal, standing on the dock and waving at me, smiling, as an icy wind traveled quickly through all of us and across the water. Ronnie in the master bedroom of 112 Ocean Avenue, buckshot flying, deafening sounds, blood. Screaming, crying. More blood, inside the rims of perfect black circles, themselves inside surfaces of otherwise undamaged skin.

I closed my eyes. I was hanging on to the tombstone, holding it off. The entity beside my mother as she lay in bed in the Surf Hotel. The house at 112. Joanne on the dock. The hotel again. The blood and the screaming. I let my arm slide off the tombstone. In the dirt beside it, I began feverishly to dig. The evil spirit would not overpower me. Not today.

The hole dug deep, I placed the coin at the bottom. But I didn't start filling the dirt back in yet. I had dug the hole extra deep because there was something else I wanted to bury along with the coin: a medicine bag with recipes of peace and protection. There are no judgments of bad or good in a battle against demons. Either everyone defeats it or everyone becomes its lawful prey. The goal wasn't to forgive Ronald DeFeo Sr. his sins; it was to keep his soul at bay.

I struggled to come back into my body. This act is seldom conscious, but, as one occasionally will have the presence to do in a horrifying dream, I was trying to will myself back. Or out. I was one spirit fighting among the dark souls of an entire family. It was the one place Ronnie feared most, not because of what it represented but because of who he knew he'd meet there.

Tremors shook my insides. Steadfastly I poured dirt into that hole. The coin was covered, but still I filled it in, filled it in faster and faster until sweat and tears mixed together and dripped from my jaw. I reached up and held on to the tombstone again with one hand, the other pushing dirt into the hole and tamping it down. My breaths came harder and faster. Tiny insects buzzed around me—gnats, or baby flies. A sprinkler clicked to life and started shooting water in circular arcs over a nearby plot.

The coin was buried. The images had begun to recede, and I could feel myself returning. In a different plot, to my east, a caretaker was planting flowers at a grave. I stood up and, with a bit of renewed strength, approached him. He looked up at me, saying nothing. I asked him if I could have some of his flowers.

"For who?" he asked.

"For my mother," I said.

He stumbled backward and dropped the flowers, a look of shock and repulsion on his face. He kept looking at me in fright while trying to scramble backward on his hands and feet.

"Take them!" he said. "Take the flowers! Leave me alone!"

He was looking past me, over my shoulder, toward Will. The man looked as though he feared for his life. When I reached out to help him, he covered his face and started to sob and pray at the same time.

"Please," he said. "Get away from me. Take your black eyes and just get away."

My eyes have always been my most distinct feature. They're light blue.

I turned away from the caretaker and staggered across the DeFeo plot toward the fuzzy shape of Will. Delirious, I collapsed into his arms.

The next thing I knew I was back in the car demanding that Will give me the phone. He had his palm on top of my hand and was urging me to just calm down and rest. I jerked my hand away and reached into his pocket, grabbing for the phone.

"Hold on," he said. "I'll get it." He handed it to me and I called home. There was no answer.

I tried Joanne's cell phone. Nothing.

I tried the business line and got only the outgoing message.

I told Will to drive faster.

It was now, suddenly, that I understood. The demon wasn't after me. He was after my daughter.

He knew, by now, that I was resilient. I had faced it at the Surf Hotel—a dark entity telling me we shall meet again. I saw my mother carted away with nothing original left inside her, and I knew then a warrior doesn't become a warrior without bloodshed. He'd watched me rise from the depths again and again, from the time I was small, building my strength.

But Joanne was the weaker of us, the more vulnerable. He had waited for the right opportunity and claimed my mother. He knew he couldn't get me. Now he wanted Joanne.

You can't run from it, Jackie, any more than you can change who you are. You have a skill and a duty. It's part of you.

Joanne, the only one not touched by evil, would be a prize indeed. If I let my soul be overtaken, the devil's path to her would be unencumbered. It was time to put the other spirits to rest and fight the true war.

Don't let anyone in that you don't have to, Jacks. Be smart and be strong.

I finally recognized why I had been placed in Ronnie DeFeo's path, or he in mine. Ours had become the same goal, but for different reasons. For him, defeating the dark evil meant owning up to the truth, cleansing his soul, and, hopefully, finding redemption. I had suspected that, for me, it meant avenging my mother. That was true. But now I realized it also meant protecting my daughter from becoming a trophy.

"Drive!" I pleaded. Will floored the gas. If a cruiser was hiding behind a billboard, we'd just have to lead it home and explain ourselves after.

When Will pulled roughly into our driveway, I jumped out of the car, racing for the house. Will caught up with me quickly and flew past, reaching the door. He was the one who found Joanne in the office, working away as diligently as always.

"Why didn't you answer the phone?" I said, panting.

"When?"

"I've been calling and calling. I tried all the lines."

"None of the phones rang," she said.

THIRTEEN

I take B12 vitamins, six a day, two, two, and two. I also take B6 once a day, first thing in the morning. I take three thousand milligrams of vitamin C, plus regular doses of vitamin E. I spread them out.

I drink vitamin drinks, too, quite a bit. I put multivitamins in my juice. I'm not steady with it all the time but mostly reliable. Recently, I also started using olive-leaf extract, which is supposed to have plenty of benefits. When I eat hummus, I add olive oil. I have, like most people, plenty of vices and bad habits, but I take care of myself, at least for the most part. I'm not big, but, then again, you probably wouldn't want to be the one to get into it with me.

Still, my strength was waning, and I knew it. No matter how strong you start out, when you allow poison into you, there can be only one of two conclusions. Either you win or the poison does.

"Jackie, it's going away," Ronnie said.

"What's going away, Ronnie?" It wasn't easy for me to talk. My throat was dry and aching.

"The hate. It's starting to go. I was full of hate before. Before I got in here, when I came here, while I been here. I hated everything and everybody. The hate side of me was getting so bad, I mean, there isn't even a word for it. It just came to a point where I had to do something. But I'm a different person now. I'm not so hotheaded and not so hateful. I was holding too much inside. I feel like it's getting out of me."

What he didn't know was that, just as the menace around his space was dwindling, the one around mine was building. The venom I was carrying inside was manifesting day and night inside our walls. My own constitution and that of my physical environment were breaking down in parallel, allowing more and more of the demon's face to show.

"Ronnie, the first few times you called me, you were really tentative. You talked a lot but didn't say much. I knew you wanted to spill, but it's like you needed to trust me before you'd let any real stuff come out," I said. "Sometimes the emotion I sensed from you meant more than the words you said. I could feel the bitterness coming through the phone."

"I was getting ready to do something. Something really bad. I'm serious. I'm not gonna talk about it, but it was gonna be a first, right here in prison. You can only drive so far before you come to the end of the road. And I was coming to the end of the road."

"Hate just grows and grows, Ronnie. If you have a leak and you don't fix it, it gets bigger and bigger. Eventually, it's going to spill over."

"I knew I wanted to talk to you, but I was buried in that hate. The only thing I felt was evil. I didn't know where to start."

"There were times when I would say to myself, *I wonder why he called—he doesn't even want to talk. He's just sitting there on the other end fuming*. But I knew you would come around. It wasn't easy, but you came around."

"I'm feeling better. I have more energy."

"I want you to do something for me, Ronnie. Stop taking medication. Anything they give you at the doctor's there, don't take it. I want you to refuse it, or pretend to take it but don't. I need you to be pure and clean. That includes drugs."

"I didn't say anything about no drugs."

"And I didn't ask. But I'm not stupid, Ronnie."

"Never mind that. How's Allison?"

"What?"

It wasn't the first time this had happened. I knew who he meant—and it worried me. He would often say Allison when he meant Joanne. It was clear by now that, just as he'd developed a soft spot for Jo, so had he held a soft spot for his youngest sister.

One morning a few weeks earlier, I'd walked into Joanne's room to find her sitting at her vanity. I had two immediate thoughts. My first thought was that Jo's room looked remarkably like the pictures of Allison's room I'd seen in the file. My second thought, when Jo turned around and smiled, was that she looked, just for a moment, jarringly like the girl herself. It chilled my blood.

Ronnie had told Joanne in a previous conversation that he had always considered Allison the innocent one. I looked at Joanne the same way: strong and smart, but pure.

Things find their way to our door all the time, from people everywhere. Often the things we receive are personal effects—objects sent by parents hoping to gain some insight or morsel of knowledge into people lost or vanished—and at other times they're simply gifts. Most of the time, the items are addressed to me. A week before, a package had come for Joanne. It was a flannel nightgown. Jo is always warm and usually wears shorts to bed. I assumed she'd put it right back in the box and, as we do with almost everything we receive, return it to sender.

Instead, I emerged from my office that evening to find Joanne twirling in front of the hallway mirror. She was wearing the nightgown. Joanne is my daughter, and I think of her as a precious doll, but twirling in front of a mirror isn't exactly her thing. She was acting like someone else.

"What are you doing?" I said.

Joanne turned to me. Her body language wasn't hers. "Do you like it?"

Will had entered from the other side of the room. He walked up very close to Joanne, looked at her directly, and said in a cautious voice, "You're going to be warm in that."

Joanne seemed to break clear of whatever abstraction

she'd been under. "I—I don't know what made me put it on," she said awkwardly. "I'm sorry. I—" She looked in the mirror and her breath caught. She ran into her bedroom shaking, and pulled off the nightgown.

A week later, another package arrived for Jo: an American Girl doll, made in her likeness—tattoos and all. We called the American Girl offices to ask who had sent it. The information was confidential, they told us. We returned the doll.

"There's one more thing I need to do, Ronnie. While I still have the strength. I need to go to the house."

"What are you talking about?"

"I need to enter that house again. I need to take the evil in."

"But you already went there."

"That's not what I mean. Not physically. Spiritually."

"What do you mean, Jackie?"

Ronnie wasn't the first person to ask me this question. As I've said, it's hard to describe. If you have the ability, you discover it early, because one moment you're as normal as can be, maybe talking to someone or exchanging a glance, and the next thing you know you're trying to deal with a surge of energy so powerful it might knock you off your feet.

In the Stephen King novel *The Green Mile*, an enormous black man named John Coffey (played by Michael Clarke Duncan in the film) has the power to take pain from others, at great cost to himself. When people ask him to explain his mysterious healing acts—like when he cures a prison guard's urinary tract infection—he says simply that he "took it back." That's about as well as I can describe it, too. My mother was still in pain, and the devil was still laughing. To get to him, and hopefully to save her, I needed to travel back to that place where the demon had played one of his most monstrous tricks.

"No, Jackie. I love you, Jackie. Don't do it. It will kill you."

"It isn't over, Ronnie. Not by a long shot. You've done your part. You told me everything. Now I have to do my part. That house is the devil's playground. I need to walk in there and turn back the clock. I need to experience it. This is my last hope for peace, and yours."

"No, Jackie!" He was yelling at me now. This was a first. "What are you doing? I felt like I was dying. I had fevers and bleeding and the fungal pneumonia, and you helped me heal. I can't let you do this. You don't understand. I'm a real bad person. I'm not supposed to have feelings. But you taught me something. I started to see and remember things. Nice things. I feel stuff I never felt before, Jackie. Yesterday, when I got off the phone with you, something strange happened. I looked down and saw my shirt move. I put my hand to my chest. It was my heart, pumping like crazy. It felt like it was going all the way up to my throat. What the fuck is this, I was saying. So I put my hands up to my eyes, and they were wet. I haven't cried since the day my family died, Jackie. I haven't cried for thirty-six years."

It wasn't just tears that had been shut off all that time.

After that terrible night, Ronnie had turned purposely numb. He dove way down into himself, to a place from which he'd hopefully never have to return.

But you can't stay in hiding forever, not even when you're hiding inside yourself.

"I said, 'Holy shit, I'm crying.' And suddenly I just bolted. I ran from the phones, didn't know where I was going, but I was so freaked out I didn't know what to do. All them COs were shocked; they're yelling, 'DeFeo, where are you going? Stop, stop!' They didn't know what the fuck was wrong with me. *I* didn't know what was wrong with me."

"You were starting to feel."

"I got to the gates, you know, those high, heavy iron gates that lead back to my cell, and I collapsed. They all knew I was messed up, Jackie. You got the most hard-core, bloodthirsty inmates starting to run over to me, yelling to get help. I swear. The guards were ready; they thought it was some kind of setup."

I didn't bother asking him how much of this story was true. He had little reason to make it up, other than maybe the combination of boredom and a captive audience. But Ronnie was in this fully now, and we were past the point where he had to fabricate stories to keep me listening. I think he knew that.

"They've got their weapons ready; they're braced for whatever might go down. And it just came out. I was balled up, my knees are at my head, and now I'm crying like a baby. I couldn't stop it. Couldn't even talk, couldn't say nothing to nobody. The guards got three other inmates to help hoist me. They had to carry back to my cell like I'm a little kid. And the tears just kept coming, just unstoppable."

"That's okay. That's good."

"There I am curled up on my cot. They just left me there and backed away, my cell door slammed shut. I couldn't stop it. My whole body was shaking. I ain't scared of nothing, Jackie—nothing alive, anyway—but this scared the piss out of me. I stayed there in my cell for two days. Didn't eat or nothing. Whatever you did, all that stuff, it just finally snuck up on me, and once it got me, it got me all the way. *Boom, bang.* But then it went bad after that. It was there again."

"What was there?"

"I was punched in the jaw, just like that, out of left field. Then a kick to the leg. Your letters start flying around my cell, and I'm still getting beat up. Then something grabs me by the throat and throws me across the floor. The guards come running down C block, calling, 'DeFeo, DeFeo!' A few of the guys are yelling, 'Help him, help him!' Now they're worried about me, they see all this shit going down. I'm up in the air a few feet. The guards back away; they're saying, 'Holy shit!' I swear this one guard was praying."

Had that happened? Maybe, maybe not. But what was clear was that Ronnie was scared. "Ronnie, look—"

"So they left me alone. Everyone was too scared to help, plain and simple. After the thing dropped me down on the floor, hard, I crumpled, I heard nothing, like a stillness, this blank, dead cold. I couldn't hear anything all of a sudden. No guards, no other inmates, voices, footsteps, nothing. Then I heard a growl, real small. And it turned into a snarl, real loud, louder and louder and louder. The snarl turns into this voice, and it says to me, like it's spitting out the words, 'Don't you want to see Mommy?' I just went frozen. They had to help me get dressed later, Jackie. The guards and two other inmates. I was a total mess; do you hear what I'm saying to you?"

"Yes, Ronnie, I do, but we can beat—"

"This thing is stepping it up. It senses me slipping away, I guess, thanks to you bringing me out, and it's pulling out the stops, okay? It's using everything it's got in its goddamn arsenal. I'm telling you, the other guys on the block are complaining now. This thing wants to get anybody who's near me, whoever they are. They're saying, 'Ronnie, you gotta do something; shit is happening to us in our cells; we're getting hit, pushed, something's holding us down in our beds, pinning us down.' One guy told me he saw a big cloud of thick black smoke in his cell. The guy grabbed his Bible and fell to his knees. And this dude is big, Jackie, about two-twenty. Fights have been breaking out on the block for no reason. These are dangerous guys in here, bad guys, but they don't fight just to prove something, like it is in the movies. Mostly the guys get along. Now there are fights all the time, sounds like goddamn rabid dogs going at each other.

"You've pissed this thing off, and now you need to stay away. You don't need to be dragged down with me. You keep trying to pull me out, but look, I made a pact with him, and now he's inside me, and I guess that's the end of it. You done enough. You made me human again. I'm at peace now, whatever happens. So save yourself and get away."

As I stood in the hallway holding the phone, I could sense its presence. The stench of rotting meat was seeping into my nostrils. The air had gone icy. Screaming voices, distant at first, started climbing on top of one another again until they were shrieks pressed up against my ears.

Somehow, I could hear Ronnie's voice over the shrieks. "Tell me you won't do nothing, Jackie. Please."

The phone went dead. There was only a loud, sustained beep. My eyes darted around. I felt it all around me, infuriating in its patience, just lying in wait. My bedroom door seemed to zoom toward me and then stop, until I stood only inches from it. Under the screaming there were moans and the sounds of voices praying in Latin. My bedroom door swung open, admitting a stench that was even worse. I slapped my hand over my nose.

Under my covers there was a lump, like the outline of a large child or small adult. The back of its head was facing me, and its hair was sticky and matted to the pillow. I couldn't move.

"Jackie," a voice said from the bed. "Come to me." The outline raised itself from the waist and threw the covers off, cackling. It was my mother, her flesh torn, her scalp bloodied, her face covered in bile.

I seldom pray, but I prayed now. *Please don't let her come near me. Please.*

I was nailed to where I stood.

"You thought I forgot you," she said. "Look what you

did. Why did you leave me? Why? You will come home. Oh, you will come home."

I collapsed to the floor.

When I opened my eyes, she was gone. My bed was untouched, the covers still pulled tightly under the edges of the mattress from that morning. It had got inside me, and it was taking over.

The phone rang again. Ronnie, calling back. I told him I didn't know why the phone had gone dead. He didn't pause. "I'm scared for you, Jackie. I'm not going to make it back to the other side, and I understand that now. I'm on the wrong side. I'm a monster, and I'm meant to die as a monster. Don't you see? I made the pact, and it's been sealed. There's no saving me. It's all over. If you do this, you won't get back to your own body. You'll die or become one of us, one of the people who are damned."

"You can be saved, Ronnie. So can my mother, and so can Joanne."

"It ain't worth it for you, Jackie. I'm a done deal. It's finished for me. But you don't have to feel bad. Look at everything you've given me. The first thing I ever asked you was to help me feel human, and you did that."

"We aren't done, Ronnie. Because you're stronger than you think you are, and you didn't sign any damn contract with Lucifer. That was only in your mind. The only weapon you have is you. It isn't holy water or empty words from fake priests. You can do things. You can be strong against this."

"It ain't worth it, Jackie. I'm scared all the time. But at least I can feel things, thanks to you."

"Ronnie, your whole family is wiped out. What do you have to lose? You're even too scared to live on the outside. You told me that. You're in prison, living with a demon inside you. You're the walking dead."

"Maybe so, but I'm still around. That's good enough for me. I don't need more than that. There's no reason for you to go where I'm going."

"Ronnie, it isn't decided where you're going yet. Your life isn't over. We all have until the very end to determine our fate. Don't give up. I know what you're feeling. When you look at yourself, you see the grown man who can reflect on the things he's done, but you also see the stupid kid who gave in to bad impulses. But there's such a thing as redemption. That kid is gone. You're a different person now."

"But I still see that kid. All the time."

"Of course you do."

"When I look in the mirror, I see a double image. I see me now, and I see me then."

"I know. And you're scared that it's the same person. But you have to believe that the person you are now is different from the person you were then."

"Before all this shit happened with my family."

"That's right, Ronnie. Before all this shit happened with your family."

"Let's talk about that house, Ronnie. Forget the Lutzes for a second. There is a presence and a spirit in that house, and it's evil. But it isn't pigs with red eyes and marching bands and all that foolishness the Lutzes wanted people to believe. The people who debunked it said it themselves—the Lutzes were trying to throw the whole kitchen sink in there. That book had every ghost and goblin you could possibly dream up. It was just silly. But they weren't wrong that there's something inside those walls. And the only way to get rid of it is for me to go there and be one with it."

"I should have burned that place down when I thought of it that day. Listen, Jackie, it's too late for me. Whatever it is that got in me got in me, and I guess it's there for good. And now it's getting to you; I know it is. So back away and leave me be. Have a regular life."

"Ronnie, if I don't do this, it will happen again. But this time it will be my house. You once told me I held the keys to hell. Maybe you're right."

"Jackie, Christ, I'm asking you this. Walk away, okay? Just walk away from me. No—run. Run as fast as you can. Leave your house. Everything. Just go, okay?"

"I can't. You're not the only one locked up. I'm in prison, too. He owes me something, and I'm planning to collect."

"Save yourself, Jackie."

"I will, Ronnie. I will. The only way I know how. By going back. And you're coming with me."

FOURTEEN

I was eight when I first learned I had the ability to travel. I'm not talking about acting as a channel for psychic energy, the spirits of those who have passed. I'm talking about actually going to another place.

It's called astral travel, and it's a technique used not only in occult practices but also in FBI training, the aim being to expand agents' minds and perspectives as they try to tease apart cases that seem like black holes. The purpose of astral travel is to go to a different time or place. Those of us who do it well can achieve full transformation. We can feel the seasons change, alterations in body temperature. I've trained countless policemen and detectives in the technique. It's grueling. The more open-minded ones are disposed to do well at it; the others never get there.

It's also a dangerous technique, for the same reason regular physical travel has its risks: you never know what you might bring back with you.

I'd been playing outside, down by the train tracks, when a dark feeling swept into my head. Something told me to rush back home. When I got through the door, I heard my mother say that my brother, Billy, wasn't feeling well. I went to his room and sat by his bed, worried. Billy was a strong, strapping kid, built like my dad. He was seventeen then, handsome in that I-don't-give-a-shit way teenage boys have. But he looked terrible. His face was pallid and his eyes were squeezed shut in pain. He kept balling up, bringing his knees toward his stomach, and crying out. My father had taught me to power through discomfort like this, and I in turn had learned to hate weakness. I hated seeing Billy giving in to this, whatever it was.

My mom and dad walked in the bedroom and looked Billy over, neither one saying a word. Finally my dad turned to my mom and said, "Go to bed." Then he picked Billy up like a rag doll and walked out. I ran over to the window to see my dad laying Billy down in the backseat of the car and placing a blanket over his body. This was a kid who played in the swamp, walked the railroad tracks with me. Now I got the terrifying feeling he might never come home. My mom didn't listen to my dad—she got in the car with him, and off they went.

Hours passed, and I didn't move from that window. I didn't care if my mother took the switch to me—a strip of bark taken from a tree and used like a belt, and one of her favorite forms of punishment. I was waiting for my brother.

The car pulled up hours later, the house now in darkness. I ran down, calling for my brother. My mom walked into the house, put her purse down, and said, "Your brother is in the hospital." I stood still, trusting nothing and nobody. The house seemed empty, matching my feeling inside. Even when my sensations were negative or frightening, I was usually sure of them. But this was a feeling I hadn't encountered, and it chilled me deep down in my bones.

My dad walked in the door and saw the look in my eyes. He crouched down to me. "You best get on now," he said, which meant I'd better do something to occupy myself because otherwise I was going to kill myself with worry, and there was nothing he could say that was going to make me feel any better.

"He's strong," I heard my mom say. That put me over. I ran to my bed, flopped onto it face-first, and started to cry. I put Billy's smile in my head. His voice. The image of us talking together, sitting, reading, taking walks down by the swamp.

And then my journey began, as though my body was being stretched in directions from the inside. My muscles were flexing, tensing, like they were bracing for flight. It was similar to the sensation of being in a plane as the engine starts to whine and the big machine starts to thunder down the runway. You feel yourself quickly giving up control of your own physical form and space, though still you have a fleeting connection to the earth. The plane accelerates, speeding along, as different forces act on your body at once. You're racing, rumbling, and then, suddenly, the feeling of lightness and air. You're traveling again, but now into a realm that feels nothing like the one you left only seconds ago. You're in flight.

This is how it felt. My body was traveling. I felt outside of myself yet aware of every sound and movement. And then I opened my eyes and I was next to Billy, lying in a hospital bed. There were tubes in his nose and an IV drip in his arm. Machines beside his bed beeped quietly. His eyes were trying to open but couldn't. At the house, Billy had looked yellow; now he looked gray.

Suddenly his hand reached out and grasped mine, and his eyes opened briefly. "I'm okay," he said. "Go back. You can't stay."

As I walked toward the door, I noticed the bed beside Billy's. It had been folded up, and an IV pole stood next to it with a half-empty bag swinging from it. I went to the elevators. The doors opened, and a red-haired kid with hair parted to the side was looking at me. He had dark circles around his eyes and white tape on his arm. He was terribly thin. And, I realized, I could see through him. "Tell my mother I love her," he said. It was the kid who had been in the bed beside Billy's. I ran out, my feet never touching the ground.

I was back in my room, in my bed. I jumped up from it and ran downstairs, calling my parents. "I saw him," I said. "I saw him. Billy. In the hospital." I started to cry.

They looked at each other. "Jackie," my mom said. "You must never leave your own body. You're too young to control what you might face."

My dad took a cold cloth to my face and said, "Calm down. Billy just had to get his appendix removed. That's all. He'll be home in a few days. There's nothing to worry about."

I lay in bed that night trying to fall asleep when the cold sweats started to attack me. Waves of nausea started to make their way through my stomach, and then I vomited something unrecognizable. As I lay moaning in bed, I registered the huge shadow of my father in my doorway. Part of me sensed him rushing to my bedside. Another part heard him yell to my mother, "Hurry, get the car! She's burning up!"

At the hospital, my father ran to the desk with me in his arms, bundled in a blanket. I was still throwing up. "You have to help me," he said. "My daughter is very ill. I also have a son in here."

I was rushed into a room and placed on a cold table. It felt as though someone was twisting a knot of pain in my side over and over. Doctors were poking at me with instruments.

"It's my brother's pain. I took it," I told them. They ignored me. "The girl's delirious," one said. "Give her something for the fever and take her home. She'll be all right." They took me home. My mom told me in no uncertain terms to stop what I was doing, it wasn't helping anyone. She, more than anyone, should have known I had no choice.

I took the pills, but the fever got worse instead of better. I couldn't hold food or water. The shakes worsened, too. By the following day, I couldn't move or speak.

My dad came to my side and took me in his arms. "Put her back in bed," my mom said.

"Like hell," my father answered, running past her to the car. He arrived at the hospital and said, "You get me a doctor. Now."

Now I really was delirious, and I couldn't make out much of what anyone was saying, though I processed the words "dying" and "*now*." I was wheeled fast down a corridor and into a room with bright lights.

People were moving around me with antlike efficiency. I was hooked up to this machine and that. I was slipping in and out. They called my parents into the room—my mom, complaining, had gotten in the car after all—and said, "We have to move fast, we don't think she's going to make it." My appendix had ruptured overnight, and the poison had attacked my small body. They would have to filter out the contaminated blood. Lots of it. One doctor told my mom she might want to make arrangements. "You just do your job," my mother said. But I died on the operating table anyway.

Ronnie had regarded his improvement the way a person who has started to get better after the worst of a bad cold sees it: prematurely. He'd hit bottom and then started to see the light, but seeing the light doesn't mean you've reached it.

"He's back," Ronnie said on the phone. There was a shudder in his voice. "I thought you'd beaten him, but he didn't go nowhere."

"He isn't back, Ronnie," I said. "He never left. Not yet. I told you that. Listen, I know you're feeling better, but that's only the first step. You need to understand this. You're on your way up, but I'm on my way down. We need to go to that house together. You have to trust me."

The truth was I didn't know if I had the strength for it. I'd taken in and passed on ruined souls before. I'd done it my whole life. But never an entire family. Never anything like the DeFeos.

"Okay," he said. "Just tell me what to do. It's getting bad again. I can't live like this anymore, and it won't let me die, so what choices do I have left? I should have been dead already. The doctors don't know how I'm still kicking. I must have lost fifty pounds since the beginning of all this shit. I'm afraid to go to sleep again. He don't like what you're doing."

"Ronnie, you told me you were happy that you could feel again. But feeling again means it hurts more."

"I need your help."

"It's going to take some work," I said. "I have to show you how to do it. But first you have to come clean with me. Is there anything you're hiding?"

"What do you mean?"

"If there's anything hidden between us, if we can't put up a united front, we've lost before we start."

It was a small feeling, but it was there. Since Ronnie had started revealing his story, I'd felt there was a break. I didn't know what it was, but it had come up again and again whenever he talked about Brother Isaac and the heart. "Ronnie? You there?"

"I don't know if she was sleeping with the priest."

"Then why did your father think she was?"

"Aw, shit. Look, I'm sorry any of this happened, okay? I wish it didn't, but it did."

"Ronnie, we can't finish this unless you tell me the truth."

"They'd brought one priest down from Saint Joseph's Oratory in Montreal. From Canada, for Christ's sake. My father had gone there on vacation, in 1970, and fell in love with the story of the guy who started it, Brother Andre or something. So he was big into that priest. The guy came and stayed in my house for a week at a time. He'd do mass on the steps on the first floor because they were so big. And he'd give out communion. I mean, I had to leave. They didn't want me there anyway."

"Why were priests invited to say mass on the porch? What was he trying to get rid of?"

"That's what I'm trying to tell you. My parents were deep into the Catholicism, okay? That means they were scared bad stuff was gonna happen all the time, and they believed in it. My father kept saying he had the devil on his back. He'd say it while looking at me. Like I was the devil. I think it was all part of his plan to knock me off."

"Was the priest from Saint Joseph's the only one?"

"The only one who was made a part of the family like that by my father. He's looking at his own son and talking about the devil and then inviting this guy in for dinner. I mean, come on. Then, when that guy apparently couldn't chase out the devil, they went and got Brother Isaac, the guy who was my gym teacher. A Jesuit. One day I overheard them talking about doing an exorcism. One guess who they were going to do it on."

"He was an exorcist?"

"Oh, it was all set. He was a real powerful priest, apparently. I used to sit in the crawl space and listen to all this nonsense. He'd done exorcisms requested by the archdiocese in Rome, if you can believe it. My mother and father both knew something evil was in that house, and I guess they decided it was me. Holding mass with the priest from Montreal didn't do it, so I guess the next choice was an exorcism. I mean, come on. So I made a comment."

"A comment?"

"My mother had dated Brother Isaac when they were teenagers. I'd heard them talk about it before, so I knew. My dad had gone to school with the guy, and my mom had gone out with him. I knew about my dad's temper, and I figured he still would be jealous of the guy. So I said it casually to him one day, something like, 'He's just another dick she's jumping on.' I couldn't remember doing that until you and I started talking. I swear."

I thought, in fact, that Ronnie was taking too much of the credit. I didn't believe someone as young and strung out as he was would have been clever enough to think up so cruel a trick and pull it off so neatly. But the dark spirit inside him would certainly have possessed that sort of cunning. A man of the cloth had entered the house, a man perhaps with the kind of strength to threaten the demon. Shifting Ronald DeFeo Sr.'s destructive focus to Brother Isaac would have been a trick of the devil indeed.

"They'd set up a room for the thing, and I heard them

talking. The idea was for my mother to get me to her room."

The demon had slipped through during a moment when Ronnie no longer had control. It had murmured the comment through Ronnie's lips, planting the seed for further pain and chaos. And how it must have enjoyed Ronnie's father going in for the kill, destroying the only man that at the time might have been strong enough to help. With Brother Isaac gone, it now had full domain over Ronnie DeFeo. The human sacrifice of a holy man, the one summoned to deliver Ronnie from evil, would only have given it strength. Seeing the heart ripped from the chest of the only man that might have saved a cursed family. The devil no longer owned a piece of Ronnie. He owned all of him.

"Anyway, I was taken to sick hall this morning. I had two black eyes and I was bleeding from the mouth. I lost a tooth. They took pictures of my hands."

"Why?"

"To show that they didn't have no marks on them. To show that I didn't do that shit to myself."

At a remove from my own consciousness, men in white coats and masks over their mouths prodded my body with cold metal instruments. Blood was everywhere. But where I was I saw only a bright tunnel and, feeling no fear, walked into it. My feet took steps along the ground, but I felt weightless. Toward the middle of the tunnel, a gentle fog settled, limiting my vision to whatever was directly in front of my eyes. A dog I didn't know scampered toward me and began turning in happy circles, his barks echoing off the tunnel walls. He licked my face and wagged his tail. A large figure approached me out of the fog, and I realized it was my grandfather. He was beating on the skin of a drum, louder and louder.

I ran over to him, the dog scurrying along beside me, and hugged his thick legs. He took a worn medicine bag from around his neck and placed it over my head. It smelled warm and familiar.

People began filling the tunnel behind my grandfather, and the mist soon melted away. It became so crowded I could no longer see the end of the tunnel, as though this crowd was blocking the way out. A very tall man dressed in black appeared at the side of the tunnel and began walking toward me. My grandfather bent down, grabbed me by the arms, and said, "You must fight this man. You must go back and follow your spirit. Never forget who you are." Then he stood up and turned around, and he and the happy dog walked back through the crowd of strangers, vanishing along with the rest of them. Before he vanished for good, I heard him say to me, "You shall win."

Though I wanted to run from the tall man, I couldn't. With a grin, he took my hand. His eyes were like twin flashlight beams. I looked down and saw his long dark fingernails. As he led me back out of the tunnel the way I'd come in, he said, "Jackie, you'll grow to realize that things are already set. If I let you go now, it will change everything else." He held up my hand and said, "Cheer up. I thought you would like a good fight. I will watch you as you watch me, and when certain deeds are done, we'll meet again." He laughed and pushed me out.

"I'm going to teach you how to leave your body, Ronnie."

"My pleasure. How?"

"It's like anything else. Training and practice. Do you trust me?"

"Just tell me what I have to do."

"We're going to visit your house. Together."

"I hope you know what you're doing."

"I hope so, too. Now listen."

I knew it would have to be a crash course. My energy was waning by the day, and the house, despite the heat being off, kept getting warmer. We'd had the thermostat checked and the boilers inspected. There was nothing wrong.

Ronnie and I began to practice on small things. I would hide a minor object in my house and then have him try to achieve a trance state to depart his body and go find it. At first, I would meet him halfway and act as his guide. Without words, I would put images in his head, giving silent direction. Learning how to travel is possible for anyone with enough intelligence and willingness to believe, but having the strength not to turn tail is a much harder achievement.

Initially, Ronnie couldn't escape his own spiritual confines. His concentration would break, or his spirit would weaken at a crucial moment, and back he would go. Those well trained in the ability to transition can achieve it just by sitting still and staring at a light. The most skilled practitioners can shift back and forth between one world and the other, touching two separate realms simultaneously. You become a visitor in one place while keeping a foot in the first.

We used objects that had been in direct contact with him. During the months we'd been speaking, he'd sent me numerous items, a whole grab bag of Ronnie DeFeo ephemera. His watch, stopped at 1:15. A lock of his hair. Nail clippings. A ring. Hospital bands. A piece of bathroom tissue he'd wiped his tears with. A tooth. Pictures of the two of us during our meeting at Green Haven. I looked at the pictures and thought, *What a pair*.

I'd hold the watch in my hand or place it somewhere else in my house and then have Ronnie try to locate it by focusing. At first he made guesses that were more or less random, and he didn't come close. But slowly, as I taught him how to block out other energies and let his natural resistance fly away, he improved. Eventually, he developed the skill of flying. He would leave his body, travel to my house, and locate the watch. It didn't matter where I placed it—on my wrist, at my bedside, even in the private space in my walk-in closet that Will had built for me, where a large painting of my grandfather hangs. He had found the ability.

"You're starting to get it," I told him. "You're starting to stretch. Soon it will be time for me to try to pull you through into my world."

"What the hell?" he said. "I thought we were looking for watches in your house."

"Don't worry. I've done this before. Stay on track with me."

"If you pull me through into your world, what about what's inside of me? Did you think of that? I don't want to pollute your atmosphere over there."

He didn't understand that his spirit was already tied up with mine, and that this was in fact the only way the two could ever be extricated. "Ronnie, shut up. I need to go to the scene as it happened and become monster and victim. Do you understand? I need to inhabit both sides. It's the only way."

"I got one question."

"What is it?"

"How do you know that you won't bring the bad stuff from that house back with you?"

"I don't."

"She made it!" I heard someone yell.

I woke up with tubes attached to me at one end, machines at the other. All around me, doctors were smiling down and saying, "You made it. You made it." One of them instructed the others to get me into ICU, stat.

During the time I had to stay in the hospital and recover, I heard them explain it again and again to my parents: a large part of my body had been poisoned by the rupture, and my body had gone into shock, giving me, they felt, approximately a 2 percent chance to live. I'd required a large on-the-spot blood transfusion—they'd had to filter out all the bad blood and replace it with good. I'd flatlined for more than three minutes.

The multiple scars across my stomach still remind me of that hospital room where I spent so many weeks of my ninth year. The procedure wasn't well known at the time, but it was the only chance they had. Maybe my parents had come to anticipate this kind of thing when I was born with the umbilical cord wrapped around my neck and a caul covering my face.

A few days later, I was allowed visitors. Doctors flowed in and out of the room constantly, as though showing off their most prized specimen. They studied me and con-gratulated each other, constantly repeating, "She made it."

I sensed something at my side and reached for it. "Oh, yes," the doctor said to my parents as he saw me reach over. "There's something here. Something I don't remem-ber her coming in with." He took from my bedside the tattered medicine bag that my grandfather had given me in the tunnel, then handed it to my father, who slowly slipped it down around my neck, smiling, saying nothing.

A professional sprinter has to be careful not to overtrain because he might pull a ligament or tear a muscle. A singer must use her voice enough to make it strong but not so much that she'll lose it. A person trying to master his psychic energy has to be careful not to bring unwelcome things back from the places he visits.

We'd been at it several days, and Ronnie was getting better. But the closer he got to being able to return to 112 Ocean Avenue, the more I had to look out for danger signs. I knew what was there waiting for both of us, and the goal was to reach ever closer without inadvertently walking through the door until he was ready. Then we'd go barreling through, hand in hand.

To begin the next stage of his training, I gave Ronnie instructions. I told him that after we got off the phone, I wanted him to take his place on his cot in prison cell block C with a picture of me in one hand and a small piece of mirror in the other. Through my loud coughs, I told him he should then lie very still, stare into the piece of mirror, and stretch his feet stiffly up and down. Then I told him he should begin replaying in his mind, slowly, as much as it might pain him to do so, the night of November 13, 1974. I asked him to focus hard until he could smell and feel the air. I told him to place himself in his car, listening to the radio.

After we'd hung up the phone, I went to my room and waited. At first, I felt his restraint. He couldn't get past the bars of his cell. Then I felt it—he was out, stretching beyond. I could feel his spirit escaping. I pulled my energy back and let him fly.

The next morning, midmorning on cue, he told me everything.

He had made it into another time. He was driving down Merrick Road in Amityville and checking himself out in the rearview mirror. The song coming from the car radio was Eddie Kendricks' "Keep On Truckin'." But then the song had morphed from his car radio into Dawn's radio at home, and now he was back in the driveway of 112 Ocean Avenue, and the piece of glass he'd held in his hands in his prison cell had now become the mirror in the bedroom of Ronald and Louise DeFeo.

It had been like walking through a movie set, Ronnie said. Like the whole thing has been built to detail for the benefit of the viewer or visitor. He touched the sleeve of his jean jacket, felt its rough denim. Then, in flashes, it all started happening around him. I had instructed him that the fear might surge, but that he had to resist it. He got frightened, Ronnie told me, but he'd held my picture close and told himself he could do it. He put his hand on the car door to open it, then looked at the boathouse, where the heart was buried, and stayed inside. Strength comes in steps.

"I looked at that sign," he said. "*High Hopes*. Then I looked up at those two windows, the eyes to hell. I saw you standing in one of them and me in the other, in my prison greens. My whole family was standing behind me."

"Did that give you comfort?"

"No. It scared the shit out of me."

He had to find the strength to walk right up to the threshold. Until then, my own family, and my whole existence, was on a tightrope.

"My hand stayed on the knob. Then a hand come down on my left shoulder like a ton of bricks. I looked down and saw the long nails—the way mine are now. Oh Christ, Lucifer. I looked up and he's got the black hair and real bright eyes. It hurt to look into them. I couldn't open my mouth. He said, 'Welcome, we've been waiting for you.' I jumped back. I know I shouldn't have, but I did."

"That's okay. You're almost prepared." He had started calling out desperately. *Bring me back, Jackie! Please, bring me back!* I'd reached my spirit out to his and he'd clung to it like a child. We traveled back together, racing in rewind, until he was back in his cell, safe again in maximum-security prison.

"I opened my eyes and saw the ceiling of my cell. Then I looked over at the clock and saw it was 3:15. For a while I couldn't move. But I think I'm ready."

"You aren't ready yet. But you need to keep going back to show him that you aren't afraid. That no matter what he does, you'll keep coming back."

We repeated the same exercise the next night, and he went a little farther. This time the perception of a movie set began to take on dimension and sensation, as it will when one begins to release himself fully, and Ronnie began to inhabit not only the setting but himself. He became the twenty-three-year-old Butch DeFeo again. As he had the first time, he saw himself in one of the house's upper windows and me in the other. This was a trick. It had worked the first time, so why not again?

"I was scared that you were stuck in my world, Jackie."

"I've been stuck in lots of places. And I always got out. You can't worry about that. The more you focus on that, the more distracted you are, and the easier it is for him to win. Stop worrying about me."

"I'll tell you the truth, I wanted to go into that house,

I wanted to confront it, but I didn't want you to have to come with me. And I didn't want to see them kids dead. Man, I can still smell the blood in my nose. I haven't thought about that in years."

"I'm sorry it's so hard."

"Yeah," he said. "It's hard. Listen, I gotta go. They're taking me to sick hall again. My fever's 104. But don't worry. I'll be okay."

Though I wanted to continue his training, this was a relief. I was slumped in my chair with a blanket over me, my temperature nearly matching Ronnie's. Joanne, Will, and Uncle Ray—who had decided, after everything, to stay—had sat me down the week before and insisted on sharing the poison spirit. I'd asked them what the hell they were talking about. "You know what we're talking about," Ray had said. "Whatever it is you have to do, do it. You can't do this yourself. It's going to get you first."

I looked in the mirror, though I didn't need to do so to know they were right. And I could see in each of their faces that they weren't going to take no for an answer. So I'd complied. We sat together, and I linked our spirits. I let it run between us until just enough had streamed out of me to allow me enough strength to do what I had to do. That evening, Ray came down with the shakes. The following night, Joanne kept bolting up out of bed and screaming, like she'd been pinched or poked, and through the disorientation of my fever I kept seeing a stretched-out black tarp above her, resembling a body bag. After that, Will's throat got so raw and his cough so bad that he winced trying to drink a glass of water. And they all did it with a proud smile.

I took the two large old mirrors out of storage. I'd used them with my mother during séances, and now seemed as good a time as any to break them in again. They hadn't been touched since Mary Palermo was alive, though when I touched them, I felt her watching me.

"What are you doing?" Will asked.

"It's time," I said.

"Is he ready?"

"Maybe."

Will and Joanne didn't question. They helped me prepare. We placed the mirrors on either side of my bed, along with some of Mary's personal effects. We drew a chalk circle with ritual symbols and voodoo signs of the gods, then filled it with offerings—liquor, cigars, perfume, fruit. Six large candles, three white, three black, were lit at the center, symbolic of the meeting of good and evil, the eternal struggle. I took out my grandfather's war bonnet—a feathered headpiece—plus my protection bag, and my grandfather's mojo bag. I also took from the storage shed a pair of old rosary beads that had been given to me in Rome by a monk I didn't know. He had placed them in my palm and said simply, "Someday you will need these."

I added as many of Ronnie's items as I could to the circle: his photos, the lock of hair, the tooth, his prison ID, hospital bands, his watch, and several pieces of clothing, including the belt he'd been wearing the day they'd brought him in thirty-seven years before. I needed everything I could to bring him through. Now that the devil knew the battle was on, there would be resistance and deception. Ronnie was the bait. I was the reinforcement.

Joanne and Will covered the windows and took everything out of the room that might be used as a weapon. I told them I felt scared. Laying your own emotions bare is part of the process. Being scared doesn't mean you don't do it. It just means you admit you're scared.

I closed my eyes and called to the spirit of my grandfather. Then we began. Joanne and Will took notes. The next morning, when I came back, they told me everything.

I had instructed them not to touch me or attempt to speak to me unless I was stuck in between. One can't always tell, but the signs will be clear eventually. The person will seem gone, and then he or she will seem to return, but neither journey will achieve completion.

They had observed and made notes during my previous travels with Ronnie. The bedroom door, they told me, had opened and slammed closed several times, and they had watched my body rise inches off the bed. I understand well that to the logical mind this may not seem acceptable. My mind is logical, too. It is possible to live in both the logical world and the spiritual. The two are not mutually exclusive.

My eyes had rolled back in my head, showing whites, and my feet had contorted. Water began to drip from the ceiling, and smoke began to billow in the room. I had told them that if they felt threatened, or if they needed to leave the room, they should. I had told them, but then again, I also knew both of them better than that. As Joanne was writing, lashes from an unseen hand came down and struck her across the wrists, staining the paper of her notebook with blood.

I had flipped over, so that I was facedown toward the bed, my shirt hanging down. Will told Joanne he didn't know if he could take it. Joanne told him he had to stay strong and follow directions. The electricity in the house died, and Will ran to get flashlights and more candles.

When I returned, they said, I'd hit the bed with a thud and started coughing immediately. The room filled with the smell of gardenias. But there was little time to enjoy that. They took me immediately to the doctor's, where I was given IV vitamin therapy to treat the dehydration and antibiotics to treat the cough.

Ronnie arrived at the doorstep moments after I did. He had accomplished the feat, left his cell, traveled. We stood together at this threshold and steeled ourselves. I took his hand.

I was about to ask him if he was ready to enter, but I didn't have time. The door flew open, letting out a stench of decay and coldness. I could feel Ronnie's hand trembling in mine.

"There's no going back," I told him. "Right?" He nodded but didn't say anything. "Be strong. You can do it."

I pulled him through the entrance and I immediately felt the souls of the DeFeo family all around me, looking for a portal. I tried to open my spirit as fully as possible to the venom, make myself the most inviting target I could. Ronnie didn't see them yet.

But as we made our way farther into the house, he began to see. We stepped into 1974, and there they all were, asleep in their beds. Louise and Ronald. Marc and John. Allison. His parents and his siblings, once more occupants of the house, figures from purgatory temporarily returned. Only Dawn and Butch were awake. Music was coming from Dawn's room, soft at first. Ronnie started shivering. I held his hand tighter. Kept myself open.

I took him up the flight of stairs, and there was the twenty-three-year-old Butch, in his room, loading the shotgun. Ronnie moved for him, wanting to pull the gun out of his hands. I yanked him back.

"No," I said. "You can't. That isn't what we're doing."

Fear coursed through me, but I couldn't show Ronnie. He couldn't be strong if he didn't believe I was strong.

I felt the spirit of the warrior suddenly rise up in me. The music grew louder. This was it. I ran to the basement and started opening doors and windows, outlets for tormented souls. I ran back upstairs and told Ronnie to execute the task I'd given him, quickly: repeat the pact he'd made all those years ago. Repeat it out loud, and bring him forth. Ronnie was still shaken. I felt their spirits start to flow into me one by one. As their dark souls rushed into me, I sank to one knee.

"Jackie!" Ronnie said.

"Ronnie, do it! Now!"

They were up, out of their beds, their cursed spirits entangled with mine. The spirits thrashed and spun. I tried to hold them there, but my strength would soon fail.

"You came to me at night, in my cell, and promised me the world!" Ronnie said. "All I got out of it was sickness and misery! I don't belong to you anymore!"

The front door slammed shut, and I heard the windows and doors I'd opened in the basement do the same, one after another. Ronnie and I both felt his presence at the same time, behind us.

We both turned, and there he was, wearing a black suit.

"You've lost a soul today," I said, falling to both knees, but still holding Ronnie's hand tightly.

"I don't belong to you anymore," Ronnie said in a trembling voice.

"You're devoted to me," he said to Ronnie.

I squeezed Ronnie's hand again.

"No," he said.

Lucifer lunged at Ronnie, knocking him to the ground and separating his hands from mine, then pounced on him like a wolverine. With fear and fire in his eyes, Ronnie shouted, "You can have my body, but not my soul! I'll never be yours!" The devil battered him, incensed.

As I collapsed backward, I realized that the fires in Ronnie's eyes were reflections of actual flames. The surge of heat first came from behind us. Then it was everywhere. The curtains caught with a sound like a deafening rip, then the fire started to climb. Heat pressed against my face, searing my eyelashes. I tried to remain strong, but I was waning. Disappearing.

Wood started peeling and splintering, and large pieces began to fall from the house. Then the whole structure began to crumble, beam by beam. The devil was still on top of Ronnie, growling and spitting, and still Ronnie was yelling that his soul was his own to keep.

Then I saw them, running, running past us and out of the house. Louise first, followed closely by Ronald DeFeo Sr. Behind them, Marc, John, and Allison. At first, I didn't see Dawn. Then she was behind them, in her nightgown, running, too. Running past the devil, out the door of 112 Ocean Avenue, forever.

They were gone. Flames hissed up the walls and across the ceiling, hungrily licking at whatever else might provide fuel. In moments, we would be engulfed. I reached my hand out to Ronnie. "Take it!" I yelled. "Take it!"

As he struggled blindly with the devil, Ronnie DeFeo stuck his hand out. I grabbed it and pulled with all my might.

We were standing on the beach of Coney Island, our hands joined. The littered boardwalk and boarded-up arcade stood sadly, the former neon sign that once flashed *Surf Hotel* long dead. Other than Ronnie and me, the beach was empty, except for a solitary figure approaching us across the hot sand. As he came nearer, I could see that the tall man in the black suit was looking at the old sign and laughing.

"Don't," I said to Ronnie. I could see him being pulled, still tempted, still vulnerable.

Lucifer walked up to us and looked me in the eye. I watched Ronnie closely.

"You may have freed these souls," he said in an elegant voice, "but you can't change the fact that my little warrior here took care of the deeds."

"It's a trick, Ronnie," I said, never averting my eyes from the devil's gaze. "Your family is free. Don't fall for it."

"No one breaks a pact with me!" Lucifer wailed. "Who do you think you are?"

I saw, out of the corner of my eye, a large wave curling toward the shore, climbing higher. I squeezed Ronnie's hand as hard as I could. "Wake up now, Ronnie. Wake up. Go back to Green Haven."

He couldn't hear me. He was still fixed by the demon's fiery eyes and thundering words.

"Ronnie, go back, dammit! *Go!*"

I didn't know if he could. But I fled, hoping he'd have the courage to do the same.

When I opened my eyes, I was in my bed, the sheets damp, the room smelling of sand and salt water. I remember Will and Joanne, who saw that I'd returned, rushing to my bedside and handing me water and a cool washcloth.

"I don't know if he made it," I said. Then I was out.

The phone rang the next day, midmorning. Just as it had happened the first time we'd spoken more than a year earlier, Joanne accepted the collect call from the operator and then, not knowing whether I was conscious or not, handed me the phone. I was groggy, but present.

"Ronnie?"

"I'm back," he said, his voice shaking. "I'm here."

He was a mere human being who happened to have been a perfect vessel for darkness. And he had fallen all the way into the black depths of evil. He wasn't the first casualty, nor would he be the last. But even for those who have committed evil, there is the possibility of redemption.

"Thank you, Jackie."

"You did it. You did it for yourself."

"He invited me to church today."

"Who?"

"Father Fernando. This morning. He asked me if I wanted to go to church. I asked him, 'What's different? Why you asking me now?' He didn't say why; he just asked me. I went."

"What did you do there?"

"I prayed. For my family. All of them."

"You're free, Ronnie. The chains are broken."

He was crying. "Thank you."

"It was you, Ronnie. I was just there to help."

"Hey," he said, his voice changing. "Why you still coughing like that? I thought if I'm better, you're supposed to be better. What's wrong?"

"It's over for you, Ronnie, but not for me. Not yet."

FIFTEEN

I had nearly finished preparing the room when Will came in. I was preparing it for travel. And for battle.

"Jackie," he said. "You need time to recover. Don't do this."

"No—it has to be now. While we have the upper hand. While he knows I'm strong."

"Jackie."

"Help me, Will. There isn't much time."

We prepared the room the same way we had for the trip to the house on Ocean Avenue—drawing a chalk circle around the bed, adding offerings to the gods of protection, calling on the spirit guides. We added conjuring items to invoke the gods, including a voodoo doll my mother had made in her own likeness, using her own hair for the doll's head.

Voodoo dolls are not used in the way one sees them used in the movies. They are summoning tools, symbols of invocation, and never used to visit harm on another. Every practitioner of the religion knows that to do so only invites the same harm right back.

The doll was more than fifty years old. It was one of the few items I'd kept of Mary's, and it had been hidden away for years, wrapped in a canvas sack. On the doll's body we drew voodoo symbols; around its neck we hung a skeleton key, said to have the power to open the door to the other side. I took a mojo bag I'd made, containing my own blood, and placed it on top of the doll. To claim her spirit, I would need to hold it down.

Will and I glued old coins from our travels around the world together in spots around the circle, symbols of the journey we'd taken and the union of our spirits. We lit the candles—three black, three white—and drew veves around the circle. I placed my grandfather's walking stick in the center of the circle. Finally, the two mirrors, the same ones we'd used before. Reflections of oneself and windows to the other side all at once.

When everything was prepared, I looked at Will and Joanne. We called Uncle Ray into the room. Then I took my place on the bed, avoiding my daughter's eyes. I didn't want her to see the slightest glimpse of trepidation in me.

I glanced at the thermostat on the bedroom wall, which had hovered around eighty-five for weeks. It read sixty-two. Will, all ten of his fingers covered in white tape, entered the circle and began pounding away at his drums, two large bongos from Brazil that he'd used in hundreds of previous rituals. Will had traveled with me before, and

I can always recognize the precise moment of his leaving. He begins to sweat heavily and his eyes flutter upward.

Joanne took her place on the floor inside the circle, turned on the ritual music, and began reciting chants from the old ritual book. She, too, had become an experienced traveler, and her brink of departure was as familiar to me as Will's. As her voice rose and its tone shifted, I knew she was beginning to take wing.

Ray stood at the opposite end of the circle, making notes. It was his task to record and bear witness.

The chandelier above me began to swing, at first in slow circles, then faster. The bedroom lights started to switch on and off. Amid the chanting and the drums, I started to feel faint.

In front of my bed, before I swooned, my grandfather materialized, summoning me. I felt myself rise above the boundaries. It's a kind of weightlessness, but more a feeling of free-floating. Something else materialized: the tunnel I'd been in as an eight-year-old clinging to life on an operating table.

I focused hard to stay away from that tunnel, and I was traveling again. The sensations around me changed, and now I heard the squawking of seagulls and the amplified sound of waves breaking against the shore, not soft lapping but loud, violent crashes.

I opened my eyes to see foamy water rushing over my bare ankles. I was lying in the sand wearing only a long white robe, one I've used often in my ceremonies and rituals. As I stood, I noticed, on my right, a brilliant light. I turned back to my left, and a swirl of sand swept across my eyes. I was back at Coney Island, on the empty beach, this time alone.

And then, as had happened with Ronnie and me, a man emerged out of nothingness, a seeming blur on the horizon one moment and the next a startling figure a few feet in front of me. He was the man who'd taken my hand in that tunnel and warned me that it was not my choice to interfere with the gears of destiny. Lucifer.

Sand continued to whip around me, but around him, everything was still. His pale white face gleamed against the black of his hair, and his eyes glimmered like sunlight on the ocean. I told myself not to be distracted by his form.

"I knew you had it in you!" he laughed. "Well, this is the day, Jackie. I've been waiting as long as you have." In his laugh there was menace and deceit, as always. But I thought I heard something else in that laugh, too. Fear. "I'll give you the chance to go back. You can't win."

He had my mother, and now he wanted Joanne. I swept the sand off my robe and looked into his eyes.

His smile turned into a scowl, then he produced a coin out of the air and tossed it. In slow motion I saw it turning over and over, droplets of blood falling from it as it spun. As I followed its turns, I felt myself becoming mesmerized.

"Mom!"

It was Joanne's voice, far away but getting through. The coin fell to earth as I turned, along with the man. There was Joanne, standing on the boardwalk, yelling. "Mom, don't!"

"Jo?"

"Don't listen to him, Mom! Follow my voice! You need to go back!"

He was drawing me into his trance, and my daughter was trying to keep me from falling into it. I shook my head, regained my sense, then turned and ran across the sand.

Joanne was gone, and I stood in front of the Surf Hotel, its facade identical to how it had looked when my mother finally succumbed to the devil's grip, decades ago. I was back in the same spot, in the same time.

I placed my hand on the doorknob, trying to stay present in this realm. The urge to travel back and wake up climbed through me again and again, and each time I pushed it back down.

A pair of pimps pushed their way past me into the hotel, just two examples of the lowlifes that now occupied it. I walked into the hotel and saw the same oily clerk I'd seen years before, seated behind a desk with iron bars protecting him from the night crawlers, drug addicts, vagrants, and thieves who now roamed the space.

I started to climb the steps, the cracks and chips in the dark-green paint of the walls emphasizing the decrepitude that had taken over. *Sometimes you can't go forward until you go back*, Mary said to me once. Now I understood.

A tortured scream issued from somewhere deep in the recesses of the floor above me. I followed the sound of the voice from which it came, pushing past the drifters and junkies stumbling their way up and down the staircase. In their stupor, they didn't notice me. Or maybe I was pushing my way through a sea of dead souls.

The more of these souls I shoved my way past, the more the stairs began to shake. Soon the entire hotel seemed to wobble, as though the ground beneath it was opening. Fear washed over me, but I didn't stop. The scared child in me wanted to stop and turn around, run back into Will's arms and never have to see the face of my demon-possessed mother again.

I was a few feet from the closed door behind which the pained screams continued to echo. The same detective I had seen all that time ago stood in front of the door. I grabbed the protection bag—my grandfather's—that hung from my neck. I closed my eyes and I squeezed it tight, asking for courage and protection. My feet carried me forward, past the detective, and, as the door swung open, into the room.

My mother's terrible screams ripped into me. There she lay, in complete possession. Bugs crept around the room, wandering past the Latin scrawls on the wall and ceiling and buzzing past the religious statues and items lying broken on the floor.

The thing occupying my mother looked up at me then, trying to catch my gaze. Forcing my eyes away from her, I instead saw an image of Joanne and Will praying and repeating the holy rite. They had traveled with me here. It wasn't enough for them to absorb my illness in the tangible world. Here they were willing to sacrifice themselves, too.

I looked back and saw that Uncle Ray, the less traveled and less experienced, had been pinned to the wall by something unseen. His arms and legs were splayed, and he couldn't move or speak. He was wearing Ronnie's army jacket, and his nails looked the way Ronnie's always did, long and manicured. As I looked, his face seemed to dissolve from his own to Ronnie's, then back again. Next to him, on the floor, was a rifle.

The thing that had been Mary reared again. "Come to me, Jackie," it said, but I held my ground, infuriating it. "What makes you so righteous!" it said. "Trying to save poor Ronnie. You couldn't even save your own mother!"

I felt myself weakening.

"Pick up that gun," it said, "and take care of the girl!" It was motioning to Joanne. "Do it!"

I was losing steadiness as the two realms fought against each other—the desire to retreat and the desire to stand firm.

"Jackie," it said, calmer now, "your mother never cared for you. You're nothing to her. Now pick up that gun! Show her the power you can have!"

"No!" I cried. "It isn't you! Stop it!"

The thing fell backward toward the rotten mattress, moaning and arching its back. "Come to Mommy, Jackie. Come on, pick up the gun!"

I forced myself to look over at Joanne and Will, and I realized what was different this time. There was no priest in the room performing the rite over my mother. They, Joanne and Will, were doing it. Together. I felt in both of them the truth and love that can alone defeat the darkest energies. Then I joined them, bending down to pick up my ritual book even though something inside me wanted to listen and pick up the gun. I looked at Will and Joanne again. My foundation. My connection. My life.

The first time, I had run to the bed, desperate to hear the voice or see the face of my mother, even though I knew she had long disappeared from this existence. Damned though she was, I'd still yearned for her love, enough to fool myself into thinking she was still somewhere inside that shell.

This time, I didn't move, and I didn't look. I knew better. She had become merely a vessel for wickedness. The demon became irate, shouting for me to pick up the gun, throwing objects across the room in a spasm of hate, goading me in every way it could think of.

From the guiding spirits of my ancestors, I summoned all the strength I could. I thought of Joanne, Will, and Ray combining their own forces to save me. Then I looked down and kicked the gun across the room. The devil howled.

I kept the pages of that ritual book open and didn't stop commanding in the name of God. It seemed to go on without end. I read and held my fist up. The demon flung its body up and down, its forked tongue whipping from one side of its mouth to the other.

As I continued to read the rite along with Will and Joanne, I thought I saw something. I had looked toward the bed accidentally and seen it. No, it must have been my mind playing tricks. Letting my resistance down, I glanced again. My mother's eyes, flashing through every few seconds, alternating with the slitted eyes of the devil. I saw them. She was in there, fighting to get out.

I ran to the side of the bed and held the book to her head. As she fell backward, I slid my grandfather's mojo bag up over my head and tried to place it on hers, but a resistant force battled me, and I couldn't get it down. Her eyes flickered through again, and the dark forked tongue became pink and rounded, surrounded by full, rose-colored lips.

"Mom! I'm here! It's Jackie!"

"No!" Will shouted. "Jackie, it's a trick! Walk away!"

Her breaths started to come in great heaving gasps, and her head swung wildly back and forth. Over my shoulder, I saw a thick fog drifting into the room. It rolled past Will and Joanne, covering them. A moment before it reached Ray, the invisible nails pinning him to the wall came loose, and he tumbled to the floor.

Suddenly I was slung back across the room, to where I'd been standing before. The book and the mojo bag had both dropped out of my hands, and now I couldn't see either one. Within moments, the fog filled the entire room, and everything was obscured. I looked back toward the bed, but it was concealed. I started to become dizzy. With what strength I had left, I called out Joanne's name, then Will's.

"We're still here!" I heard Joanne shout, though I didn't know from which part of the room. "Don't stop!" In my daughter's voice there was no fear. Only strength.

From the other side of the room, out of the fog, a

figure emerged. It was a man. A large man, with a distinctive side-to-side walk that projected ease and power at the same time.

My father. As he walked across the room, the fog began to lift and separate. I stopped talking. I could see my mother's bed again. He walked over to the side of it and put his hand out. A hand reached out from the bed, and right away I noticed the luster of its skin. The hand was smooth and milky, attached to an arm that was the same. I looked at her face, which bore the same striking light of youth. My mother was there, new again.

Mary took my father's hand and got up out of the bed. My father looked toward me and grinned, the corners of his eyes welling. My mother, pure, unmarred, smiled, too. They turned together and walked into what remained of the fog, which swirled powerfully for a moment and then, with the slightest whisper, vanished. In its place came a beautiful, fresh scent, filling the room.

"Look!" Will yelled, pointing out the window. A wrecking ball on a thick chain swept down in an arc and smashed into the wall like a bomb, shattering the concrete and brick.

We all raced for the stairs as the walls around them started to buckle. Uncle Ray held Joanne's hand and went as quickly down the steps as he could, Will in front of them, taking the steps two and three at a time. I was in the rear. Will stopped, retreated, and pulled Ray and Joanne in front of him. "Don't stop!" he told them. "Keep going! Go, go!" Then he grabbed me by the arms and yelled, "Jackie, wake up!"

I was trying to get us out, but something was restricting my flight. I focused, tried to get us back, but I was blocked.

"Wake up!" Will yelled. Just like I'd implored Ronnie to do.

I sprinted for the door. The wrecking ball came sweeping down again and smashed the remaining wall to pieces just as I ran through the doorway. Ahead of me I saw Will, Joanne, and Ray running for the car. We were getting out. I headed toward them.

"Not so fast," I heard, and then a hand was around my neck. "The score is *not* settled," Lucifer said, bringing his face close to mine and clamping his hand tighter around my throat. I swatted at it in vain as he pushed me back into the hotel. "You interfered when you shouldn't have. I warned you." He squeezed my windpipe. I started to see black spots. "Now you must take your mother's place."

"Hey."

It was Joanne. I looked to the side to see her standing there, defiant.

"Let my mother go. It's me you want, isn't it?"

The demon turned to Joanne and smiled, relaxing his grip on my throat.

"Joanne—no!" I said in a gasp as my windpipe sought air.

"An exchange?" he said.

"*JOANNE!*"

But I was too late. The air hadn't come back in fast enough. I fell away, back into my body, back to the other side.

* * *

Sometimes the student is the best teacher.

I was back in my bed, sitting up, disoriented. The six candles had burnt to the bottom of their wicks, and the room was quiet apart from the soft sounds of a man weeping. It was Uncle Ray, in the corner of the room, frightened, but returned. He'd made it back through.

And as I came back into myself fully, I saw them: Will and Joanne, each standing at a mirror on either side of the circle and holding a thick canvas down over the glass. From somewhere between two dimensions, the voice of the demon, though muffled, tried to press through, accompanied by loud scratching noises. Will and Joanne pressed the canvases down harder. The voice, and the noises, started to recede, then, after a few seconds, shrank away to nothing.

I looked at Joanne. Around her neck was the mojo bag I had tried to slide over my mother's head. I jumped off the bed, ran over to my daughter, and hugged her. Will walked over and wrapped both of us in his big arms. Ray staggered across the circle and leaned himself against us as a group, still crying, but now tears of joy and relief.

Joanne slid the mojo bag up over her head and placed it in my hands, smiling. She had come full circle. She knew who she was and the bloodline she shared.

Maybe that's all any of us really wants: to know who we are, and, for better or for worse, where we came from.

SIXTEEN

"The greatest trick the devil ever pulled was convin-cing the world he didn't exist." That's a line from the movie *The Usual Suspects*. I think about it often, because I wouldn't mind being one of those people—the ones who aren't aware. I've been aware of him all my life, and I suppose I always will be. I can't say I've won the war. I can say only that I've won the most recent battle.

Ronnie still calls, of course. Delivered from the entity that haunted him or not, he's still an inmate, and inmates still like to talk, perhaps none more than him. Except now, he's mostly quiet on the phone. I'd almost describe him as serene, though that would be false. He's free from the evil that tortured his days and nights, yes, but free is not the same thing as pure. We are pristine only at the beginning.

I try not to think about the evil spirit lurking some-where in wait, but one tries not to continue watching horror movies or gawking at car accidents, too. Will, Joanne, Ray, and I are a more resilient team than ever, but we know that in the gaps of our conversations there are things unsaid that none of us wants to broach. I lay my head down at night and the distant voices still whisper—souls lost or in pain, seeking rescue. Sometimes, in the middle of washing dishes or doing laundry, I'll look up and think I see someone watching me. Each of us hears the doorbell ring at odd hours, followed by knocking. We don't get up to answer. We let the game play out, then we try to roll back over and find sleep. Every one of us in life is continually building up our spiritual suit of armor. Yours just looks different from mine.

I still ask why I was chosen for this. Does connecting the living with the dead truly represent a higher responsibility? I've crossed the two lines so often that half the time I barely know which world I'm occupying. I feed the homeless with two legs and with four, dry the eyes of those whose spirits have been darkened or broken. People call me generous. They call me charitable. I'm not. I'm just trying to relieve myself from ever wanting. It's a continuous act of freedom. The more one gives up materially, the better she feeds her own soul. We all have our chains to drag, but we can make them lighter. We can shed old skin and start new.

I look in the mirror and can still see, somewhere in there, the face of the little person I once was. I wasn't little for very long, but she's there, and I still hold on to her. She's the innocent part of me, the part who only got to stay that way for a few years. The young shall indeed lead the old, as Mr. Gramp liked to say. I cling to that little girl with something like desperation but more like love. She's the part of me that can move through the days unfettered and unafraid. She has no thought of heaven or hell, no fear of hurt or evil. As long as she lives, I live.

On one side of the road, the sun shines; on the other, it rains fire. You can't always choose which side of the road you end up on. There isn't anyone born in this world for whom the two sides of the road don't sometimes converge. The question for all of us is whether we can make it from one side back to the other. I didn't choose my path, Mother, but I also didn't run from it.

I don't know where my journey, nor that of Ronnie DeFeo, will lead. But I do know that darkness exists, and that I will continue, forever, to seek light.

Dear Jackie,

And they say the Devil doesnt exeit, Oh do I have a Story to tell. One Can't Believe in God without the Devil, isn't that what the Holy Church Believe's In? We Both Know the Truth! People Only Believe in what they see. That's where they all go Wrong. That's Why the Door Swung Open and all the Demons walked, Looking for the Right Person moving un-noticed like the wind, Knowing the next move Before its made. Just Think of all the Damage I Know You remember. You always did! And You will never forget. I remember this Dream Of a little Girl. I Didn't Know Her Name but I do now, in my Dream She saw me I was just a Guy, my Family was Alive. I was a Teenager Standing in a Room I Couldent move. She was sitting on the Floor with Her back to me, She turned around and walked over, Just Staring at me Screaming Coming from the Walls, I Couldent look away. She showed me my life I saw my faith and it wasnt good. A Cold Dark Prison Cell, She was You Jackie, it always ended with a Tear falling from Your Eye it hit the Floor like a Blast, Years later I understood. I would see You Growing Becoming a warrior I was always there, You saw Heaven and Hell and Nothing is Going to change that. Even those dream's of the burnt down land, trees black and still smoking fire. Fire all around, You Remember Jackie?

The Devil you and me, all Face to Face. 2 things the Public will never understand, 1- Those weren't Dreams we went to Hell! 2- We Both waited a life time to Seal the deal, the Devil Knows Your Name and so do I. I will never forget the Battle, the War will always remain. The Secret of the Amityville will always be with You and who knows maybe in You along with the pact that I signed so long ago. I know the Devil isn't done you will meet Him again a different person a Different Place. If only they Know What we do. You have givin me a great peace in what life I have Left, I wish the same for You, Your going to need it! See Ya in those Dreams HA HA HA! If Only they Knew !!!!

Your Truly
From Hell and Back
"Ronald DeFeo 75A4053"
RONALD DeFeo

I know the devil isn't done...

For more than two decades, world-renowned psychic Jackie Barrett has been astounding television, radio, and guest audiences with her ability to communicate with the dead. Unlike a typical medium, Jackie's unique ability allows her clients to interact directly with the dead. Her client list includes A-list celebrities, notable politicians, professional athletes, and business leaders.She has a legion of faithful believers, including various crime fighting units all over the globe, and her sterling reputation has gained her an honorary captain's badge from the New York Police Department. Jackie is a leading expert on occult crimes, which has taken her to the darkest corners of humanity. Jackie has appeared on A&E, Bio, WE, MTV, Lifetime, E!, and the Travel Channel, as well as in numerous newspapers, magazines, and radio shows. You can visit her website at www.jackiebarrett.com.